War and Laws
– a Changing Scenario

War and Laws

Changing Scenario

Col. (Retd.) S.C. Narang

Prashant Publishing House
DELHI - 110094 (INDIA)

PRASHANT PUBLISHING HOUSE
C-34, 28 Foota Road, Gali No. 3
West Karawal Nagar, Delhi-110094
Phone : 9810396373, 22963970

War and Laws : Changing Scenario

First Published : 2010

ISBN : 978-93-80565-02-6

PRINTED IN INDIA

Published by Mr. R. K. Jha M/s. Prashant Publishing House, Delhi and Printed at H.S. Offset Press, Delhi.

Preface

The laws of war are the rules of international law that govern the conduct of war between nation-states, and are especially concerned with whether a use of force is allowed, when a state of war exists, the weapons and conduct of war, and the treatment of opponents, prisoners, neutrals, and noncombatants. They apply to the United States through enactments by Congress, the president, the Department of Defense, and specific commanders—as well as through the ratification of treaties including the Charter of the United Nations, and through those obligations of international custom binding according to the U.S. Constitution. There have been limits on the conduct of war throughout military history. These limits persist even though they are frequently violated, often without punishment. The degree to which a nation complies with them is the degree to which that nation is perceived as civilized, just as compliance on the part of a nation's military is what distinguishes it as professional. Furthermore, in the twentieth century, principles of state and personal responsibility have led to the possibility of effective criminal enforcement. Ancient laws of war dealt mostly with immunity from combat and with the commencement of hostilities.

More than 5000 years ago India recognized that the person of the ambassador was inviolable. This was a great service that ancient Hinduism rendered to the cause of international law. It was the religious force that invested the person of the herald or ambassador with an inviolable sanctity in the ancient world. The Mahabharata rules that the king who killed an envoy would sink into hell with all his ministers. As early as the 4th century B.C. Megasthenes noticed a peculiar trait of Indian warfare.

The vaunted theory, so beloved in the Rumsfeld-era Pentagon, of a "network-centric" revolution in military affairs can now be seen more clearly as a byproduct of the 1990s dotcom boom. The Internet has certainly affected how people shop, communicate, and date. Amid this ecstatic hype, it is not surprising that many security studies experts, both in and out of the defense establishment, latched onto the notion that linking up all our systems via electronic networks would "lift the fog of war," allow war to be done on the cheap, and even allow the United States to "lock out" competition from the marketplace of war, much as they saw Microsoft doing to Apple at the time. Nor is it surprising that now analysts are writing off high-tech warfare altogether in the wake of Afghanistan and Iraq. Insurgents armed with crude conventional weapons have proved frequently to flummox their well-equipped American foes.

Despite these difficulties, the available records allow an informed study of War and Laws, and they suggest that its activities made a valuable contribution.

—Author

Contents

Contents

1 Introduction

The value and importance of the army were realized very early in the history of India, and this led in course of time to the maintenance of a permanent militia to put down dissensions. War or no war, the army was to be maintained, to meet any unexpected contingency. This gave rise to the Kshatriya or warrior caste, and the *ksatram dharman* came to mean the primary duty of war. To serve the country by participating in war became the *svadharma* of this warrior community.

The necessary education, drill, and discipline to cultivate militarism were confined to the members of one community, the Kshatriyas. This prevented the militant attitude from spreading to other communities and kept the whole social structure unaffected by actual wars and war institutions.

Says the *Arthva Veda:* "May we revel, living a hundred winters, rich in heroes."

The whole country looked upon the members of the Kshatriya community as defenders of their country and consequently did not grudge the high influence and power wielded by the Kshatriyas, who were assigned a social rank next in importance to the intellectual and spiritual needs of the society.

The ancient Hindus were a sensitive people, and their heroes were instructed that they were defending the noble cause of *God, Crown* and *Country*. Viewed in this light, war departments were 'defense' departments and military expenditure were included in the cost of defense. In this, as in many cases, ancient India was ahead of modern ideas.

Chivalry, individual heroism, qualities of mercy and nobility of outlook even in the grimmest of struggles were not unknown to the soldiers of ancient India. Thus among the laws of war, we find that,

(1) a warrior (Khsatriya) in armour must not fight with one not so clad.

(2) one should fight only one enemy and cease fighting if the opponent is disabled.

(3) aged men, women and children, the retreating, or one who held a straw in his lips as a sign of unconditional surrender should not be killed.

It is of topical interest to note that one of the laws enjoins the army to leave the fruit and flower gardens, temples and other places of public worship unmolested. Terence Duke, author of The Boddhisattva Warriors: The Origin, Inner Philosophy, History and Symbolism of the Buddhist Martial Art Within India and China, martial arts went from India to China. Fighting without weapons was a specialty of the ancient *Ksatreya warriors of India.*

TERRITORIAL IDEAL OF A ONE-STATE INDIA

Imperial sway in ancient India meant the active rule of an individual monarch who by his ability and prowess brought to subjection the neighboring chieftains and other rulers, and proclaimed himself the sole ruler of the earth. This goes by the name of digvi-jaya. It is not necessary that he should conquer all States by the sword. A small state might feel the weight of a conquering king and render obeisance of its own accord.

According to the Sangam classics, each of the respective rulers of the chief Tamil kingdoms, the Cera, Cola and Pandya, carried his sword as far north as the Himalayas, and implanted on its lofty heights his respective crest the bow, the tiger and the fish. In these adventures which the Tamil Kings underwent for their glorification, they did not lag behind their northern brethren. The very epithet *Imayavaramban* shows that the limits of the empire under that Emperor extended to the Himalayas in the north.

This title was also earned by Ceran Senguttuvan by his meritorious exploits in the north. Names like the Cola Pass in the Himalayan slopes, which in very early times connected Nepal and Bhutan with ancient Tibet, give a certain clue to the fact that once

Tamil kings went so far north as the Himalayas and left their indelible marks in those regions.

If in the epic age a Rama and an Arjuna could come to the extremity of our peninsula, and in the historical period of a Chandragupta or a Samudragupta could undertake an expedition to this part of our country, nothing could prevent a king of prowess and vast resources like the Cera king Senguttuvan from carrying his armies to the north. The route lay through the Dakhan plateau, the Kalinga, Malva, and the Ganga. Perhaps it was the ancient Daksinapatha route known to history from the epoch of the Rig Veda Samhita.

The king who became conqueror of all India was entitled to the distinction of being called a Samrat. In the Puranic period the great Kartavirya Arjuna of the Haihaya clan spread his arms throughout the ancient Indian continent and earned the title of Samrat. The same principle of glory and distinction underlay the performance of the sacrifice, Asvamedha and Rajasuya, which were intended only for the members of the Kshatriya community. This bears testimony to ' the existence of the territorial ideal of a one-State India' (Cakravartiksetram of Kautalya). These kings were called Sarvabhaumas and Ekarats.

Vedic kings aimed at it, and epic rulers realized it. The idea of ekarat, continued down to Buddhist times and even later. The Jatakas which are said to belong to the fifth and sixth century B.C., make pointed reference to an all-Indian empire. This concept of an all-India empire stretching from Kanyakumari to the Himalayas, according to Kautalya receives further support from another important political term: ekacchatra, or one-umbrella sovereignty.

Hindus have given shelter to the persecuted people from many lands and in all ages. But what is most important, they have always regarded their own homeland as the only playfield for their chakravartins, and never waged wars of conquest beyond the borders of Bharata-varsha.

THE LAWS OF WAR

When society became organized and a warrior caste (Kshatriya) came into being, it was felt that the members of this caste should be governed by certain humane laws, the observance of which, it was believed, would take them to heaven, while their non-observance would lead them into hell. In the post Vedic epoch, and especially before the epics were reduced to writing, lawless war had been supplanted, and a code had begun to govern the waging of wars. The ancient law-givers, the reputed authors of the Dharmasutras and the Dharmasastras, codified the then existing customs and usages for the betterment of mankind. Thus the law books and the epics contain special sections on royal duties and the duties of common warriors.

It is a general rule that kings were chosen from among the Kshatriya caste. In other words, a non-Kshatriya was not qualified to be a king. And this is probably due to the fact that the kshatriya caste was considered superior to others in virtue of its material prowess. Though the warrior's code enjoins that all the Kshatriyas should die on the field of battle, still in practice many died a peaceful death. There is a definite ordinance of the ancient law books prohibiting the warrior caste from taking to asceticism.

Action and renunciation is the watch-word of the Kshatriya. The warrior was not generally allowed to don the robes of an ascetic. But Mahavira and Gautama protested against these injunctions and inaugurated an order of monks or sannyasins. When these dissenting sects gathered in strength and numbers, the decline of Kshatriya valour set in. Once they were initiated into a life of peace and prayer, they preferred it to the horrors of war. This was a disservice that dissenting sects did to the cause of ancient India. When a conqueror felt that he was in a position to invade the foreigner's country, he sent an ambassador with the message: 'Fight or submit.'

More than 5000 years ago India recognized that the person of the ambassador was inviolable. This was a great service that ancient Hinduism rendered to the cause of international law. It was the religious force that invested the person of the herald or ambassador with an inviolable sanctity in the ancient world. The Mahabharata rules that the king who killed an envoy would sink into hell with all his ministers. As early as the 4th century B.C. Megasthenes noticed a peculiar trait of Indian warfare.

"Whereas among other nations it is usual, in the contests of war, to ravage the soil and thus to reduce it to an uncultivated waste, among the Indians, on the contrary, by whom husbandmen are regarded as a class that is sacred and inviolable, the tillers of the soil, even when battle is raging in their neighborhood, are undisturbed by any sense of danger, for the combatants on either side in waging the conflict make carnage of each other, but allow those engaged in husbandry to remain quite unmolested. Besides, they never ravage an enemy's land with fire, nor cut down its trees."

The modern "scorched earth" policy was then unknown. " Professor H. H. Wilson says: "The Hindu laws of war are very chivalrous and humane, and prohibit the slaying of the unarmed, of women, of the old, and of the conquered."

At the very time when a battle was going on, he says, the neighboring cultivators might be seen quietly pursuing their work,- " perhaps ploughing, gathering for crops, pruning the trees, or reaping the harvest." Chinese pilgrim to Nalanda University, Hiuen Tsiang affirms that although the there were enough of rivalries and wars in the 7th century A.D. the country at large was little injured by them.

WEAPONS OF WAR AS GATHERED FROM LITERATURE

Dhanur Veda classifies the weapons of offence and defense into four-the mukta, the amukta, the mukta-mukta and the yantramukta. The *Nitiprakasika,* on the other hand, divides them into three broad classes, the mukta (thrown), the amukta (not thrown), and the mantramukta (discharged by mantras).

The bows and arrows are the chief weapons of the mukta group. The very fact that our military science named Dhanur Veda provides sufficiently clearly that the bow and arrow were the principle weapons of war in those times. It was known by different terms as sarnga, kodanda, and karmuka. Whether these are synonyms of the same thing or were different is difficult to say. The Rig vedaic smith was not only a steel worker but also an arrow maker.

Fire-Arms: It would be interesting to examine the true nature of the agneya-astras. Kautalya describes agni-bana, and mentions three recipes-agni-dharana, ksepyo-agni-yoga, and visvasaghati. Visvasaghati was composed of 'the powder of all the metals as red as fire or the mixture of the powder of kumbhi, lead, zinc, mixed with the charcoal and with oil wax and turpentine.' From the nature of the ingredients of the different compositions it would appear that they were highly inflammable and could not be easily extinguished.

A recent writer remarks: 'The Visvasaghati-agni-yoga was virtually a bomb which burst and the fragments of metals were scattered in all directions. The agni-bana was the fore-runner of a gun-shot.....

Sir A. M. Eliot tells us that the Arabs learnt the manufacture of gunpowder from India, and that before their Indian connection they had used arrows of naptha. It is also argued that though Persia possessed saltpetre in abundance, the original home of gunpowder was India. It is said that the Turkish word top and the Persian tupang or tufang are derived from the Sanskrit word dhupa. The dhupa of the Agni Purana means a rocket, perhaps a corruption of the Kautaliyan term natadipika. (source: Fire-Arms in Ancient India-By Jogesh Chandra Ray).

Heinrich Brunnhofer (1841-1917), German Indologist, also believed that the ancient Aryans of India knew about gunpowder. Gustav Oppert (1836-1908) born in Hamburg, Germany, he taught Sanskrit and comparative linguistics at the Presidency College, Madras for 21 years. He was the Telugu translator to the Government and Curator, Government Oriental Manuscript Library. Translated *Sukraniti*, statecraft by an unknown author. He attempted to prove that ancient Indians knew firearms.

In his work, *Political Maxims of the Ancient Hindus*, he says, that ancient India was the original home of gunpowder and fire-arms. It is probable that the word *Sataghni* referred to in the Sundara Kanda of the Ramayana refers to cannon.

The word astra in the Sukraniti is interpreted by Dr. Gustav Oppert as a bow. The term *astra* means a missile, anything which is discharged. *Agneya astra* means a fiery arm as distinguished from a firearm. Dr. Oppert refers to half a dozen temples in South India to prove the use of fire-arms in ancient India. The Palni temple in the Madurai District contains on the outer portion in an ancient stone mantapa scenes of carved figures of soldiers carrying in their hands small fire-arms, apparently the small-sized guns mentioned in the Sukranitisara. Again in the Sarnagapani temple at Kumbakonam in the front gate of the fifth story from the top is the figure of a king sitting in a chariot drawn by horses and surrounded by a number of soldiers. Before this chariot march two *sepoys* with pistols in their hands. In the Nurrukkal mantapam of the Conjeevaram temple is a pillar on the north side of the *mandapa*. Here is a relief vividly representing a flight between two bodies of soldiers. Mounted horsemen are also seen. The foot-soldier is shown aiming his fire-arm against the enemy. Such things are also noted in the Tanjore temple and the temple at Perur, in the Coimbatore District. In the latter there is an actual representation of a soldier loading a musket.

The Borobudar in Java where Indian tradition is copied wholesale. They are ascribed roughly to the period 750-850 A.D. There is a striking relief series PL. I, representing a battle in which two others are seen on each side, one wearing a curved sword in the right hand and a long shield, and the other a mace and a round shield resembling a wheel, all apparently made of iron. The story of the Ramayana is also given as in the Tadpatri temple from Rama's going to the forest down to the killing of Ravana. There is also a wonderful sculpture of an ancient Hindu ship. Medhatithi remarks thus "while fighting his enemies in battle, he shall not strike with concealed weapons nor with arrows that are poisoned or barbed on with flaming shafts."

Sukraniti while referring to fire-arms, (*agneyastras*) says that before any war, the duty of the minister of war is to check up the total stock of gunpowder in the arsenal. Small guns is referred as *tupak* by Canda Baradayi. The installation of yantras (engines of war) inside the walls of the forts referred to by Manasollasa and the reference of Sataghni (killer of hundreds of men) pressed into service for the protection of the forts by Samaranganasutradhara clearly reveals the frequent use of fire arms in the battle-field.

In the light of the above remarks we can trace the evolution of fire-arms in the ancient India. There is evidence to show that *agni* (fire) was praised for vanquishing an enemy. The Arthava Veda shows the employment of fire-arms with lead shots. The *Aitareya Brahmana* describes an arrow with fire at its tip. In the Mahabharata and Ramayana, the employment of agnyastras is frequently mentioned, and this deserves careful examination in the light of other important terms like ayah, kanapa and tula-guda. The agnicurna or gunpowder was composed of 4 to 6 parts of saltpetre, one part of sulphur, and one part of charcoal of arka, sruhi and other trees burnt in a pit and reduced to powder. Here is certain evidence of the ancient rockets giving place to actual guns in warfare. From the description of the composition of gunpowder, the composition of the Sukraniti can be dated at the pre-Gupta age. Bow and Arrow: In the words of H. H. Wilson: "the Hindus cultivated archery most assiduously and were very Parthians in the use of the bow on horse-back." One feature of this weapon was that it could be handled by all the four classes of warriors.

Other Weapons: The Bindipala and the nine following are minor weapons of this class. Probably this was a heavy club which had a broad and bent tail end, measuring one cubit in length. It was to be used with the left foot of the warrior placed in front. The various uses of this weapon were cutting, hitting, striking and breaking.

It was like a kunta but with a big blade. It was used by the Asuras in their fight with Kartavirya Arjuna. The Nalika is a hand gun or musket rightly piercing the mark. It was straight in form and hollow inside. It discharged darts if ignited. As has been already said, Sukracarya speaks of two kinds of nalika, one big and the other small. The small one, with a little hole at the end, measured sixty angulas (ie. distance between the thumb and the little finger) dotted with several spots at the muzzle end.

Through the touch hole or at its breach which contained wood, fire was conveyed to the charge. It was generally used by foot-soldiers. But the big gun had no wood at the breach and was so heavy that it had to be conveyed in carts. The balls were made of iron, lead or other material. Kamandaka uses the word *nalika* in the sense of firing gun as a signal for the unwary king. Again in the Naisadha, a work of the medieval period, Damayanti is compared to the two bows of the god of love and goddess of love, and her two nostrils to the two guns capable of throwing balls. Thus there is clear evidence of the existence and use of firing guns in India in very early times.

The Cakra, the next weapon in the category, is a circular disc with a small opening in the middle. It was of three kinds of eight, six and four spokes. It was used in five or six ways. It resembled the quoid of the Sikhs today. Lord Vishnu is popularly addressed as Sankha-cakra-gada-pani, that is having Sankha or conch, Cakra or disc, and Gada or mace in three of his four hands.The various uses of a disc were felling, whirling, rending, breaking, severing, and cutting. It is one of the instruments peculiar to Lord Vishnu. Kautalya speaks of it as a movable machine. The Cakra belongs to the category of a missile. According to the Vamanapurana, the Cakra has lustrous and sharp edges. The Tomara is another weapon of war frequently mentioned in all kinds of warfare. It was of two kinds, an iron club (sarvayasam) and a javelin.. According to the Agni Purana it was to be with the help of an arrow of straight feathers, and was powerful in dealing blows to the eyes and hands of an enemy. The Dantakanta, is another weapon of war, perhaps the shape of a tooth, made of metal, of strong handle and a straight blade. It had two movements. The Pasa, which is a noose killing the enemy at one stroke, of two or tree ropes used as a weapon attributed to the god Varuna. It was triangular in shape and embellished with balls of lead. It was associated with three kinds of movements. In the Agni Purana are described eleven ways of turning it to one's own advantage by dexterity of hand. The Masundi, was probably an eight sided cudgel. It was furnished with a broad and strong handle. It apparently comes from the root-meaning to cleave or break into pieces, and perhaps akin to the Musala. All these and more found used in one battle or another both in the Mahabharata and the Ramayana.

AMUKTA WEAPONS

The first of the Amukta weapons was the Vajra or the thunderbolt. The origin of this weapon is given in the Rirthayatra portion of the Mahabharata. It was made out of the backbone of the Rishi Dadhichi which was freely given by him to Indra. Originally perhaps it had six sides and made a terrible noise when hurled.

- The Parasu is the battle-axe attributed to Parasu-rama, of great fame. Its blade was made of steel and it had a wooden handle. There were six ways of manipulating it to one's own advantage.

- The Gada is a heavy rod of iron with one hundred spikes on the top. One of the four cubits was able to destroy elephants and rocks. It could be handled in twenty different ways. By means of gun powder it could be used as a projectile weapon of war. Its principal use was to strike the enemy either from a raised place or from both sides and strike terror into the enemy especially of the Gomutra array.
- The Mudgara was a staff in the shape of a hammer. It was used to break heavy stones and rocks* This is again a movable machine according to Kautalya.
- The Sira was a bucket-like instrument curved on both sides and with a wide opening made of iron. It was as long as a man's height. The Pattisa is a razor like weapon.
- The Sataghni, literally means that which had the power of killing a hundred at a time. It looked like a Gada and is said to be four cubits in length. It is generally identified with modern cannon and hence was a projectile weapon of war.

  * "sataghni tu catustala lohakantaka samcita yastih! iti Kesavah."
- It was generally placed on the walls of a fort and is included among the movable machines by Kautalya.
- Asi or the Swords-The best sword measured fifty inches. They were usually made of Pindara iron found in the Jangala country, black iron in the Anupa, white iron in the Sataharana, gold colored in the Kalinga, oily iron in the Kambhoja, blue-colored in Gujarat, grey-colored in the Maharashtra and reddish white in Karnataka. The asi si also known as Nistrimsa, Visamana, Khadga, Tiksnadhara, Durasada, Srigarbha, Vijaya and Dharmamula, meaning respectively cruel, fearful, powerful, fiery, unassailable, affording wealth, giving victory, and the source of maintaining dharma. And these are generally the characteristics of a sword.

It was commonly worn on the left side and was associated with thirty-two different movements. It measured 50 thumbs in length and four inches in width. In the Santi-parva (166,3 ff; 82 ff). Bhisma being asked as to which weapon in his opinion was the best for all kinds of fighting, replies that the sword is the foremost among arms (agryah praharananam), but the bow is first (adyam).

B.K. Sarkar says that the secret of manufacturing the so-called Damascus blade was learnt by the Saracens from the Persians, who, in their turn, had learnt it from the Hindus. Early Arabic literature provides us with a curious illustration of the esteem with which Indian swords were looked upon in Western Asia.

An early Arabic poet, Hellal, describing the flight of the Hemyarites, says: "But they fled under its (ie. the clouds) small hail of arrows quickly, whilst hard Indian swords were penetrating them." and again: "He died and we inherited him; one old wide (cuirass) and a bright Indian (sword) with a long shoulder-belt."

The original Damascus steel-the world's first high-carbon steel-was a product of India known as *wootz*. Wootz is the English for *ukku* in Kannada and Telugu, meaning steel. Indian steel was used for making swords and armour in Persia and Arabia in ancient times. Ktesias at the court of Persia (5th c BC) mentions two swords made of Indian steel which the Persian king presented him. The pre-Islamic Arab word for sword is 'muhannad' meaning from Hind. So famous were they that the Arabic word for sword was Hindvi-from Hind.

Wootz was produced by carburizing chips of wrought iron in a closed crucible process. "Wrought iron, wood and carbonaceous matter was placed in a crucible and heated in a current of hot air till the iron became red hot and plastic. It was then allowed to cool very slowly (about 24 hours) until it absorbed a fixed amount of carbon, generally 1.2 to 1.8 per cent," said eminent metallurgist Prof. T.R. Anantharaman, who taught at Banares Hindu University, Varanasi. "When forged into a blade, the carbides in the steel formed a visible pattern on the surface."

To the sixth century Arab poet Aus b. Hajr the pattern appeared described 'as if it were the trail of small black ants that had trekked over the steel while it was still soft'. In the early 1800s,

Europeans tried their hand at reproducing wootz on an industrial scale. Michael Faraday, the great experimenter and son of a blacksmith, tried to duplicate the steel by alloying iron with a variety of metals but failed.

Some scientists were successful in forging wootz but they still were not able to reproduce its characteristics, like the watery mark. "Scientists believe that some other micro-addition went into it," said Anantharaman. "That is why the separation of carbide takes place so beautifully and geometrically."

The crucible process could have originated in south India and the finest steel was from the land of Cheras, said K. Rajan, associate professor of archaeology at Tamil University, Thanjavur, who explored a 1st century AD trade centre at Kodumanal near Coimbatore. Rajan's excavations revealed an industrial economy at Kodumanal. Pillar of strength The rustless wonder called the Iron Pillar near the Qutb Minar at Mehrauli in Delhi did not attract the attention of scientists till the second quarter of the 19th century.

The inscription refers to a ruler named Chandra, who had conquered the Vangas and Vahlikas, and the breeze of whose valour still perfumed the southern ocean. "The king who answers the description is none but Samudragupta, the real founder of the Gupta empire," said Prof. T.R. Anantharaman, who has authored *The Rustless Wonder*. Zinc metallurgy travelled from India to China and from there to Europe. As late as 1735, professional chemists in Europe believed that zinc could not be reduced to metal except in the presence of copper.

The alchemical texts of the mediaeval period show that the tradition was live in India. In 1738, William Champion established the Bristol process to produce metallic zinc in commercial quantities and got a patent for it. Interestingly, the mediaeval alchemical text *Rasaratnasamucchaya* describes the same process, down to adding 1.5 per cent common salt to the ore.

ARTILLERY—INDIA TAUGHT EUROPE

Artillery was introduced into Europe by the Roma (Gypsies), who were none else than *the Jats* and *Rajputs* of India. This has been revealed in a study by a reputed linguist, Weer Rajendra

Rishi, after an extensive tour of Roma camps in Europe. He explains that the Romas, who are the Gypsies of Europe, also taught the use of artillery to Europeans. These Roma belonged to the Jat and Rajput clans who left India during the invasions by Mohamud Ghaznavi and Mohammad Ghori between the 10th and 12th centuries of the Christian era. He says the use of artillery was known in Asia, notably in India, from time immemorial, while it was introduced to the Europeans much later.

Mr. Rishi reveals that the Roma had helped different countries of Europe in making artillery. "Evidence of this is given as early as 1496 by a mandate of that date granted by Wadislas, King of Hungary, wherein it is said that Thomas Polgar, chief of 25 tents of wandering Gypsies had, with his people, made at Funfkirchen musket-balls and other ammunition for Bishop Sigismond. "In 1546 when the English were holding Boulogne against the French the latter took the help of two experienced Romas of Hungary to make great number of cannons of greater caliber than earlier guns. The Hungarian Roma of the 16th century possessed fuller knowledge of fabricating artillery than the races of Western Europe.

There were also records that the Roma were employed as soldiers by some countries of Europe. Dr. W. R. Rishi, is the author of the book, *Roma-The Panjabi Emigrants in Europe, Central and Middle Asia, the USSR, and the Americas*-published 1976. Mr. Rishi is a well-known linguist of India and was awarded the honour of 'Padmashri' by the President of India in 1970 for his contributions in the field of linguistics. He is also the Founder Director of the Indian Institute of Romani Studies

To conclude with the words of Sir George Birdwood: "For a variety, extent, and gorgeousness, and ethnological and artistic value, no such collection of Indian arms exists in this country (England) as that belonging to the Prince of Wales. It represents the armorer's art in every province of India, from the rude spear of the savage Nicobar islanders to the costly damascened, sculptured, and jewelled swords, and shields, spears, daggers, and match-locks of Kashmir, Kutch and Vizianagaram. The most striking object in the collection is a suit of armour made entirely of the horny scales of the Indian armadillo, or pangolin, encrusted with gold, and turquoise, and garnets."

MARTIAL ARTS—FIGHTING WITHOUT WEAPONS

"Fighting without weapons was a specialty of the Ksatreya (caste of Ancient India) and foot soldier alike. For the Ksatreya it was simply part and parcel of their all around training, but for the lowly peasant it was essential. We read in the Vedas of men unable to afford armour who bound their heads with turbans called Usnisa to protect themselves from sword and axe blows.

"Fighting on foot for a Ksatreya was necessary in case he was unseated from his chariot or horse and found himself without weapons. Although the high ethical code of the Ksatreya forbid anyone but another Ksatreya from attacking him, doubtless such morals were not always observed, and when faced with an unscrupulous opponent, the Ksatreya needed to be able to defend himself, and developed, therefore, a very effective form of hand-to-hand combat that combined techniques of wrestling, throws, and hand strikes. Tactics and evasion were formulated that were later passed on to successive generations. This skill was called Vajramukhti, a name meaning "thunderbolt closed-or clasped-hands." The tile Vajramukti referred to the usage of the hands in a manner as powerful as the vajra maces of traditional warfare. Vajramukti was practiced in peacetime by means of regular physical training sessions and these utilized sequences of attack and defense technically termed in Sanskrit nata."

Kalaripayattu, literally "the way of the battlefield," still survives in Kerala, where it is often dedicated to Mahakali. The Kalari grounds are usually situated near a temple, and the pupils, after having touched the feet of the master, salute the ancestors and bow down to the Goddess, begin the lesson. Kalari trainings have been codified for over 3000 years and nothing much has changed. The warming up is essential and demands great suppleness. Each movement is repeated several times, facing north, east, south and west, till perfect loosening is achieved. The young pupils pass on to the handling of weapons, starting with the "Silambam", a short stick made of extremely hard wood, which in the olden times could effectively deal with swords. The blows are hard and the parade must be fast and precise, to avoid being hit on the fingers!

They continue with the swords, heavy, and dangerous, even though they are not sharpened any more, as they are used. Without guard or any kind of body protection; they whirl, jump and parry, in an impressive ballet. Young, fearless girls fight with enormous knives, bigger than their arms and the clash of irons is echoed in the ground. The session ends with the big canes, favourite weapons of the Buddhist traveller monks, which they used during their long journey towards China to scare away attackers. The "Urimi" is the most extraordinary weapon of Kalari, unique in the world. This double-edged flexible sword which the old-time masters used to wrap around the waist to keep coiled in one hand, to suddenly whip at the opponent and inflict mortal blows, is hardly used today in trainings, for it is much too dangerous.

This indigenous martial arts, under the name of Kalari or Kalaripayit exists only in South India today. Kalarippayat is said to be the world's original martial art. Originating at least 1,300 years ago, India's Kalaripayit is the oldest martial art taught today. It is also the most potentially violent, because students advance from unarmed combat to the use of swords, sharpened flexible metal lashes, and peculiar three-bladed daggers. More than 2,000 years old, it was developed by warriors of the Cheras kingdom in Kerala. Training followed strict rituals and guidelines. The entrance to the 14 m-by-7 m arena, or kalari, faced east and had a bare earth floor. Fighters took Shiva and Shakti, the god and goddess of power, as their deities. From unarmed kicks and punches, kalarippayat warriors would graduate to sticks, swords, spears and daggers and study the marmas—the 107 vital spots on the human body where a blow can kill. Training was conducted in secret, the lethal warriors unleashed as a surprise weapon against the enemies of Cheras. Father and founder of Zen Buddhism (called C'han in China), Boddidharma, a Brahmin born in Kacheepuram in Tamil Nadu, in 522 A.D. arrived at the courts of the Chinese Emperor Liang Nuti, of the 6th dynasty. He taught the Chinese monks Kalaripayattu, a very ancient Indian martial art, so that they could defend themselves against the frequent attacks of bandits. In time, the monks became famous all over China as experts in bare-handed fighting, later known as *the Shaolin boxing art.*

The Shaolin temple which has been handed back a few years ago by the communist Government to the C'han Buddhist monks, inheritors of Boddhidharma's spiritual and martial teachings, by the present Chinese Government, is now open to visitors. On one of the walls, a fresco can be seen, showing Indian dark-skinned monks, teaching their lighter-skinned Chinese brothers the art of bare-handed fighting. On this painting are inscribed: "Tenjiku Naranokaku" which means: "the fighting techniques to train the body (which come) from India..." *Kalari payatt* was banned by the British in 1793.

SILAMBAM – INDIAN STICK FIGHTING

The art *Nillaikalakki Silambam,* which exists for more than five thousand years, is an authentic art which starts with the stick called *Silambamboo* (1.68 meters long). It originates from the Krunji mountains of south India, and is as old as the Indian sub-continent itself.

The natives called Narikuravar were using a staff called Silambamboo as a weapon to defend themselves against wild animals, and also to display their skill during their religious festivals. The Hindu scholars and yogis who went to the Krunji mountains to meditate got attracted by the display of this highly skilled spinning Silambamboo. The art Nillaikalakki Silambam therefore became a part of the Hindu scholars and yogis training, as they were taught by the Narikuravar. They brought the art to the royal court during the reign of the Cheran, Cholan and Pandian emperors, once powerful rulers of India.

ARMY AND ARMY DIVISIONS

The Game of Chess and the Four-Fold Force

Owing to peculiar geographical features, with her vast plains interspersed with forests, the ancient Indian States had to make extensive use of mounted forces which comprised cavalry, chariots, and elephants. This does not mean that infantry was neglected. Hindu India possessed the classical fourfold force of chariots, elephants, horsemen, and infantry, collectively known as the *Caturangabala.*

Students also know that the old game of chess also goes by the name of Caturanga. Chess is a game of war, and in each game there are a king, a councilor, two elephants, two horses, two chariots, and eight foot-soldiers. From the references to this game in the Rig Veda and the Atharva Veda and in the Buddhists and Jaina books, it must have been very popular in ancient India. The Persian term Chatrang and the Arabic Shatrang are forms of the Sanskrit *Chaturanga*. The famous epic Mahabharata narrates an incidence where a game called *Chaturang* was played between two groups of warring cousins. In some form or the other, the game continued till it evolved into chess.

H.J.R. Murray, in his work titled "A History of Chess", has concluded that, "chess is a descendant of an Indian game played in the 7th century AD". The Encyclopedia Britannica states that "we find the best authorities agreeing that chess existed in India before it is known to have been played anywhere else."

On the whole the board is 8 X 8 squares. According to Taylor, the game of chess was the invention of some Hindu who devised a game of war with the astapada board as his field of battle. From the reference to the game in the Rig Veda and the Arthava Veda and in the Buddhist and Jaina books, it must have been very popular in ancient India. It is to be noted that the relative values of the chess pieces were analogous to or identical with the relative values of different arms as laid down by Kautalya, Sukra, and Vaisampayana. The organization of the Indian army which came to be known as *Caturanga*, both in epic Sanskrit and Pali literature, was based on the ancient game.

The Chariots

Chariots were used in warfare from very remote times. There are many references to chariots in the Samhitas and in the Brahmanas. The chariot was an indispensable instrument of war in the days of the Vedas, and on its possession depended victory. In the Rig Veda there is a hymn addressed to the war chariot: ' Lord of the wood, be firm and strong in body: be bearing as a brave victorious hero. Show forth thy strength, compact with straps of leather and let thy rider win all spoils of battle.' Chariots were of different types and materials. In the Ramayana and the Mahabharata their use is largely in evidence. Each chariot was marked off by its ensign and banner. Besides flags, umbrellas (chattra, atapatra), and fans were a part of the paraphernalia of the war chariot.

Sukra mentions an awe-inspiring chariot of iron with swift-moving wheels, provided with good seats for the warriors and a seat in the middle for the charioteer; the chariot was also equipped with all kinds of offensive and defensive weapons.

The conception of the sun-god in Indian tales is of value to the student of ancient Indian military history. The idea is that the sun-god wants to destroy darkness. Therefore he dons a lustrous armour and marching in his swift flying chariot drawn by seven powerful *steads*, Aruna (dawn) being his charioteer. The whole image presents a life-like portrait of the military dress as well as the march against an enemy.

Elephants

The next important force of war consisted of elephants. The numerous representations of the animal on coins and in architectural sculptural works from Gandhara to Ramesvaram as well as bronze figures in Indonesia are an indication of the esteem in which it was held by the ancient Indians, clearly on account of its usefulness. There is a reference in the Rig Veda to two elephants bending their heads and rushing together against the enemy, which is a fairly early reference to the animal being used in war. By the time of the Yajur Veda Samhita the art of training elephants had become common. The Arthashastra mentions a special officer of the State for the care of elephants and lays down his duties.

Megasthenes explains how the elephants were hunted, and how their distempers were cured by simple remedies such as cow's milk for eye-disease and pig's fat for sores. A Jataka story throws some light on how fire-weapons were used in ancient India. "Once a king mounted on an elephant and led an attack on the city of Benares. The soldiers who offered defenses from within the city gates discharged a shower of missiles against the enemy at which the elephant was frightened a little." The use of burning naphtha balls thrown against on rushing elephants to frighten them and make them turn back on their own side, is mentioned by early Mohammadan historians as a feature of the warfare between the Rajputs and the Turkish invaders from the North-West.

Cavalry

We hear from the Kautaliya and Megasthenes that there was a well-organized and efficient cavalry force in the army of Chandragupta. In the ArthaVeda we hear of dust-raising horsemen. In this connection it is interesting to consider the oft-repeated statement that horses are non-Indian. It is not the whole truth. They were known to the Asuras of Vedic literature. There is a legend narrated in the third book of the Hariharacaturanga (though this is work of the late 12th century A.D., the tradition recorded is very ancient). In the epoch of the epics and the Arthashastra, we find that the cavalry occupied as important a place in the army as any other division.

Megasthenes corroborates the evidence of the Arthashastra. There was a special department in the State for the cavalry. The horses of the State were provided with stables and placed under the care of good grooms and *syces*. There were several trained horsemen who could jump forward and arrest the speed of galloping horses. But the majority of them rode their horses with bit and bridle. When horses became ungovernable they were placed in the hands of professional trainers who made the animals gallop round in small circles. In selecting horses of war, their age, strength, and size were taken into account. We may remark in passing that Abhimanyu's horses were only three years old. In the *Mahabharata* war the Kambojans (Cambodians) were enlisted. The steeds of Bahalika were also highly esteemed. Horses had names and so did elephants. Unlike the chariot horse, the cavalryman drove his animal with a whip which was generally fixed to the wrist. This allowed his hand free play. The cavalryman was armed with arrow or spear or sword. He wore breastplate and turban (unsnisa). Worth noting is the fact that horses were made to drink wine before actually marching to battle.

The tactical use of the cavalry was to break through the obstacles on the way, to pursue the retreating enemy, to cover the flanks of the army, to effect speedy communication with the various parts of the army unobserved (bahutsara) and to pierce the enemy ranks from the front to the rear. The cavalry was responsible, in a large measure, for the safety and security of the army in entrenched positions, forests or camps. It obstructed movements of supplies and reinforcements to the enemy. In short, the cavalry was indispensable in situations requiring quickness of movement.

Infantry

The next important division of the army was the infantry, or foot-soldier. The Arthashastra speaks of the infantry as a separate army department under the charge of a special officer of the State. This receives confirmation from Megasthenes statement. Besides the *maula* or hereditary troops which formed a considerable portion of the army, there were,

- the *bhrta* or mercenaries
- the *sreni* or soldiers supplied by the different group and guild organizations
- the mitra or soldiers supplied by allies
- the *amitra* or deserters from the enemy ranks
- the *atavi* recruited from forest tribes

According to the Sukraniti and the Kamandakanitsara, the army was to be made as imposing as possible to frighten the enemy by its size. The Agni-purana says that victory ever attends the army where foot-soldiers are numerically strong. The Sukraniti also mentions that foot-soldiers possessed fire-arms when they fought. When these foot-soldiers equipped themselves for war Arrian says that, 'they carry a bow made of equal length with the man who bears it. This they rest upon the ground and pressing against it and their left foot, thus discharge the arrow having drawn the string backwards: the shaft they use is little short of being three yards long, and there is nothing which can resist an Indian Archer's shot-neither shield nor breast-plate, nor any stronger defense if such there be.' In their left hand they carry bucklers made of undressed ox-hide which are not so broad as those who carry them but are about as long. If we turn to the ancient nations and especially the ancient Egyptians we meet with almost a similar description.

The Commissariat

The *Caturanaga* was a classical division of the army accepted by tradition. But in the epoch of the epic we hear of a Sadanga or the six-fold army, including commissariat and admiralty. The use of commissariat can be traced to the epic age. This belonged to the category of administrative division of troops as against the combatant. We are told that this division of the army into two categories was first seen in the battle of Mansikert (1071 A.D.)

But, centuries before, the Indian army leaders had realized the value of such a division. It is said that when the Pandava army marched to Kurukshetra it was followed by 'carts and transport cars, and all descriptions of vehicles, the treasury, weapons and machines and physicians and surgeons, along with the few invalids that were in the army and all those that were weak and powerless. This was purely a civil department attached to the army. Care was also given to wounded animals. The numerous references in our authorities to the Commissariat demonstrate beyond doubt that wars were planned methodically and conducted systematically.

The Admiralty

The Admiralty as a department of the State may have been a creation of *Chandragupta* but there is evidence to show that the use of ships and boats was known to the people of the Rig Veda. In the following passage we have reference to a vessel with a hundred oars. "This exploit you achieved, Asvins in the ocean, where there is nothing to give support, nothing to rest upon, nothing to cling to, that you brought Bhujya, sailing in a hundred-cared ship, to his father's house."

Cartography

There is no special word in Sanskrit for a 'a map.' There is, however, reason to believe that in ancient India a map or chart was regarded as a *citra* or *alekhya*, i.e., 'a painting, a picture, a delineation'. That maps were made in ancient India seems to be quite clear from the evidence of the New History of the T'ang Dynasty which gives an account of the Chinese general Wang Hiuen-tse's exploits in India in the year 648 A.D. With reference to the knowledge of map-making among the people of India, especially the Dravidians of the South: "The charts in use by the medieval navigators of the Indian Ocean-Dravidas, Arabs, Persians, were equal in value, if not superior, to the charts of the Mediterranean. Marco Polo (1498) found them in the hands of his Indian pilot, and their nature is fully explained in the Mohit or 'the Encyclopaedia of the Sea'"

Hindu Valour

The Hindus were declared the by the Greeks to be the bravest nation they ever came in contact with. It was the Hindu King of Magadha that struck terror in the ever-victorious armies of Alexander. Abul Fazal, the minister of Akbar, after admiring their noble virtues, speaks of the valour of the Hindus in these terms:

"Their character shines brightest in adversity. Their soldiers (Rajputs) know to what it is to flee from the fields of battle, but when the success of the combat becomes doubtful, they dismount from their horses and throw away their lives in payment of the debt of valour."

Francois Bernier, a 17th century traveller says that: "The Rajputs embrace each other when on the battlefields as if resolved to die."

The Spartans, as is well known, dressed their hair on such occasions. It is well known that when a Rajput becomes desperate, he puts on garments of saffron color, which act, in technical language, is called *kesrian kasumal karna* (donning saffron robes).

AERIAL WARFARE

"The ancient Hindus could navigate the air, and not only navigate it, but fight battles in it like so many war-eagles combating for the domination of the clouds. To be so perfect in aeronautics, they must have known all the arts and sciences related to the science, including the strata and currents of the atmosphere, the relative temperature, humidity, density and specific gravity of the various gases..." ~ Col. Henry S Olcott (1832 – 1907)

"No question can be more interesting in the present circumstances of the world than India's contribution to the science of aeronautics. There are numerous illustration in our vast Puranic and epic literature to show how well and wonderfully the ancient

Indians conquered the air. To glibly characterize everything found in this literature as imaginary and summarily dismiss it as unreal has been the practice of both Western and Eastern scholars until very recently. The very idea indeed was ridiculed and people went so far to assert that it was physically impossible for man to use flying machines. But today what with balloons, airplanes….."

Turning to Vedic literature, in one of the Brahmanas occurs the concept of a ship that sails heavenwards. The ship is the *Agnihotra* of which the *Ahavaniya* and *Garhapatya* fires represent the two sides bound heavenward, and the steersman is the Agnihotrin who offers milk to the three Agnis. Again in the still earlier Rig Veda Samhita we read that the Asvins conveyed the rescued Bhujya safely by means of winged ships. The latter may refer to the aerial navigation in the earliest times. In the recently published *Samarangana Sutradhara of Bhoja,* a whole chapter of about 230 stanzas is devoted to the principles of construction underlying the various flying machines and other engines used for military and other purposes.

The various advantages of using machines, especially flying ones, are given elaborately. Special mention is made of their use at one's will and pleasure, of their uninterrupted movements, of their strength and durability, in short of their capability to do in the air all that is done on earth. Three movements are usually ascribed to these machines,-ascending, cruising thousands of miles in different directions in the atmosphere and lastly descending.

It is said that in an aerial car one can mount up to Suryamandala, 'solar region' and the Naksatra mandala (stellar region) and also travel throughout the regions of air above the sea and the earth. These cars are said to move so fast as to make a noise that could be heard faintly from the ground. The evidence in its favour is overwhelming. An aerial car is made of light, wood looking like a great bird with a durable and well-formed body having mercury inside and fire at the bottom. It had two resplendent wings, and is propelled by air. It flies in the atmospheric regions for a great distance and carries several persons along with it. The inside construction resembles heaven created by Brahma himself. Iron, copper, lead and other metals are also used for these machines. All these show how far art and science was developed in ancient India in this direction. Such elaborate description ought to meet the criticism that the vimanas and similar aerial vehicles mentioned in ancient Indian literature should be relegated to the region of myth.

The ancient writers could certainly make a distinction between the mythical which they designated as daiva and the actual aerial wars designated as manusa. After the great victory of Rama over Lanka, Vibhisana presented him with the Puspaka vimana which was furnished with windows, apartments, and excellent seats. It was capable of accommodating all the vanaras besides Rama, Sita and Lakshmana. Again in the Vikramaurvaisya, we are told that king Puraravas rode in an aerial car to rescue Urvasi in pursuit of the Danava who was carrying her away.

Similarly in the Uttararamacarita in the flight between Lava and Candraketu (Act VI) a number of aerial cars are mentioned as bearing celestial spectators. There is a statement in the Harsacarita of Yavanas being acquainted with aerial machines. The Tamil work Jivakacintamani refers to Jivaka flying through the air. Kathasaritsagara refers to highly talented woodworkers called Rajyadhara and Pranadhara. The former was so skilled in mechanical contrivances that he could make ocean crossing chariots. And the latter manufactured a flying chariot to carry a thousand passengers in the air. These chariots were stated to be as fast as thought itself.

2 Laws of War

The law of war is law concerning acceptable practices relating to war. In cases other than civil wars, it is considered an aspect of public international law (the law of nations). The laws of war are divided into two categories:

- *Jus in bello,* law concerning acceptable conduct in war.
- *Jus ad bellum,* law concerning acceptable justifications to use armed force.

SOURCES OF THE LAWS OF WAR

Attempts to define and regulate the conduct of individuals, nations, and other agents in war and to mitigate the worst effects of war have a long history. The earliest known instances are found in the Hebrew Bible (Old Testament). For example, Deuteronomy 20:19 limits the amount of collateral and environmental damage: "If you besiege a city for a long time while attempting to capture it, you must not chop down its trees, for you may eat fruit from them and should not cut them down. A tree in the field is not human that you should besiege it! However, you may chop down any tree you know is not suitable for food, and you may use it to build siege works against the city that is making war with you until that city falls." (NET) Similarly Deuteronomy 21:10-15 requires that female captives be treated in a manner that in the ancient world (although of course not by present-day standards) was unusually humane. In the early 7th century, the first Caliph, Abu Bakr, whilst instructing his Muslim army, laid down the following rules concerning warfare:

Stop, O people, that I may give you ten rules for your guidance in the battlefield. Do not commit treachery or deviate from the right path. You must not mutilate dead bodies. Neither kill a child, nor a woman, nor an aged man. Bring no harm to the trees, nor burn them with fire, especially those which are fruitful. Slay not any of the enemy's flock, save for your food. You are likely to pass by people who have devoted their lives to monastic services; leave them alone.

These rules were put into practice during the early Muslim conquests of the 7th and 8th centuries. After the expansion of the Caliphate, Islamic legal treatises on international law from the 9th century onwards covered the application of Islamic military jurisprudence to international law, including the law of treaties; the treatment of diplomats, hostages, refugees and prisoners of war in Islam; the right of asylum; conduct on the battlefield; protection of women, children and non-combatant civilians; contracts across the lines of battle; the use of poisonous weapons; and devastation of enemy territory.

These laws were put into practice by Muslim armies during the Crusades, most notably by Saladin and Sultan al-Kamil. For example, after al-Kamil defeated the Franks, Oliverus Scholasticus praised the Islamic laws of war, commenting on how al-Kamil supplied the defeated Frankish army with food: Who could doubt that such goodness, friendship and charity come from God? Men whose parents, sons and daughters, brothers and sisters, had died in agony at our hands, whose lands we took, whom we drove naked from their homes, revived us with their own food when we were dying of hunger and showered us with kindness even when we were in their power.

In medieval Europe, the Roman Catholic Church also began promulgating teachings on just war, reflected to some extent in movements such as the Peace and Truce of God. The impulse to restrict the extent of warfare, and especially protect the lives and property of non-combatants continued with Hugo Grotius and his attempts to write laws of war.

Positive international humanitarian law consists of treaties (international agreements) which directly affect the laws of war by binding consenting nations and achieving widespread consent—see the section below called "International treaties on the laws of war". The opposite of positive laws of war is customary laws of war, many of which were explored at the Nuremberg War Trials. These laws define both the *permissive* rights of states as well as *prohibitions* on their conduct when dealing with irregular forces and non-signatories.

In addition, the Nuremberg War Trial judgment on "The Law Relating to War Crimes and Crimes Against Humanity" held, under the guidelines Nuremberg Principles, that treaties like the Hague Convention of 1907, having been widely accepted by "all civilised nations" for about half a century, were by then part of the customary laws of war and binding on all parties whether the party was a signatory to the specific treaty or not.

Interpretations of international humanitarian law change over time and this also affects the laws of war. For example Carla Del Ponte, the chief prosecutor for the International Criminal Tribunal for the former Yugoslavia pointed out in 2001 that although there is no specific treaty ban on the use of depleted uranium projectiles, there is a developing scientific debate and concern expressed regarding the effect of the use of such projectiles and it is possible that, in future, there will be a consensus view in international legal circles that use of such projectiles violate general principles of the law applicable to use of weapons in armed conflict.

This is because in future it may be the consensus view that depleted uranium projectiles breaches one or more of the following treaties: The Universal Declaration of Human Rights; the Charter of the United Nations; the Genocide Convention; the United Nations Convention Against Torture; the Geneva Conventions including Protocol I; the Convention on Conventional Weapons of 1980; the Chemical Weapons Convention; and the Convention on the Physical Protection of Nuclear Material.

Purposes of the laws

It has often been commented that creating laws for something as inherently crimeful and lawless as war seems like a lesson in absurdity. However, based on the adherence to what amounted to customary international law by warring parties through the ages, it was felt that codifying laws of war would be beneficial.

Some of the central principles underlying laws of war are:

- Wars should be limited to achieving the political goals that started the war (e.g., territorial control) and should not include unnecessary destruction;

- Wars should be brought to an end as quickly as possible;
- People and property that do not contribute to the war effort should be protected against unnecessary destruction and hardship;

To this end, laws of war are intended to mitigate the evils of war by:

- Protecting both combatants and noncombatants from unnecessary suffering;
- Safeguarding certain fundamental human rights of persons who fall into the hands of the enemy, particularly prisoners of war, the wounded and sick, and civilians;
- Facilitating the restoration of peace.

Conduct of Warfare

Among other issues, the laws of war address declaration of war, acceptance of surrender and the treatment of prisoners of war; military necessity along with *distinction* and *proportionality;* and the prohibition of certain inhumane weapons which cause unnecessary suffering. It is a violation of the laws of war to engage in combat without meeting certain requirements, among them the wearing of a distinctive uniform or other distinctive signs visible at a distance, and the carrying of weapons openly. Impersonating soldiers of the other side by wearing the enemy's uniform is allowed, though fighting in that uniform, like fighting under a white flag, is perfidy which is forbidden, as is the taking of hostages.

Land Warfare

The Law of Land Warfare is that part of the Laws of War applicable to the conduct of warfare on land (territory) and to relationships between belligerents and neutral states. The conduct of armed hostilities on land is regulated by the law of land warfare which is both written and unwritten. The transition from unwritten to written began in 1856. In fact, historian Geoffrey Best has called the period from 1856 to 1909 the law of war's "epoch of highest repute." The defining aspect of this epoch was the establishment, by states, of a positive legal or legislative foundation (i.e., written) superseding a regime based primarily on religion, chivalry, and customs. It is during this "modern" era that the international conference became the forum for debate and agreement between states and the "multilateral treaty" served as the positive mechanism for codification.

While many point correctly to the Lieber Code, which was promulgated by the Union during the American Civil War, as critical in the development of the laws of land warfare, one researcher who analyzed the evolution of these laws concludes that "following the publication of Lieber's code as General Orders 100 in 1863, the United States did not effectively contribute anything to The Hague Laws relating to land warfare as they evolved during this period." This was probably because the United States was involved in only one armed conflict (the Spanish-American War) in the time period immediately following the Lieber Code and the coming into force of 4th Hague. As the Lieber Code was a comprehensive written recital of the customary law of war in force at the time between the civilized nations and peoples, and 4th Hague was essentially a written recital of the Lieber Code, the United States had nothing further to contribute, having already "written the book" on the laws of war, so to speak.

Prohibitory Effect

The law of war places limits on the exercise of a belligerent's power mentioned under *Purposes* and requires that belligerents refrain from employing any kind or degree of violence which is not actually necessary for military purposes and that they conduct hostilities with regard for the principles of humanity and chivalry.

Binding both on States and Undividuals

The law of war is binding not only upon States as such but also upon individuals and, in particular, the members of their armed forces.

Sources of the Law

The law of war is derived from two principal sources:

- *Lawmaking treaties* (or *conventions*) — see the section below called "International treaties on the laws of war".

- *Custom*. Not all the law of war derives from or has been incorporated in such treaties, which can refer to the continuing importance of customary law. Such customary international law is established by the general practice of nations together with their acceptance that such practice is required by law.

Declaration of War

Some treaties, notably the UN charter (1945) Article 2, and some other articles in the charter, seek to curtail the right of member states to declare war; as does the older Kellogg-Briand Pact of 1928 for those nations who ratified it. The Kellogg-Briand Pact was used against those charged at the Nuremberg War Trials in Germany post-World War II for waging an aggressive war.

Violations and Applicability

Parties are bound by the laws of war to the extent that such compliance does not interfere with achieving legitimate military goals. For example, they are obliged to make every effort to avoid damaging people and property not involved in combat, but they are not guilty of a war crime if a bomb mistakenly hits a residential area. By the same token, combatants that use protected people or property as shields or camouflage are guilty of violations of laws of war and are responsible for damage to those that should be protected.

Prohibitory Effects

Well-known examples of such laws include the prohibition on attacking doctors, ambulances or hospital ships displaying a Red Cross, a Red Crescent or other emblem related to the International Red Cross and Red Crescent Movement (this sometimes leads to confusion when the British military is involved, where certain regiments use the English flag, which is also a red cross). It is also prohibited to fire at a person or vehicle bearing a white flag, since that indicates an intent to surrender or a desire to communicate. In either case, the persons protected by the Red Cross or white flag are expected to maintain neutrality, and may not engage in warlike acts; in fact, engaging in war activities under a white flag or red cross is itself a violation of the laws of war known as perfidy. Failure to follow these requirements can result in the loss of protected status and make the individual violating the requirements a lawful military target.

Remedies for Violations

During conflict, punishment for violating the laws of war may consist of a specific, deliberate and limited violation of the laws of war in reprisal. Soldiers who break specific provisions of the laws of war lose the protections and status afforded as prisoners of war, but only after facing a *"competent tribunal"*. At that point they become an unlawful combatant but they must still be *"treated with humanity and, in case of trial, shall not be deprived of the rights of fair and regular trial"*, because they are still covered by GC IV Art 5. For example in 1976 foreign soldiers fighting for FNLA were captured by the MPLA in the civil war that broke out when Angola gained independence from Portugal in 1975. In the Luanda Trial, after *"a regularly constituted court"* found them guilty of being mercenaries, three Britons and an American were shot by a firing squad on July 10, 1976. Nine others were imprisoned for terms of 16 to 30 years.

Spies and terrorists may be subject to civilian law or military tribunal for their acts and in practice have been subjected to torture and/or execution. The laws of war neither approve nor condemn such acts, which fall outside their scope. However, nations that have signed the *UN Convention Against Torture* have committed themselves not to use torture on anyone for any reason. Citizens and soldiers of nations which have not signed the Fourth Geneva Convention are also not protected by it, whether they are spies or terrorists. Also, citizens and soldiers of nations which have not signed and do not abide by the Third and Fourth Geneva Conventions are not protected by them.

If someone is (or is suspected to be) a citizen or soldier of a nation which has signed or abides by the Fourth Geneva Convention, or is (or is suspected to be) a "prisoner of war" (POW) per the definitions of such *"protected persons"* in the Third Geneva Convention, the following applies: A POW who breaks specific provisions of the laws of war may be penalized, but not penalized worse than the tribunal would penalize its own soldiers for the same offense (and usually a disciplinary, not judicial, punishment if its own soldiers normally wouldn't be brought to trial for a particular offense) and POW's may not be penalized based on rank or gender, nor with corporal punishment, collective punishments for individual acts, lack of daylight, or torture/ cruelty.

After a conflict has ended, persons who have committed or ordered any breach of the laws of war, especially atrocities, may be held individually accountable for war crimes through process of law. Also, nations which signed the Geneva Conventions are required to search for, then try and punish, anyone who has committed or ordered certain *"grave breaches"* of the laws of war. History has shown that the laws of war are traditionally more strictly applied to those defeated, as the victorious faction are placed in the role of policing themselves.

While it can be argued that the victors may be less strict on their own forces, it can also be argued that the signing of the treaties involved in the laws of war implies a good-faith promise to adhere to them equally. As with many facets of war, the aftermath and subsequent legal proceedings depend heavily on circumstance, and are different for each conflict. There is an emerging trend in the US to hold private corporations civilly liable for aiding and abetting in war crimes, by knowingly providing substantial assistance in the commission of the crimes.

Under international law, the mens rea element is knowledge, not intent that the crimes be carried out. This opens the door not only to hold private security contractors liable, but also other kinds of corporations which employ violent mercenary or terrorist groups as private security forces. Although conflict zones often lack functioning legal systems, and government may even have passed laws immunizing private mercenaries from criminal liability, aiding and abetting a war crime can still be the basis for civil liability in a foreign court with jurisdiction over the defendant corporation.

International Treaties on the Laws of War

List of declarations, conventions, treaties and judgements on the laws of war:

- 1856 Paris Declaration Respecting Maritime Law abolished privateering
- 1864 First Geneva Convention "for the Amelioration of the Condition of the Wounded and Sick in Armed Forces in the Field"
- 1868 St. Petersburg Declaration Renouncing the Use, in Time of War, of Explosive projectiles Under 400 grams Weight
- 1874 Project of an International Declaration concerning the Laws and Customs of War (Brussels Declaration). Signed in Brussels 27 August. This agreement never entered into force, but formed part of the basis for the codification of the laws of war at the 1899 Hague Peace Conference.
- 1880 Manual of the Laws and Customs of War at Oxford. At its session in Geneva in 1874 the Institute of International Law appointed a committee to study the *Brussels Declaration* of the same year and to submit to the Institute its opinion and supplementary proposals on the subject. The work of the Institute led to the adoption of the Manual in 1880 and it went on to form part of the basis for the codification of the laws of war at the 1899 Hague Peace Conference.
- 1899 Hague Conventions consisted of four main sections and three additional declarations (the final main section is for some reason identical to the first additional declaration):
    * Pacific Settlement of International Disputes
    * Laws and Customs of War on Land
    * Adaptation to Maritime Warfare of Principles of Geneva Convention of 1864
    * Prohibiting Launching of Projectiles and Explosives from Balloons
    * Declaration I-On the Launching of Projectiles and Explosives from Balloons
    * Declaration II-On the Use of Projectiles the Object of Which is the Diffusion of Asphyxiating or Deleterious Gases

  * Declaration III-On the Use of Bullets Which Expand or Flatten Easily in the Human Body
- 1907 Hague Conventions had thirteen sections, of which twelve were ratified and entered into force and two declarations
  * The Pacific Settlement of International Disputes
  * The Limitation of Employment of Force for Recovery of Contract Debts
  * The Opening of Hostilities
  * The Laws and Customs of War on Land
  * The Rights and Duties of Neutral Powers and Persons in Case of War on Land
  * The Status of Enemy Merchant Ships at the Outbreak of Hostilities
  * The Conversion of Merchant Ships into War-Ships
  * The Laying of Automatic Submarine Contact Mines
  * Bombardment by Naval Forces in Time of War
  * Adaptation to Maritime War of the Principles of the Geneva Convention
  * Certain Restrictions with Regard to the Exercise of the Right of Capture in Naval War
  * The Creation of an International Prize Court
  * The Rights and Duties of Neutral Powers in Naval War
  * Declaration I-extending Declaration II from the 1899 Conference to other types of aircraft
  * Declaration II-on the obligatory arbitration
- 1909 London Declaration concerning the Laws of Naval War largely reiterated existing law, although it showed greater regard to the rights of neutral entities. Never went into effect.
- 1922 The Washington Naval Treaty, also known as the *Five-Power Treaty*
- 1923 Hague Draft Rules of Aerial Warfare
- 1925 Geneva protocol for the Prohibition of the Use in War

of Asphyxiating, Poisonous or Other Gases, and of Bacteriological Methods of Warfare

- 1927-1930 Greco-German arbitration tribunal
- 1928 Kellogg-Briand Pact (also known as the *Pact of Paris*)
- 1929 Geneva Convention, Relative to the treatment of prisoners of war
- 1930 Treaty for the Limitation and Reduction of Naval Armament
- 1936 Second London Naval Treaty
- 1938 Amsterdam Draft Convention for the Protection of Civilian Populations Against New Engines of War.
- 1938 League of Nations declaration for the "Protection of Civilian Populations Against Bombing From the Air in Case of War"
- 1945 United Nations Charter
- 1946 Judgment of the International Military Tribunal at Nuremberg
- 1947 Nuremberg Principles. formulated under UN General Assembly Resolution 177 21 November 1947
- 1948 United Nations Convention on the Prevention and Punishment of the Crime of Genocide.
- 1949 Geneva Convention I for the Amelioration of the Condition of the Wounded and Sick in Armed Forces in the Field
- 1949 Geneva Convention II for the Amelioration of the Condition of Wounded, Sick and Shipwrecked Members of Armed Forces at Sea
- 1949 Geneva Convention III Relative to the Treatment of Prisoners of War
- 1949 Geneva Convention IV Relative to the Protection of Civilian Persons in Time of War
- 1954 Hague Convention for the Protection of Cultural Property in the Event of Armed Conflict
- 1971 Zagreb Resolution of the Institute of International Law on Conditions of Application of Humanitarian Rules of Armed Conflict to Hostilities in which the United Nations Forces May be Engaged

- 1977 United Nations Convention on the Prohibition of Military or Any Other Hostile Use of Environmental Modification Techniques
- 1977 Geneva Protocol I Additional to the Geneva Conventions of 12 August 1949, and Relating to the Protection of Victims of International Armed Conflicts
- 1977 Geneva Protocol II Additional to the Geneva Conventions of 12 August 1949, and Relating to the Protection of Victims of Non-International Armed Conflicts
- 1978 Red Cross Fundamental Rules of International Humanitarian Law Applicable in Armed Conflicts
- 1980 United Nations Convention on Prohibitions or Restrictions on the Use of Certain Conventional Weapons Which May be Deemed to be Excessively Injurious or to Have Indiscriminate Effects (CCW)
    * 1980 Protocol I on Non-Detectable Fragments
    * 1980 Protocol II on Prohibitions or Restrictions on the Use of Mines, Booby-Traps and Other Devices
    * 1980 Protocol III on Prohibitions or Restrictions on the Use of Incendiary Weapons
    * 1995 Protocol IV on Blinding Laser Weapons
    * 1996 Amended Protocol II on Prohibitions or Restrictions on the Use of Mines, Booby-Traps and Other Devices
    * Protocol on Explosive Remnants of War (Protocol V to the 1980 Convention), 28 November 2003, entered into force on 12 November 2006
- 1994 San Remo Manual on International Law Applicable to Armed Conflicts at Sea.
- 1994 ICRC/UNGA Guidelines for Military Manuals and Instructions on the Protection of the Environment in Time of Armed Conflict
- 1994 UN Convention on the Safety of United Nations and Associated Personnel
- 1996 The International Court of Justice advisory opinion on the Legality of the Threat or Use of Nuclear Weapons

- 1997 Convention on the Prohibition of the Use, Stockpiling, Production and Transfer of Anti-Personnel Mines and on their Destruction (Ottawa Treaty)
- 1998 Rome Statute of the International Criminal Court entered into force on 1 July 2002.
- 2000 Optional Protocol on the Involvement of Children in Armed Conflict, entered into force on 12 February 2002.

WAR AND ENVIRONMENTAL LAW

War can heavily damage the environment, and warring countries often place victory ahead of environmental concerns for the duration of the war. Some international law is designed to limit this environmental harm.

Environmental Impact of War

War and military activities have obvious detrimental impacts on the environment. Weaponry, troop movements, land mines, creation and destruction of buildings, destruction of forests by defoliation or general military usage, poisoning of water sources, target-shooting of animals for practice, consumption of endangered species out of desperation etc., are just some of the examples of how both war and peacetime military activities (such as training, base construction, and transportation of weaponry) harm the environment.

Law

From a legal standpoint, environmental protection during times of war and military activities is addressed partially by international environmental law. Further sources are also found in areas of law such as general international law, the laws of war, human rights law and local laws of each affected country. However, this article is chiefly focused on the environment and as soon as two countries are battling it out, the issue becomes one of international concern. Thus, international environmental law is the appropriate focus here. The law of armed conflict is not very well developed in comparison to other areas of international law.

This is because there are no international institutions in place to deal with its development and implementation, or to monitor its observance. Relying on the parties to implement it during the most heated time of a country's history is a little like asking the thief to guard a jewellery store-the temptation to ignore the obligation and to overstep the mark is enormous. Military restraint is often theoretical rather than real and the promise of punishment for environmental damage does not appear to weigh heavily on the minds of military commanders. National laws dealing with environmental degradation caused by military activities during peacetime are also not very strong.

Many countries regard military activities as sacrosanct, permitting environmental destruction in the name of country protection. However, there are indications in some countries that national governments are taking their environmental responsibilities more seriously in relation to military activities and it is perhaps from these national experiences in controlling excesses that future international controls may be better modelled and implemented.

UN Treaties

Several United Nations treaties, including the Fourth Geneva Convention, the 1972 World Heritage Convention and the 1977 Environmental Modification Convention have provisions to limit the environmental impacts of war or military activities.

1977 Environmental Modification Convention

This treaty makes explicit reference to the environment. It prohibits the hostile use of environmental modification techniques having "widespread, long-lasting or severe effects." This treaty is in force and has been ratified (accepted as binding) by leading military powers.

Additional Protocol I & Protocol II

Additional Protocols I and II are amendments to the Fourth Geneva Convention. It prohibits methods of warfare intended to or expected to cause "widespread, long-term and severe damage to the natural environment", or to prejudice the health or survival of the civilian population. The understanding behind this obligation is that this is aimed directly at those capable of unleashing the use of unconventional weapons that cause biological and chemical warfare (e.g. herbicides, fungicides, chemical agents etc). Under this Protocol, parties must take care to protect the natural environment.

In addition, the Protocol provides for limits on the situations during which a warring side can make use of "works or installations containing dangerous forces" as an object of attack. This is aimed squarely at such potentially devastating sites as nuclear power plants, power plants and large dams or waterworks. Protocol II has the same limitations but in relation only to non-international armed conflict. Although both Protocols have been ratified widely, there are many major Western military powers missing from the ratification.

1972 World Heritage Convention

Although not related to armed conflict, the obligations under this convention to protect cultural or ecologically significant sites is of potential usefulness. This is especially important in relation to military activities during peacetime but may also become relevant during armed conflict to deter direct attacks on such sites. Partly this will depend on raising the awareness of soldiers during both peace and war times that there are some sites in our world of such significance that their destruction is absolutely forbidden ethically, culturally and morally.

Proposed Fifth Geneva Convention

Attempts have been made to get a specific Geneva convention dealing with protection of the environment during times of armed conflict but so far this has not been successful.

Customary international law

Customary international law also has something to say about protection of the environment during times of armed conflict and military activities.

- Under the Rio Declaration, Principle 24 provides: "States shall... respect international law providing protection for the environment in times of armed conflict and cooperate in its further development, as necessary."
- UN General Assembly Resolution 47/37 (1992) provides:

> "[D]estruction of the environment not justified by military necessity and carried out wantonly is clearly contrary to existing international law."

Case Law

In the case of the Nuclear Weapons Advisory Opinion, the ICJ found that as a matter of general international law that States must take the environment into account when deciding on what is necessary and proportionate in pursuing legitimate military objectives. The ICJ stated that there must be a respect for the environment and that this will be a factor that is weighed when considering the legitimacy or otherwise of the military actions.

Organisations

The international organisations with environmental mandates may be called upon during times of armed conflict to assist with mediating or remedying damage caused by armed conflict. Such agencies as the UN Environment Programme, the World Health Organization and the IMO will be of relevance here. The UN Security Council has also demonstrated environmental concern in deliberations on recent conflicts, for example, during the 1991 Gulf War.

UNEP and IMO were also involved in this conflict, attempting to remedy the most serious of the environmental impacts. The role of international organisations in relation to protection of the environment during armed conflict needs to be expanded and better developed. It is hoped that greater understanding by the international community of this need will compel more attention to creating this role at the international level.

3 War and Laws: Rules of International Law

The laws of war are the rules of international law that govern the conduct of war between nation-states, and are especially concerned with whether a use of force is allowed, when a state of war exists, the weapons and conduct of war, and the treatment of opponents, prisoners, neutrals, and noncombatants. They apply to the United States through enactments by Congress, the president, the Department of Defense, and specific commanders—as well as through the ratification of treaties including the Charter of the United Nations, and through those obligations of international custom binding according to the U.S. Constitution.

EARLY LIMITS ON WAR

There have been limits on the conduct of war throughout military history. These limits persist even though they are frequently violated, often without punishment. The degree to which a nation complies with them is the degree to which that nation is perceived as civilized, just as compliance on the part of a nation's military is what distinguishes it as professional. Furthermore, in the twentieth century, principles of state and personal responsibility have led to the possibility of effective criminal enforcement. Ancient laws of war dealt mostly with immunity from combat and with the commencement of hostilities.

By custom and treaties, the city-states of ancient Greece respected truces, armistices, peace treaties, alliances, flags of truce and the immunity of heralds, truces to bury the dead, surrender conditions, and the inviolability of victory monuments. The neutrality of religious temples, the Olympic games and, sometimes, third-party states were ordinarily respected. Conformity to these rules was thought necessary to be civilized, to obey the gods, and to justify similar treatment from opponents. The Roman *iustum bellum* required that attacks could not be made unless there had been a prior declaration of war or unless prior demands had not been satisfied.

Roman law did not, of course, limit conquest, although the treatment of conquered lands and people was closely regulated. Religion and manners were the sole limits on medieval warfare. Both Christianity and Islam placed limits on treatment of their faithful in war that did not apply to heretics or infidels. Both cultures evolved forms of chivalry that constrained the forms of battle and the treatment of prisoners, although such rules were often beneficial only to those with high rank. Neither could enslave a captured enemy of the same religion.

The Christian church evolved a doctrine of just war and doctrines protecting noncombatants from death in war. These doctrines were reflected in canon law but not in national legal systems, which tended to follow the view associated with Niccolò Machiavelli and Carl von Clausewitz, that war is justified as a rational instrument of national policy, even for the purpose of conquest. Various attempts were made by popes and kings to improve the treatment of civilians in surrendered towns and to limit the horrors of war by banning devious or inhumane weapons, such as the crossbow or, later, the bayonet. While these attempts yielded no means of enforcement, still, armies often followed some humanitarian customs of war for the ancient reason of ease to the army, particularly by limiting looting.

The Seventeenth through Early Twentieth Centuries

The modern law of war was invented during the age of the English colonies in North America. During the Thirty Years' War (1618–1648), Dutch jurist and ambassador Hugo Grotius published *On the Law of War and Peace*, an extended and systematic argument that nations are bound by natural law to respect other nations, that they should only engage in wars justified by grounds that would be satisfactory as claims for legally cognizable harms, and that they must respect the rights of noncombatants. This argument gained much attention but slow acceptance. During the American

Revolution, the guiding principle was not a law of war but the customs of the armies and navies of Europe; however, these customs were often violated, as with the American habit of sharpshooting enemy officers.

One custom that was honored was the execution of spies. The U.S. Army's Articles of War (1775) did, however, codify many customs, such as the requirements of uniforms and organization. By the mid-nineteenth century, there was both more formal organization of the U.S. military and greater agreement about the rules. In the Mexican War, General Winfield Scott created military commissions to prosecute U.S. soldiers and Mexican civilians for violations of the rules of war. The first codification of the law of war by the United States was General Order 100, issued at the direction of President Lincoln by General-in-Chief Henry Halleck, enacting the rules set forth in a report by Francis Lieber, a German-American law professor at Columbia College in New York.

Entitled *Instructions for the Government of Armies of the United States in the Field,* it augmented the 1775 articles but went much further, setting humane standards for the handling and exchange of prisoners, the freeing of slaves, the treatment of people and property in occupied territory, and the treatment of opposing combatants. With the notable exception of Sherman's surprise bombardment of Atlanta, the union Army appears to have complied with Lieber's Code, and the Southern armies seem to have emulated it. The U.S. Supreme Court acknowledged it as federal law in *Ex parte Vallandigham,* 68 US 243 (1863). Lieber's Code immediately influenced international law.

Translated into German by Johann Bluntschli, it formed the basis of his *Das Moderne Kriegsrecht* (1866) and was reprinted whole in most international law texts for the next fifty years. Its terms and ideas influenced the European powers at the first Geneva Convention (1864) to agree to standards of treatment for wounded prisoners of war. International conferences at The Hague in 1899 and 1907 codified much of the Code regarding the definition of combatants and treatment of neutrals into the international laws of war. The Crimean War, the U.S. Civil War, and the Franco-Prussian War all provoked codification of the laws of war. The Declaration of Paris of 1856 outlawed privateering, made naval warfare a matter for state professionals, and established clearer rules regarding blockades and the rights of neutral shippers.

The Geneva Convention of 1864 drafted the first code for the treatment of the enemy's wounded. The 1868 Declaration of Saint Petersburg announced that the only legitimate use of war is to weaken an enemy's military, and it restricted the use of small explosive or incendiary projectiles. A convention at The Hague in 1899 rejected the use of expanding bullets and asphyxiating gasses. While the great states of Europe negotiated and signed conventions, the United States was slow to do so, although it abided by these norms separately.

Only during World War I did the U.S. agree to abide by the Declaration of Paris of 1856. The U.S. did not sign the convention of 1864, the declaration of St. Petersburg, the 1899 Hague Convention, or the first Geneva Convention. Even so, the Hague Conventions of 1899 and 1907 were both derived from Lieber's *Instructions,* which the United States reissued in 1898, and in 1914 the U.S. Army first compiled *The Rules of Land Warfare,* a handbook for soldiers in battle. American interest in international regulation of law increased dramatically with the presidency of Theodore Roosevelt.

In 1904 Roosevelt called a meeting under terms of the 1899 convention, seeking to codify and extend the earlier conventions. The resulting Second Hague Peace Conference ended in 1907 with fourteen treaties, setting forth standards for the commencement of hostilities, customs and duties of warfare on land and sea, and the standards of neutrality. The U.S. signed and ratified these conventions, making them the first significant international laws of war to be law in the U.S. through treaty. This was not the only method by which the laws of war became U.S. law, however, and in *The Paquete Habana,* 175 US 677 (1900), the U.S. Supreme Court had recognized that the customary international law of war was enacted into U.S. law by the Constitution.

World Wars I and II and Their Consequences

The horrors of World War I, including the widespread violation of earlier pacts, led interwar peace conferences toward attempts at the prevention of war and the limiting of inhumane tactics and weapons, but these efforts met with only moderate success. The 1923 Hague Convention, on the rules of aerial warfare, failed to achieve sufficient ratification to come into force.

The Geneva Gas Protocol (1925) prohibited the use in war of asphyxiating, poisonous, or other gases and of bacteriological methods of warfare. The Geneva Conventions of 1929 detailed the treatment of prisoners of war and of the enemy sick and wounded. The Washington Disarmament Conference (1921–1922) and the Treaty of London of 1930 limited submarine warfare against noncombatant ships.

Despite occasional breaches, it is notable that there was widespread compliance with these treaties in the subsequent world war. The great exceptions to this tendency toward compliance were the peace treaties, commencing with the Bryan Treaties of 1913 and 1914, and the controversial Versailles Treaty of 1919, all of which promoted limits on the grounds for commencing war, including requirements for investigation, arbitration, and peaceful settlement of disputes.

This process culminated in the Kellogg-Briand Pact of 1928. Named for French foreign minister Aristide Briand and U.S. secretary of state Frank B. Kellogg, this initially bilateral treaty was eventually signed by nearly all of the nations then on earth, each renouncing war as an instrument of national policy and agreeing to settle all disputes by peaceful means.

A surfeit of qualifications allowed wars in defense of the Covenant of the League of Nations, other military treaties, the Monroe Doctrine, and for self-defense. More damning, there was no mechanism for enforcement, and the treaty was ineffective as a prior restraint to aggression. It was, however, one of the key bases for trials after World War II on charges of waging aggressive war in violation of international law. Even so, none of these instruments prevented the horrors of World War II.

At the war's end, the allies established tribunals at Nuremberg and Tokyo to try defeated leaders, soldiers, and sailors accused of war crimes, mainly crimes against peace, which included the planning, initiating, and waging of wars of aggression in violation of international law; crimes against humanity, including exterminations, deportations, and genocide; war crimes on the battlefield; and conspiring to commit the criminal acts of the first three counts.

Of twenty-four major German defendants, three were acquitted, four imprisoned from ten to twenty years, three imprisoned for life, and twelve sentenced to hang. (Two were not tried, one owing to suicide and one to physical incapacity.) Of twenty-five major defendants in Japan, two received prison terms, sixteen life imprisonment, and seven were sentenced to hang. Both tribunals adopted the "Nuremberg principle," which held the individual and not just the state liable for violations of the laws of war.

This principle was soon a maxim of military training in most developed nations. With the adoption of the United Nations Charter in 1945, almost all the nations of the world committed to the peaceful settlement of disputes and agreed to renounce war except in self-defense.

Under the sponsorship of the United Nations, additional conventions have been adopted outlawing genocide and crimes against humanity; further limiting the use of weapons of mass destruction, such as nuclear and biological weapons, and of particular inhumanity, such as exploding bullets; and further refining standards for the treatment of prisoners and the wounded.

The Geneva Conventions of 1949 refined duties to the wounded and sick on land, to the wounded, sick, and shipwrecked at sea, to prisoners of war, and to civilians. Conventions in 1954 and 1977 sought to protect property of great cultural significance and to end deliberate acts of war that harm the environment.

The Cold War and After

The Cold War between the U.S. and the Soviet Union, the Korean War, and the American war in Vietnam raised new questions about the nature and application of the laws of war. The laws of war traditionally applied only to conflicts between de jure states, and controversies arose over the legality of U.S. actions when war was not declared, as with U.S. involvement in Vietnam and Cambodia in the 1960s. The Vietnam War also led to debates over the legal definition of war as a civil war, guerrilla war, or national war; the applicability of the laws of war in the absence of a uniformed enemy; the adherence of the parties to the laws and conventions of war; and the tactics used by the belligerents, particularly the American use of carpet bombing and defoliants, which damaged noncombatant areas. Blame in these disputes was not one-sided.

The North Vietnamese and Vietcong used terrorism and refused to adhere to the 1949 Geneva Convention—they did not, for example, permit the International Red Cross to inspect prisoner-of-war camps. Greater agreement on matters of international law and the law of war followed the end of the Cold War in the 1990s. With American support, the U.N. Security Council created the International Criminal Tribunal for the Former Yugoslavia in 1993 and the International Criminal Tribunal for Rwanda in 1994.

Both tribunals applied the Nuremberg principle and actively investigated and convicted individuals, including former Yugoslav president Slobodan Milosevic, for violations of the Geneva Convention of 1949.

They were charged to investigate and prosecute genocide, violations of the laws and customs of war, and crimes against humanity. The violation of the laws and customs of war included using poisonous weapons or other weapons calculated to cause unnecessary suffering; wanton destruction of civilian areas not justified by military necessity; attack or bombardment of undefended towns; seizing or harming buildings dedicated to religion, charity, or education, or to the arts and sciences, or historic monuments and works of art and science; and plundering public or private property.

At Rome in 1998 a U.N. conference opened for signature a treaty establishing an International Criminal Court, with global jurisdiction to try individuals whose governments are unwilling to try them when they have been accused of any of various "crimes against humanity"—the definitions of which are similar to those established by the Yugoslavia and Rwanda tribunals.

To become effective the treaty needed the ratification of sixty states, a goal that was achieved in April 2002. The United States had signed in 2000, but withdrew its signature in 2002. On 11

September 2001 an attack by a terrorist organization undirected by any state, but apparently sheltered by a theocratic de facto government in Afghanistan, destroyed the towers of the World Trade Center in New York, one of the largest office buildings in history and a center of the commercial world.

The attack killed nearly three thousand people, mainly Americans but including people from many nations. The response of the United States and its allies was to demand surrender of the leaders of the attack, and, in the absence of satisfaction, to attack the armies of the Afghan government while seeking to arrest the terrorists. As much criminal enforcement as military action, this response further signaled a comprehensive change in the structure of the laws of war, which now include an element of the enforcement of international criminal law.

4 Terrorist Laws and the War on Terror

We are celebrating a hundred years of the concept of Satyagraha, which we practiced tardily during the freedom movement and those that practiced did not fiercely believe in the concept as Gandhiji did, for they knew that they were likely to be the power wielders and their faith in the concept could only be a short term strategy than an article of faith. When Gandhiji started his defiant non-violent protest against the racist South African regime, lethal force was the monopoly of state power and individuals and groups could not command sufficient lethal force to either confront or hold out against the violent assault by the State and its minions. 11th September was the day a hundred years back and that was against British imperialism in South Africa to begin with. He brought to politics a new approach which lays emphasis on ethical relationship between means and ends, a debate, which he commenced with Tolstoy, and the latter's use of passive resistance was transformed into Satyagraha a concept with insurgent potentialities. A hundred years later on the same day in the month of September 2001 Osama Bin Ladin as an act of defiance of the Super Power embarked on the unprecedented attack on the world trade center by ramming fuel filled planes on to the twin towers of the World Trade Center which led to horrendous deaths of quite a few thousand trapped in the towers.

In an interview to the CNN in the year 1997 he said: The US Government has committed acts that are extremely unjust, hideous and criminal through its support of the Israeli occupation of Palestine. Due to its subordination to the Jews, the arrogance of the United States have reached a point that they have occupied Arabia, the holiest place of the Muslims. For this and other acts of aggression and injustices, we have declared jihad against the

United States." Some described this as "morally Neanderthal pursuit of this strain of jihad". What is to be noticed is the qualitative transformation of politics and war. A handful of terrorists were able to humiliate the most powerful nation in the world. Both were acts of defiance.

One gave the world the concept of Satyagraha, non-violent protest against Imperial domination and the other terrorism as an act of defiance against impervious entrenched power and authority, hegemonic or otherwise. Against both acts of defiance the response of the State is the same.

Gandhiji's non-cooperation and civil disobedience movement were countered by extensive arrests and by the introduction of a repressive legal structure. Independent India proudly uses these very laws for dealing with democratic protests. The impervious Indian Leviathan invited, by its own governance terror as acts of defiance and pronouncedly after 9/11 at the prompting of US has been passing terrorist laws again and again. While Gandhi's legacy may not have much relevance to running a government, was the latter abiding by the Constitution or has it adopted the dual character of the British policy of criminal justice system? In dealing with terrorism the new form of defiance, which does shake ones faith in public tranquility, special laws are enacted with special procedures, special evidentiary rules which makes the Indian Penal Code look very liberal. This is what we can call the Rowlatt tradition.

After terrorism this is the tradition which has occupied the center stage of all legal and political debate in the world of Anglo Saxon jurisprudence. The war on terror was politically declared on 9/11 but officially commenced on 9/12/'94 when the United Nations General Assembly passed Resolution 49/60 delineating the measures to eliminate all forms of Terrorism. The Resolution recalled the Principles of International Law concerning Friendly Relations and Cooperation in accordance with the Charter of the United Nations, and goes on to refer to various other Resolutions including International Covenant on Civil and Political Rights and the Covenant on Economic, Social and Cultural Rights. The reference to the last two Covenants is to assure the World Public opinion that rights ensured by these Covenants will not be trampled upon and that this War on Terror shall not impede the forces of social change.

Pursuant to this, a solemn declaration was made containing twelve clauses divided into three sections simultaneously. One of the clauses calls upon the member states "to fulfil obligations under the Charter of the UN and other provisions of International law with respect to combating international terrorism and are urged to take effective and resolute measures in accordance with relevant provisions of International law and international standards of human rights for the speedy and final elimination of international terrorism."

The resolution itself is very cleverly worded. It refers to the international standard and not according to the Covenants or the clauses in the Declaration of Human Rights. If we work out among various member countries the average respect for human rights the result will haunt us with pessimism and the prospect of a better world will appear very bleak. After the attempt at destroying the Ram Temple located in the disputed site by same terrorists, who were immediately shot by the security forces Terrorism has again occupied the center stage replacing the ongoing peace process. This was followed by blasts in Varanasi, trains in Mumbai and the latest being Malegaon in Maharashtra. Along with Advani, who considers himself the author of POTA, Arun Jetley and other important leaders and the electronic media are feeling the absence of effective terrorist laws to counter the onslaught by terrorists.

They accused the UPA of hastily repealing the POTA of which the National Democratic alliance was the architect. Congress is the holding company of Indian parliamentary politics. They were the persons who authored the first terrorist legislation. Terrorism is no longer the nation's field of legislation. It is a Directive from the United Nations International that directives have to be fitted into the scheme of adversarial power play. There was an election promise that POTA will be repealed by the UPA, and therefore enacted a law to repeal POTA with a saving clause providing for review of all pending cases under POTA. No terrorist law was introduced while repealing POTA, which was not the usual the legislative practice. Such a course would have invited vociferous adverse criticism and the alliance would have cut a sorry figure.

After some time lag an existing law was amended to introduce the terrorist provisions. They verbatim copied Chapter II to VI of the POTA into Chapter IV to VII of the Unlawful Activities (Prevention) Act 1967 by amending the long title by adding after the word "association" the words "for dealing with terrorist activities'. By plagiarizing POTA they gain the advantage of avoiding litigation about the constitutional validity of the law.

There is no intellectual property right in law making. Nor is there any freedom for nations in law making in this uni-polar world after 9/11 and after we joined US in the War on Terrorism. By choosing to be with US we have surrendered our legislative independence and there is a necessity to resurrect our legislative and policy decision making process from the thralldom of Western hegemonic dominance. It would be interesting to study the steady erosion of the objectives of the UN.

It is necessary to advert to Article (1) of the United Nations Charter: "To maintain international peace and security, and to that end to take effective collective measures for the prevention and removal of threats to peace, and for the suppression of acts of aggression or other breaches of peace, and bring about by peaceful means, in conformity with the principles of justice and international law, or adjustment or settlement or situation which may lead to breach of peace". We also believe that peace is a collective human right of societies in the world. Then came the United Nations Millennium Declaration, which not only reiterated the continuing faith in the Charter with promises to improve and democratize the functioning of the World Body and its principal ancillaries.

Special provision is made to strengthening the UN. The Heads of State met between 6 & 8 September 2000. The States gathered there affirmed their faith in the Charter expressed their resolve to establish lasting peace all over the world and support all efforts to uphold the sovereign equality of all states, respect for their territorial integrity and political independence, resolution of all disputes by peaceful means and in comity with principles of justice etc. And then came the attack on the twin towers on 9/11 and thereafter the scene shifted to the Security Council and from that date to 15/1/2002 around 20 resolutions were passed to justify and for preemptive ratification of US large scale intervention into the territories of other states.

The event of 9/11 itself beggars description and analysis. As Jean Baudrillard describes it "With attack on the World Trade Center in New York, we might even be said to have before us the absolute event, the mother of all events, the pure event uniting within itself all the events that have ever taken place" The event disrupted, as he points out, the play between history and power. The tragedy also brought about rejoicings from people who were suffering from the violence generated all over the world by the hegemonic US interventions, Gore Vidal, the writer, has recorded 200 armed interventions all over the globe between 1948 to 2002 resulting in quite a huge loss of life in all these interventions. This Hegemonic power was rendered totally helpless by at the most 18 individuals with their hijacked planes felled twin towers and the victory march of globalization overnight had to change its tune to one of self-defense and defending its democratic faith. The War on Terrorism is unlike all the wars preceding it.

There were wars for imperial acquisitions; then there were ideological wars and then we experienced the Cold War, which led ultimately to the collapse of the Communist systems in the world and in this process what is called a uni-polar world led by the United States emerged and for a long time it was believed that there is no state tall enough to contest the hegemony of the US and its satellites. This belief and assumption was rudely disturbed on 9/11. The terrorist attack on 7/7 and later on 21/7 on London again informed us the character of the declared war on terrorism. There is a qualitative change in this war in which all of us are engaged in. All conventions regulating the conduct of war were rendered at one stroke null and void. This war does not respect territorial integrity or the sovereignty of nations. The invasion of alien territory is not out of disrespect of sovereignty but it is in search a wanted terrorist(s). It is asserted that there are only two options.

Either you are with the US and fight the terrorist or you are with the terrorist. In search of Osama Afghanistan was almost bombed out of existence. This is the battle cry after 9/11. This war not only erases the territorial boundaries which define the sovereignty of states, but this war brings abut a change in our understanding of the concept of sovereignty. This war on terrorism is forcing a change in our criminal legal structure and this specter is leading us to terrorize ourselves, by introducing statutes, which looks upon Rule of Law as inconvenient to carry on this war.

As happened in London on 7/7 an angry and frenzied police force would pump bullets into an innocent person and the angry protest would lead to a half-hearted apology for an act, which is hardly qualitatively different from the act of the terrorists. The state of continued belligerence will be toward the Muslim population around the world and they will be marked as suspects and in all further attacks the articulate among them will be rounded up. The state of war that comes into existence will be genocidal and for the present the Muslims as a religious community will continue to be targeted. We need not look at it as the United States presented it to the world. We need not approve of Huntingdon's thesis that what we are witnessing is a clash of civilizations. Almost all public utility services are privatized. State is distancing itself slowly but surely from peoples problems and therefore from the people. The World Bank or the US stipulates legislation.

Foreign policy decisions by the Government are taken under dictation or in consultation with the US. If FDI role is made unrestricted the picture will be complete. When we entered our era of independence we were confronted with the Cold War and the nations of the world were presented with the choice of either to be with the Western bloc or the Soviet Bloc.

On 9 December 1958 Pandit Nehru who played a leading role in enunciating the policy of nonalignment and for campaigning for it set down what it meant "It is said that there are only two ways of action in the world today, and that one must take this way or that. I repudiate this attitude of mind. If we accept that there are two ways, then we have to join the Cold War – if not an actual military bloc, at least a mental military bloc. I do not see why the possession of great armed might or great financial power should necessarily lead to right decisions or a right mental outlook. The fact that I have got the atom bomb with me does not make me any the more intelligent, wiser or more peaceful than I otherwise might have been. I say this with all respect to the great countries. But I am not prepared even as an individual, much less as a Foreign Minister of this country to give up my right to independent judgment to anybody else in other countries. This is the essence of our policy." We have after the collapse of the Soviet Union what emerged was the US domination and the general indebtedness of the governments of all the countries to the International Financial Institutions, mainly funded by the USA.

We are politically emasculated and therefore unable to chalk out an independent line for ourselves. The United Nations, as it is constituted is unequal in its representative capacities as also in terms of power relationship inter se. To make the UN more responsive and democratic seems to be impossible. The broad objective of the Charter and the Declaration of Human Rights remain rhetoric because many of the members of the World Body are themselves not democracies and many have very weak claims to represent its people. There is the added difficulty of restructuring the Body by reforms for the power to bring about amendments for restructuring the Body can be vetoed by one or the other members of the Security Council. The United Nations is entrusted with three tasks. Two of these are inter national responsibilities. To mediate between states with opposing interests and the second is to restrain the members from violating the rights of its citizens. These tasks have been imperfectly performed. The third task that has been assigned to this Body is the global responsibility to represent the common interests of all the people of the world. It is equipped to discharge the first of its aforementioned obligation. In context of Terrorism it is the global responsibility to ensure peace and security to all the peoples of the world.

The existing institutions set up by the UN will have to be innovatively used. The General Assembly comprising of 186 member states should undertake the responsibility of chalking a 'way out' of this 'either/or' impasse. This responsibility the member state should undertake in the General Assembly defying the Security Council, if necessary and set out an independent approach to the problem posed by the Terrorists. Such an approach would enable the General Assembly or the collective of the member states who are gathered in the United Nations keep the channels for a dialogue with them open. Octavio Paz, sees history as dialogue. Yet time and time again this dialogue has been broken off, drowned out by the din of violence or interrupted by the monologue of ranting leaders. Violence exacerbates differences and keeps both parties from speaking and hearing; monologue denies the existence of the other; dialogue allows differences to remain yet at the same time creates an area in which the areas of otherness coexist and interweave.

Since dialogues eliminate the ultimate, it is a denial of absolutes and their despotic pretensions to totality: we are relative, and what we say and hear is relative. But this relativism is not surrender: in order for there to be dialogue, we must affirm what we are and at the same time recognize the other in all his irreducible difference. Dialogue keeps us from denying ourselves and from denying the humanity of our adversary." Perhaps terrorist violence is the only way left to people to fight hegemonic power whether it be Western or Islamic. Later, whether it be domestic or international. To dismiss them as criminals or people having ambition to proselytize the world to Islam appears to be an unfounded inference. It may still be possible to hold a dialogue with terror. One sure method appears to be of holding a dialogue is, to hold a dialogue with the people whom it assumes to represent and shall for the moment call them its constituency. We should dialogue with the constituency, the terrorist assumes he represents and that can be done only when we accord them an equal status. allow them the growth, we are fighting to acquire for ourselves, if we make them feel that they are participating partners in the socio-economic processes they will grow in the main stream as intellectuals as academics as entrepreneurs.

All these years we have not allowed "the other people" the space to grow in the main stream and so they grew into Dawood Ibrahim, Tiger Memon, Chota Shakeel and the like of them in various gradations. Relieve them of the reason to turn (to) terrorist and try to build up a plural society where equality reigns in all walks and all facets of life. Penal statutes cannot remedy social imbalances. Despite the presence of penal laws social imbalances trigger political turbulence and intelligent governance consists in addressing the reasons for these social imbalances.

5 Kautilya's Arthashastra on War and Diplomacy in Ancient India

Kautilya was the key adviser to the Indian king Chandragupta Maurya (c. 317-293 B.C.E.), who first united the Indian subcontinent in empire. Written about 300 B.C., Kautilya's *Arthashastra* was a science of politics intended to teach a wise king how to govern. In this work, Kautilya offers wide-ranging and truly fascinating discussions on war and diplomacy, including his wish to have his king become a world conqueror, his analysis of which kingdoms are natural allies and which are inevitable enemies, his willingness to make treaties he knew he would break, his doctrine of silent war or a war of assassination against an unsuspecting king, his approval of secret agents who killed enemy leaders and sowed discord among them, his view of women as weapons of war, his use of religion and superstition to bolster his troops and demoralize enemy soldiers, the spread of disinformation, and his humane treatment of conquered soldiers and subjects.

Kautilya's *Arthashastra* was one of the greatest political books of the ancient world. Max Weber recognized this. "Truly radical 'Machiavellianism,' in the popular sense of that word," Weber said in his famous lecture "Politics as a Vocation," "is classically expressed in Indian literature in the *Arthashastra* of Kautilya (written long before the birth of Christ, ostensibly in the time of Chandragupta [Maurya]): compared to it, Machiavelli's *The Prince* is harmless." Although Kautilya proposed an elaborate welfare state in domestic politics, something that has been called a socialized monarchy, he proved willing to defend the general good of this monarchy with harsh measures.

A number of authors have explored these domestic policies, but very few scholars have focused on Kautilya's discussions of war and diplomacy. And yet, his analyses are fascinating and far-reaching, such as his wish to have his king become a world conqueror, his evaluation of which kingdoms are natural allies and which are inevitable enemies, his willingness to make treaties that he knew he would break, his doctrine of silent war or a war of assassination and contrived revolt against an unsuspecting king, his approval of secret agents who killed enemy leaders and sowed discord among them, his view of women as weapons of war, his use of religion and superstition to bolster his troops and demoralize enemy soldiers, his employment of the spread of disinformation, and his humane treatment of conquered soldiers and subjects.

HISTORICAL BACKGROUND

Kautilya was the key adviser to—and the genius of the strategy undertaken by—the Indian king Chandragupta Maurya (c. 317-293 B.C.), who defeated the Nanda kings (several related kings trying unsuccessfully to rule India together), stopped the advance of Alexander the Great's successors, and first united most of the Indian subcontinent in empire. Kautilya—sometimes called chancellor or prime minister to Chandragupta, something like a Bismarck —composed his *Arthashastra,* or "science of politics," to show a wise king how to defeat his enemies and rule on behalf of the general good.

He was not modest in his claims as to how much he helped Chandragupta, noting "This science has been composed by him [Kautilya], who... quickly regenerated the science and the weapon and [conquered] the earth that was under control of the Nanda kings." Just after Alexander's death in 323 B.C., Chandragupta and Kautilya began their conquest of India by stopping the Greek invaders.

In this effort they assassinated two Greek governors, Nicanor and Philip, a strategy to keep in mind when I later examine Kautilya's approval of assassination. "The assassinations of the Greek governors," wrote Radha Kumud Mookerji, "are not to be looked upon as mere accidents." By taking much of western India (the Punjab and the Sindh) from the Greeks and concluding a treaty with Seleucus (Alexander the Great's Greek heir to western

India), Chandragupta and Kautilya succeeded in bringing together almost all of the Indian subcontinent.

As a result, Chandragupta was, and is now, considered the first unifier of India and the first genuine emperor or king of India. The Mauryan Empire established by Chandragupta and continued by his son Bindusara (c. 293-268 B.C.)—whom Kautilya also advised—and by his grandson Ashoka (c. 268-232 B.C.) was, and still is, astonishing.

With a population of about fifty million people, the Mauryan Empire was larger than the Mughal Empire two thousand years later and even larger than the British Empire in India, extending in fact all the way to the border of Persia and from Afghanistan to Bengal. (The map on the previous page shows the extent of the Mauryan Empire under Ashoka.) Pliny—borrowing from Megasthenes, the ambassador of Seleucus to Chandragupta—wrote that Chandragupta's army totaled about six hundred thousand infantry, thirty thousand calvary, eight thousand chariots, and nine thousand elephants.

Chandragupta's capital was Pataliputra, which he apparently seized from the Nandas sometime between 324 and 322 B.C. Pataliputra was probably the largest city in the world at that time, a city eight miles long and a mile and one-half wide, with 570 towers and sixty-four gates, all surrounded by a moat six hundred feet wide and forty-five feet deep. Also protecting the city were wooden walls—stone was very scarce—with slits to be used by archers. Pataliputra "was about twice as large as Rome under Emperor Marcus Aurelius." Chandragupta Maurya consolidated an empire and passed it down intact to his son Bindusara, about whom we know little, and to his grandson Ashoka.

Some argue that the extreme measures that we will see Kautilya advocate, and some of which Chandragupta surely must have employed, were necessary to bring order and the rule of law out of chaos, making possible the emergence of Ashoka, who was widely regarded as one of the finest kings in world history. M. V. Krishna Rao contends, "As a result of the progressive secularisation of society due to the innovations contemplated by [the *Arthashastra*] and the administration of Chandragupta, the country was prepared for the reception of the great moral transformation ushered in by A's-oka and his administration." K. A. Nilakanta Sastri has written, in a fairly typical statement, "The reign of A's-oka forms the brightest page in the history of India." After witnessing the suffering that occurred during his invasion of the kingdom of Kalinga, Ashoka turned toward Buddhism and nonviolence.

He declared that in the future he would conquer only by morality or by *dhamma*—which is a Prakrit word, often replaced by the more familiar Sanskrit word *dharma*—a word meaning right conduct, duty, religion, law, social justice, and responsibility. *Dhamma,* or *dharma,* was Ashoka's all-encompassing principle. In his First Pillar Edict, he announced, "For this is my principle: to protect through *Dhamma,* to administer affairs according to *Dhamma,* to please the people with *Dhamma,* to guard the empire with *Dhamma.*" What specific reforms did Ashoka make in his wish to conquer the world by morality or *dharma*?

These included tolerance and respect for others, even those with different religions and backgrounds, or, as the Twelfth Rock Edict states, "other sects ought to be duly honoured in every case"; love of the family; compassion, which includes respect for others, kindness even toward slaves and prisoners, "reverence toward elders, and gentleness to animals"; honesty; liberality toward relatives, friends, and neighbours; moderation and self-control, or as the Seventh Rock Edict says, "but even one who practises great liberality but does not possess self-control, purity of mind, gratitude, and firm devotion, is very mean"; a system of social welfare, including medical centers for human beings and animals, the construction of roads for good communication, along with the digging of wells and the planting of trees for shade, and so on, all policies that he thought best carried out by the centralized administration of government; an unusual concern for the poor in rural areas, a concern that led him to tour the countryside frequently; and *ahimsa* or nonviolence, which prohibited both the slaughter and sacrifice of animals. According to V. R. R. Dikshitar, in the Sixth Rock Edict Ashoka said he was promoting *dharma* for "the common good of the world," and in the Tenth Rock Edict, Ashoka stated plainly that he put forth the doctrine of *dharma* for "happiness in the next world." Many Indian historians are proud to embrace Kautilya's *Arthashastra* as a practical book of rugged political realism—instead of the impotent idealism of, say, Plato—that actually shaped history.

D. D. Kosambi notes, "The Greeks make excellent reading; the Indian treatise [*Arthashastra*] worked infinitely better in practice for its own time and place." Ram Sharan Sharma maintains, "Kautilya furnishes us as full and complete [a] definition of the state as was possible in ancient times. The Greek thinkers hardly discuss the constituent elements of the state." Kautilya's *Arthashastra* is thus a book of political realism, a book analyzing how the political world does work and not very often stating how it ought to work, a book that frequently discloses to a king what calculating and sometimes brutal measures he must carry out to preserve the state and the common good.

One important question lurks in discussions of Kautilya. Were the harsh actions he often recommended necessary for the common good of India? Did Chandragupta and Bindusara have to act in a violent and sometimes brutal fashion to defend India, bring order, and establish unity? With the old order crumbling, with the Nanda kings having proved cruel and inept, with enemies on India's borders, and with the threat of anarchy within, were not Kautilya's harsh measures necessary and have not his critics failed "to note the nature of the times in which he lived"? In defense of Chandragupta and Kautilya, Bhargava says, "all kinds of means might have been considered necessary to restore peace with honour." Put more bluntly, did India need the harsh measures of Kautilya the realist in order to enjoy the luxury of Ashoka the idealist?

KAUTILYA AND HIS "SCIENCE OF POLITICS"

R. P. Kangle translates the word *Arthashastra* as "science of politics," a treatise to help a king in "the acquisition and protection of the earth." Others translate *Arthashastra* in slightly different ways: A. L. Basham says it is a "treatise on polity," Kosambi emphasizes the economic importance of the word in calling it a "science of material gain," and G. P. Singh labels it a "science of polity." I happen to prefer to translate *Arthashastra* as a "science of political economy," but however one translates the word,

Kautilya claimed to be putting forth what Heinrich Zimmer rightly calls "timeless laws of politics, economy, diplomacy, and war." Because he was offering his readers a science with which they could master the world, Kautilya believed that having a passive stance toward the world—for example, trusting in fate or relying on superstition—was outlandish.

"One trusting in fate," noted Kautilya, "being devoid of human endeavour, perishes." His philosophy called for action, not resignation: "The object slips away from the foolish person, who continuously consults the stars;... what will the stars do?" In urging the king to rely on science and not the precepts of religion, Kautilya separated political thought from religious speculation. Like Thomas Hobbes, Kautilya believed the goal of science was power.

His statements "Power is (possession of) strength" and "strength changes the mind" show that Kautilya sought the power to control not only outward behaviour, but also the thoughts of one's subjects and enemies. Probably his science could not promise all of that, but the power offered by this science was extensive: "An arrow, discharged by an archer, may kill one person or may not kill (even one); but intellect operated by a wise man would kill even children in the womb." Having as his first and primary goal to "destroy the enemies and protect his own people," the king could certainly accomplish this with Kautilya's science; in fact, "he, who is well-versed in the science of politics,... plays, as he pleases, with kings tied by the chain of his intellect." Beyond protecting the kingdom, the king who uses Kautilya's science can bring to himself and his subjects the three goods of life—"material gain, spiritual good and pleasures." Wealth is the key to raising successful armies and having a peaceful and just kingdom, and Kautilya's political science brings wealth: "The source of the livelihood of men is wealth, in other words, the earth inhabited by men. The science which is the means of the attainment and protection of that earth is the Science of Politics."

Put another way, Kautilya's book is the greatest weapon a king can have, and political science is more important than—or at least brings about—wealth, armies, and conquests. In the world of international politics, it is only "natural" that nations interact with each other through "dissension and force." A political realist typically argues that there will always be conflict in international relations and, in effect, rule by the strongest. Kautilya was writing about 300 B.C.E., a century after Thucydides composed his *History of the Peloponnesian War* and several decades after the Sophists Callicles and Thrasymachus said to Plato that rule by the stronger was "natural." Kautilya, in the boldest of his promises, claimed that one who knows his science of politics can conquer the world, that "one possessed of personal qualities, though ruling over a small territory... conversant with (the science of) politics, does conquer the entire earth, never loses."

There is no modesty here. Kautilya's science brings an abundance of wealth and details correct strategies in politics and war. With this science anyone can succeed: "And winning over and purchasing men of energy, those possessed of might, even women, children, lame and blind persons, have conquered the world." Kautilya did not see this conquest as something unjust. A king who carries out his duties, rules according to law, metes out only just punishment, applies the law equally "to his son and his enemy," and protects his subjects not only goes "to heaven" but "would conquer the earth up to its four ends."

Whereas Kautilya did not talk of glory, I do believe he was thinking of something we might call "greatness," but this would come only with social justice and the morally correct ordering of the world. The king, "after conquering the world, should enjoy it divided into *varnas* [classes, sometimes castes] and *asramas* [Hindu stages of life] in accordance with his own duty." Kautilya apparently meant by the phrase "conquering the world" something like conquering up to what Indians regarded as the natural borders of India, from the Himalayas all the way south to the Indian Ocean, and from the Arabian Sea to the Bay of Bengal, although Kautilya said, "the region of the sovereign ruler extends northwards between the Himavat and the sea, one thousand *yojanas* [about nine thousand miles!] in extent across." As Kangle puts it, in the Indian tradition, the world conqueror, or *cakrava-rtin,* was not one who conquered "regions beyond the borders of India." In short, India did not include the land of "barbarians" or *mlecchas,* those outside of Indian culture. *Cakra* means wheel; it is possible that the Indian concept of the world conqueror involved someone who ruled as far as his chariots could roll, without obstacles or opposition. At any rate, surely Dikshitar is correct in saying that this ideal of a world conqueror in ancient India led to an "imperialism" that was "one of the causes of chronic warfare," although the Mauryan dynasty did bring comparative peace for more than a century. As Narasingha Prosad Sil notes, "For Kautilya a world conquest is the true foundation for world peace."

DIPLOMACY AND FOREIGN POLICY AS EXTENSIONS OF WARFARE

As a political realist, Kautilya assumed that every nation acts to maximize power and self-interest, and therefore moral principles or obligations have little or no force in actions among nations. While it is good to have an ally, the alliance will last only as long as it is in that ally's as well as one's own self-interest, because "an ally looks to the securing of his own interests in the event of simultaneity of calamities and in the event of the growth of the enemy's power." Whether one goes to war or remains at peace depends entirely upon the self-interest of, or advantage to, one's kingdom: "War and peace are considered solely from the point of view of profit."

One keeps an ally not because of good will or moral obligation, but because one is strong and can advance one's own self-interest as well as the self-interest of the ally, for "when one has an army, one's ally remains friendly, or (even) the enemy becomes friendly." Because nations always act in their political, economic, and military self-interest, even times of peace have the potential to turn abruptly into times of war, allies into enemies, and even enemies into allies. Burton Stein notes correctly that Kautilya was describing a foreign policy not of a great empire like that of the Mauryas, but of small warring states in incessant conflict, such as India experienced before the Mauryan empire. Kautilya probably assumed that peaceful empires cannot last forever, and that conflict among smaller states is more common in history. For Kautilya, this principle of foreign policy—that nations act in their political, economic, and military self-interest—was a timeless truth of his science of politics, or *Arthashastra*.

He did not believe that nations never act in an altruistic manner—indeed, Kautilya advocated humanitarian acts that also coincided with one's self-interest—but he did believe that one must assume, if entrusted with political or military power, that one's neighbours will eventually act in their own interests. Put another way, one would be betraying one's own people if one did not assume a worst-case scenario. A nation forced to rely on the kindness of neighboring states is weak and, unless it can change rapidly, doomed to destruction. This same assumption can be seen in the work of Thucydides, who discussed foreign policy a century before Kautilya, and in the thoughts of the Chinese Legalist Han Fei Tzu, who wrote about fifty years after Kautilya's *Arthashastra.* Kautilya is most famous for outlining the so-called Mandala theory of foreign policy, in which immediate neighbours are considered as enemies, but any state on the other side of a neighboring state is regarded as an ally, or, the enemy of my enemy is my friend.

Imagine a series of states to one's west, and then number them starting with oneself. States numbered 1, 3, 5, 7, and so on will likely be friends, whereas states 2, 4, 6, 8, and so on will probably be enemies. (The same thing can be done with concentric circles, which would look more like a mandala, but it is difficult to envision these circles as states.) Kautilya put this basic principle in a number of different ways, but most simply as, "One with immediately proximate territory is the natural enemy." Elsewhere he stated this Mandala theory of foreign policy in more detail: "With respect to the middle king [he himself], the third and the fifth constituents are friendly elements. The second, the fourth, and the sixth are unfriendly elements." Kautilya assumed that he lived in a world of foreign relations in which one either conquered or suffered conquest.

He did not say to himself, "Prepare for war, but hope for peace," but instead, "Prepare for war, and plan to conquer." Diplomacy was just another weapon used in the prolonged warfare that was always either occurring or being planned for. After analyzing a king's unique configuration of potential enemies and allies, Kautilya then coldly calculated how that king must think and act. "The king, endowed with personal excellences and those of his material constituents, the seat of good policy, is the would-be conqueror. Encircling him on all sides, with territory immediately next to his is the constituent called the enemy. In the same manner, one with territory separated by one (other territory) is the constituent called the ally." This much just repeats the principles of foreign policy discussed above, but then notice how Kautilya regarded neighboring states: "A neighboring prince possessed of the excellences of an enemy is the foe; one in calamity is vulnerable; one without support or with weak support is *fit to be exterminated*; in the reverse case, fit to be harassed or weakened. These are the different types of enemies." When Kautilya wrote of "exterminating" an enemy, he meant killing only the leaders.

As we will see in more detail later, he thought the best policy toward ordinary soldiers and subjects was to treat them well and recruit them. In his excellent discussion of Kautilya's Mandala theory of foreign policy, Singh continues by correctly stating that this is ancient India's most notable contribution to political theory. Although Singh analyzes Kautilya's theory well, he makes a mistake in labeling the Mandala theory an argument based on the doctrine of the balance of power. Kautilya, in fact, was not offering a modern balance of power argument. In the twentieth century, international relations theorists have defended the doctrine of the balance of power, because equally armed nations will supposedly deter each other, and therefore no war will result. One does find this argument occasionally in Kautilya: "In case the gains [of two allies of equal strength] are equal, there should be peace; if unequal, fight," or, "the conqueror should march if superior in strength, otherwise stay quiet."

Whereas these balance of power theorists suggest that a nation arm itself so that it can ensure peace, Kautilya wanted his king to arm the nation in order to find or create a weakness in the enemy and conquer, even to conquer the world, or at least the subcontinent of India. In reading his *Arthashastra,* we find no moral considerations other than a king doing what is right for his own people. Rather, we discover merely what Kautilya regarded as the nature of power. The king, he wrote, "should march when by marching he would be able to weaken or exterminate the enemy." And Kautilya assumed that every other state would act in a like manner because "even the equal who has achieved his object tends to be stronger, and when augmented in power, untrustworthy; prosperity tends to change the mind." Just as did Thucydides, Kautilya regarded a request for negotiations as a sign of weakness, indeed a desperate act of a weak nation trying to survive: "A weaker king may bargain with a stronger king with the offer of a gain equal to his troops, when he is in a calamity or is addicted to what is harmful [that is, women, wine, or gambling] or is in trouble.

He with whom the bargain is made should fight if capable of doing harm to him; else he should make the pact." Whereas Carl von Clausewitz said that war is just an extension of domestic politics, Kautilya argued that diplomacy is really a subtle act of war, a series of actions taken to weaken an enemy and gain advantages for oneself, all with an eye toward eventual conquest. A nation's foreign policy should always consist of preliminary movements toward war: "In this way, the conqueror should establish in the rear and in front, a circle (of kings) in his own interest.... And in the entire circle, he should ever station envoys and secret agents, becoming a friend of the rivals, maintaining secrecy when striking again and again. The affairs of one, who cannot maintain secrecy,... undoubtedly perish, like a broken boat in the ocean." In Kautilya's foreign policy, even during a time of diplomacy and negotiated peace, a king should still be "striking again and again" in secrecy. Consider some of the measures Kautilya supported during times of peace.

If opposed by an alliance of nations, a king should secretly "sow dissensions" within the alliance until one or more of the parties in the alliance becomes weak. When he has weakened a neighbor, the king "should violate the treaty." Or, in another example, "The wise (conqueror), making one neighboring king fight with another neighboring king, should seize the territory of another, cutting off his party on all sides." In Kautilya's view, two kinds of kingdoms confront any king—those weak kingdoms fit to be exterminated and those strong kingdoms that, over a long period of time, one can only secretly harass and hope to weaken. He advised, "As between an enemy fit to be harassed and an enemy fit to be exterminated, acquisition of land from an enemy fit to be exterminated is preferable. For, the king fit to be exterminated, being without support or with a weak support, is deserted by his subjects when, on being attacked, he wishes to flee taking with him the treasury and the army." It is best to attack an enemy that is "disunited," rather than an enemy in which the subjects have organized themselves into "bands." During times of peace and negotiations, Kautilya wanted spies and secret agents to exploit the divisions within a country. Most countries, he maintained, have four kinds of unhappy subjects—the enraged, the frightened, the greedy, and the proud. Secret agents can widen and deepen these divisions by inciting these four types of people to act against their king. The opposing king "should win over the seducible in the enemy's territories by means of conciliation and gifts and those not seducible by means of dissension and force." Because a king abides by a treaty only for so long as it is advantageous, Kautilya regarded all allies as future conquests when the time is ripe.

He wrote, for example, "That ally who remains common to the enemy (and himself), he should divide that rogue from the enemy (and) when divided, exterminate him, thereafter (exterminate) the enemy." Kautilya also sought to take a nation trying to remain neutral or "indifferent" and secretly provoke war between that nation and a neighboring kingdom, until the neutral nation sought his help. Then Kautilya's king could "place him under (his) obligations." Kautilya himself had no moral qualms about breaking obligations or trust: "That ally who might do harm or who, though capable, would not help in times of trouble, he should exterminate him, when trustingly, he comes within his reach." Because foreign policy is just an extension of a nation's wars, the goal of foreign policy is not to end wars, but rather to ward off defeats and to make sure one is successful in subsequent warfare. For Kautilya, all ambassadors were potential spies with diplomatic immunity. Indeed, he wrote an entire section about how to "fight with the weapon of diplomacy."

War

Kautilya thought there was a "science" of warfare, presumably part of a larger science of politics. The Commandant of the Army, he suggested, should be "trained in the science of all (kinds of) fights and weapons, (and) renowned for riding on elephants, horses or in chariots." Just as Machiavelli advised his prince to attend to matters of warfare constantly, so did Kautilya advise the king not to leave military matters entirely to others: "Infantry, cavalry, chariots and elephants should carry out practice in the arts outside (the city) at sun-rise.... The king should constantly attend to that, and should frequently inspect their arts." Just as the king's agents spied on officials in the state bureaucracy, so too must the king have spies to assess the loyalty of soldiers. What greater threat is there to a king than having a military coup remove him from power? Kautilya recommended that "secret agents, prostitutes, artisans and actors as well as elders of the army should ascertain with diligence, the loyalty or disloyalty of soldiers." In his section on foreign policy, Kautilya wrote a startling sentence: "Of war, there is open war, concealed war and silent war."

Open war is obvious, and concealed war is what we call guerrilla warfare, but silent war is a kind of fighting that no other thinker I know of has discussed. Silent war is a kind of warfare with another kingdom in which the king and his ministers—and unknowingly, the people—all act publicly as if they were at peace with the opposing kingdom, but all the while secret agents and spies are assassinating important leaders in the other kingdom, creating divisions among key ministers and classes, and spreading propaganda and disinformation. According to Kautilya, "Open war is fighting at the place and time indicated; creating fright, sudden assault, striking when there is error or a calamity, giving way and striking in one place, are types of concealed warfare; that which concerns secret practices and instigations through secret agents is the mark of silent war." In silent warfare, secrecy is paramount, and, from a passage quoted earlier, the king can prevail only by "maintaining secrecy when striking again and again." This entire concept of secret war was apparently original with Kautilya. Open warfare, Kautilya declared, is "most righteous," but he was willing to use any and all kinds of warfare to achieve consolidation and expansion of the kingdom.

There is no question of morality here—other than the general good of one's kingdom—but only of strategy. Kautilya advised the king that "When he is superior in troops, when secret instigations are made (in the enemy's camp), when precautions are taken about the season, (and) when he is on land suitable to himself, he should engage in an open fight. In the reverse case, (he should resort to) concealed fighting." How different all this is from the image of war, certainly exaggerated, found in the Hindu epics, the *Mahabharata,* or the *Ramayana,* of the central figure being the great hero in the chariot who frightened all before him. In Book 12, Kautilya faced the situation in which one rules a weak kingdom and is about to be attacked by a stronger king.

He maintained that "there are three kings who attack: the righteous conqueror, the greedy conqueror and the demoniacal conqueror." Whereas one can satisfy a righteous conqueror simply by submitting to his rule, one must surrender "land and goods" as well as money in order to satisfy a greedy conqueror. The demoniacal conqueror, however, will stop only when he has seized "land, goods, sons, wives and life." (Kautilya apparently saw himself as advising a righteous conqueror, although he did seek some tribute from defeated peoples.) A weak king must give up everything if it is inevitable, but he must find a way to survive to fight another day, preserving "his body, not wealth; for, what regret can there be for wealth that is impermanent?"

However, Kautilya did not advocate giving in to a conqueror without countermeasures and recommended that the king use "diplomatic or concealed warfare"; attempt to conciliate his enemy with gifts; direct secret agents to wield "weapons, poison or fire" to destroy the enemy's fort or camp; instruct secret agents to promote a coup by a "pretender from his family or a prince in disfavour"; send the demoniacal king listless elephants, which had been poisoned; give to the enemy king treasonable or alien troops; surrender to an entirely different king and give him all but the capital city; have secret agents instigate a revolt among the subjects of the enemy king, "employ assassins and poison-givers"; use an astrologer to persuade a "high officer" of the enemy king to try a coup; command secret agents to declare that the Regent of the king is about to take power, while the agents kill leaders at night and blame the murders on the Regent of the enemy king; use secret agents in the countryside to protest oppression of the enemy king's bureaucracy and kill agents of the king hoping to start a revolt; or finally, set fire to palaces and stores of grain and blame this on the Regent of the enemy king. Kautilya often advocated using women as weapons of war.

He certainly regarded women as a source of satisfaction for troops at war, writing that when setting up camp for the army, "courtesans (should be encamped) along the highways." And Kautilya certainly saw women as an addictive source of pleasure, worse than wine or gambling, that a good king must enjoy only in moderation: "Deliverance is possible in gambling, without deliverance is addiction to women. Failure to show himself, aversion from work, absence of material good and loss of spiritual good by allowing the right time to pass, weakness in administration and addiction to drink (result from addiction to women)." Precisely because women are such a powerful addiction, a king can use them against an enemy; for example, if a king is trying to undermine a ruling oligarchy, he "should make chiefs of the ruling council infatuated with women possessed of great beauty and youth. When passion is roused in them, they should start quarrels by creating belief (about their love) in one and by going to another." A woman supposedly in love with one leader should go to another, profess her love for him, urge him to murder the first leader, and "then she should proclaim, 'My lover has been killed by so and so.'" Obviously such tactics create mistrust among leaders of an oligarchy and also bring about the death of key enemies.

In the chapters about how a weak king can stave off disastrous conquest by a stronger king, Kautilya again turned, as just one possible tactic among many, to women as weapons of war, stating that "keepers of prostitutes should make the (enemy's) army chiefs infatuated with women possessed of great beauty and youth. When many or two of the chiefs feel passion for one woman, assassins should create quarrels among them." Secret agents can destroy high officers in the enemy army either with poison or with "love-winning medicines." Speaking of justice to an enemy about to conquer is the last tactic of the weak, just as Thucydides showed in his recreation of the debate about Melos. In Thucydides's *History of the Peloponnesian War,* the Melians try to talk about justice and fair play when facing the prospect of conquest by the Athenians, who contend that such arguments are the last, desperate tactic of those facing defeat, which the Melians "know as well as we do." The Athenians tell the Melians "that, when these matters are discussed by practical people, the standard of justice depends on the equality of power to compel and that in fact the strong do what they have the power to do and the weak accept what they have to accept."

After that both the Melians and the Athenians debate only what is in the self-interest of Athens. Similarly, willing to try all tactics, even desperate ones, Kautilya made up a powerful speech to be given by a weak king to the king about to conquer, a speech offering a mixture of moral exhortation and arguments based on the self-interest of the conqueror. In this speech, Kautilya depicted an envoy saying to the conquering king that he should accept a treaty and "pay regard to [his] spiritual and material well-being"; that conquering a kingdom willing to surrender on reasonable terms is an "impious act"; that battle is not in the conquering king's self-interest, since "to fight with brave men who have given up all hope of life is a rash deed" and the conqueror will lose troops and "material good"; that such a conquest will only unite his enemies all the more; that the conquering king's enemies are only waiting for him to be weakened in order to attack; that he himself is risking death; that war itself in which men on each side die is "an impious act"; and that he should not listen to "enemies masquerading as friends" who are giving him false advice as to his real self-interest.

In much the same way as Thucydides, only more dramatically, Kautilya demonstrated the realities of diplomacy and war as well as the ineffectiveness of moral pleas when confronted by a superior power. Machiavelli longed for the legions of ancient Rome; Kautilya wanted legions, but he wanted them preceded by elephants, which acted in the ancient world a bit like modern tanks. So valuable were they that Kautilya wrote, "destruction of an enemy's forces is principally dependent on elephants."

As shown earlier, Kautilya considered the treasury most valuable in raising an army, procuring equipment (including elephants), and preparing for war. After the treasury and the army, Kautilya focused on the importance of the fort, on which depends "the treasury, the army, silent war, restraint of one's own party, use of armed forces, receiving allied troops, and warding off enemy troops and forest tribes. And in the absence of a fort, the treasury will fall into the hands of enemies.... those with forts are not exterminated." Kautilya was inconsistent in ranking the importance of the treasury, the army, and forts, but it seems that the people, or a popular army, are the most important of all.

As he put it, "one should seek a fortress with men." Well before Machiavelli defended a republican army, well before Mao Zedong defended a people's war as invincible, Kautilya urged the king to be popular with the people and rely on the countryside. "If weak in might, [a king] should endeavor to secure the welfare of his subjects. The countryside is the source of all undertakings; from them comes might." The "undertakings" of forts, the treasury, and the army all depend ultimately on the people of the countryside, where are found "bravery, firmness, cleverness and large numbers."

Kautilya here was cautiously making a revolution in warfare, relying not quite as much on the warrior class of *kshatriyas*. India was divided into four classes or castes (*varnas*): *brahmins* or priests; *kshatriyas* or warriors and rulers; *vaishyas* or farmers and traders; and *sh-udras* or labourers. The *Dharmas-utras*, or law codes, writtenbefore Kautilya, urged an army of *kshatriyas* and, in an emergency, also *brahmins* (priests) and *vaishyas* (farmers or merchants). Kautilya had no use for *brahmin* troops—"by prostration, an enemy may win over Brahmana troops"—but he liked the energy, numbers, and strength of *sh-udras*, agricultural labourers treated much like serfs.

Kautilya's praise of ordinary men from the lower two *varnas* was unusual in the ancient world. He wrote, "As between land with the support of a fort and one with the support of men, the one with the support of men is preferable. For, a kingdom is that which has men. Without men, like a barren cow, what could it yield?" Says Sharma, "Kautilya alone holds that the army made up of vaishyas and sudras is important." Kautilya apparently believed that an army of *kshatriyas* was best; warriors were supposed to find their "highest duty and pleasure" by dying in battle. Megasthenes, a Greek ambassador to Chandragupta

Maurya's court, suggested that as much as one-fifth of the population under Chandragupta's empire were warriors or *kshatriyas*. In addition, Kautilya clearly argued that sections of the army should consist "mostly of persons from the same region, caste or profession."

Using a little common sense, we can see that he is suggesting that men of an army should know one another, that an army of friends fighting side by side is the most difficult to defeat. On the subject of the king's location during battle, for example, he wrote: "A bare army, without standards, consisting of warriors related as fathers, sons and brothers, should be the place for the king. An elephant or a chariot should be the vehicle for the king, guarded by cavalry." (Kautilya wanted a man who looked like the king to lead the army into battle.) And thus, a king's power, for Kautilya, is in the end tied to the power and popular energy of the people, without which a king can be conquered, for "not being rooted among his subjects, [a king] becomes easy to uproot."

Although Kautilya wrote of using money to raise an army and even of "purchasing heroic men," he was not advocating mercenaries who fought only for pay, but he was merely outlining the cost of paying, supplying, and feeding soldiers. He believed that "hereditary troops are better than hired troops"; in other words, troops made of men born in the kingdom and thus loyal to the king since birth are better than strangers fighting for money, as Machiavelli noted so often later. It is not at all clear, remarked Kautilya, that "inviting alien troops with money" is an advantage or a disadvantage.

Which States to Attack

In Kautilya's view of the world, expansion by a prosperous kingdom was inevitable, natural, and good, and as a consequence, moral considerations did not enter into his deliberations, only what was for the good of the kingdom. If a king can win, then he should go to war. As Kangle says, the *Arthashastra* "preaches an ideal of conquest." But who should be attacked? This is not an ethical question. The decision takes only careful calculation and observes the principle that a king should attack weakness. Certain states are vulnerable. If a state is unjust, then its people will welcome a deliverer from a tyrannical king; if a kingdom is weakened from a poor economy, or if a state has experienced some kind of calamity ranging from fires to flood or famine, then a king "should make war and march." As Rajendra Prasad says, Kautilya believed that "whenever an enemy king is in trouble, and his subjects are exploited, oppressed, impoverished and disunited, he should be immediately attacked after one proclamation of war." Every adjacent kingdom should be looked upon as an enemy and classified.

If a kingdom is strong, Kautilya called it a "foe"; if a kingdom is suffering calamity, then it is "vulnerable"; if a kingdom has weak or no popular support, then "it is fit to be exterminated." Even if one cannot attack a strong neighbor or "foe," one can harass it silently and weaken it over time.

What Kautilya called an enemy "fit to be exterminated" was an enemy with little or no popular support, an enemy whose subjects quite likely would desert to Kautilya's attacking army. And Kautilya argued, or perhaps assumed, that imperial expansion was the correct goal: "After conquering the enemy's territory, the conqueror should seek to seize the middle king, after succeeding over him, the neutral king. This is the first method of conquering the world.... And after conquering the world he should enjoy it divided into *varnas*... in accordance with his own duty." In Kautilya's mind, treaties were agreements between kingdoms of roughly equal power, agreements a king should break if they are no longer advantageous, and thus, believing that a treaty will provide a wall of protection against a strong enemy would be a foolish act.

If an ally with whom a king has a treaty becomes weakened, that is, if the treaty is no longer to a king's advantage, then the king "should violate the treaty," or, "when after making a pact he intends to violate it,... he should demand a gain not received or more." Because Kautilya thought that promises or agreements were strategies and not moral obligations, he had no moral qualms about violating a promise and recommended that "The commander of a frontier fort, by offering the surrender of the fort, should get part of the (enemy's) troops inside and destroy [them] *when full of trust*." To protect his own people, a king has an obligation to weaken or destroy any potential enemy: "That ally who might do harm or who, though capable, would not help in times of trouble, he should certainly exterminate him, *when trustingly, he comes within his reach.*" Charles Drekmeier is certainly correct in saying that, "In outlining military campaigns Kautilya disregards the traditional humanitarian principles laid down to regulate the conduct of war." In Book 9, Kautilya listed various "hindrances to gain"; among them were pity, piousness, and "regard for the other world." In short, in waging war, compassion and morality and religious principles have no place, unless they are useful for bringing victory. In another way, moral considerations did enter into Kautilya's calculations.

Whereas it is best to wage war against an unjust king who has no public support, it is wise to avoid war with a righteous king whose subjects will fight energetically on his behalf. Kautilya noted that if one has a choice about where to attack, it is always best to attack an unjust kingdom, because "The subjects help the king who is justly behaved.... Therefore, [a king] should march only against [an enemy] with disaffected subjects." Once more, morality is sometimes advantageous and in one's self-interest, for "The unjustly behaved [king] would cause even settled land to be laid waste." By being unjust, a king loses all popular support, thereby weakening the kingdom and making it easily conquered: "The king fit to be exterminated, being without support or with weak support, is deserted by his subjects when, on being attacked, he wishes to flee taking with him the treasury and the army." If a king has a choice of attacking a strong king who is unjust or a weak king who is just, he should actually attack the stronger king, because the stronger king's subjects, weary of injustice, will not help the strong king and might even join the war against him. An unjust state is really two states, already at war with one another, the rulers and the ruled. Kautilya paused to remind a king how practical it was to be just toward his subjects because "Subjects, when impoverished, become greedy; when greedy they become disaffected; when disaffected they either go over to the enemy or themselves kill the master. Therefore, [a king] should not allow these causes of decline, greed and disaffection among the subjects to arise, or, if arisen, should immediately counter-act them."

A domestic political policy of social justice is, in the long run, the best defence against outside enemies, because "one attacking a righteous king is hated by his own people and by others; one attacking an unrighteous king is liked (by them)." Kautilya maintained that a humanitarian policy toward a defeated people was practical. If a king massacres those whom he has defeated, then he frightens all those kingdoms that surround him and terrifies even his own ministers. Rather, one gains more land and new and loyal subjects if one treats the defeated in a magnanimous manner. Certainly a conquering king must silently kill those former leaders loyal to the defeated king, but those who approach him promising loyalty should be treated generously: "He should not use towards them insults, injuries, contemptuous words or reproaches. And after promising them safety, he should favour them like a father." Because a conquering king intends to expand his territory and acquire new subjects, he must treat a defeated people well. The victor, "after gaining new territory,... should cover the enemy's faults with his own virtue, his virtues with double virtues. He should carry out what is agreeable and beneficial to his subjects by doing his own duty as laid down, granting favours, giving exemptions, making gifts and showing honour." Indeed, the conquering king should "order the release of all prisoners and render help to the distressed, the helpless and the diseased." It is sound military policy to "establish a righteous course of conduct." What is moral is once more practical.

Just as one can kill a traitor, but cannot use force "against a multitude of people," so one can kill the leaders of a defeated kingdom, but must bring the great majority of the citizens peacefully into one's own kingdom. In this instance, Kautilya was following the traditional advice given in the *Dharmas-utras* that "Aryans condemn the killing of those who have thrown down their weapons, who have dishevelled hair, who fold their hands in supplication, or who are fleeing." And by these actions, Kautilya fit his own definition of a righteous conqueror who sought victory and the submission of the enemy, but not greedy pillaging or lawless killing. Kautilya demanded much of his soldiers, because they had to be brave and fierce in battle, but gentle and kind toward those whom they had defeated: "When attacking the enemy's fort or camp, they should grant safety to those fallen down, those turning back, those surrendering, those with loose hair, those without weapons, those disfigured by terror and to those not fighting." After a king has subdued the country and taken care of the people, he should "grant safety to the countryside," settle subjects down to farm the land, and "induce" even those who had fought against him to settle down and farm (even by giving tax exemptions), all because the countryside needs farmers and the new kingdom wants prosperity. "For," according to Kautilya, "there is no country without people and no kingdom without a country," meaning a prosperous—not a ravished—countryside.

Both Sun Tzu (c. 400-320 B.C.) and Machiavelli, in books entitled *The Art of War*, pointed out that a general should always give an enemy the hope of escape and never surround a nearly defeated enemy completely. Enemy soldiers who have hope of living will eventually run for safety, and they are easily killed, but soldiers surrounded with no choice but to fight or die will fight with an unimagined ferocity. Kautilya was arguing something similar, to let the enemy soldiers know that the king will be generous in victory, will allow defeated soldiers to return to their land, and will take no reprisals except toward the leaders of the opposing kingdom, against whom "he should act as in 'the infliction of (secret) punishment.'" After such humanitarian policies toward the defeated populace have become widely known, ordinary enemy soldiers will surrender in great numbers. By contrast, if a king announces that he will massacre every soldier, then all will fight to the death. Said Kautilya, "The vehemence of one returning again to the fight and despairing of his life becomes irresistible; therefore, [a king] should not harass a broken enemy." Similarly, he advised that "to fight with brave men who have given up all hope of life is a rash deed." A conquering king should reassure a defeated people that not much, except their rulers, will change.

The king who has triumphed "should adopt a similar character, dress, language and behaviour (as the subjects). And he should show the same devotion in festivals in honour of deities of the country, festive gatherings and sportive amusements." He should keep his promises, especially to those who helped him win, he should honour the local "deities," and he should make grants of land and money to men distinguished in wisdom and piety. And the conquering king should show his goodwill toward the defeated by instituting "a righteous custom, not initiated before." While the victorious king is reassuring the general population with generous policies, he must continue to kill anyone who is dangerous and those who are disgruntled: "He should put down by silent punishment those capable of injuring [him] or those brooding on the master's destruction." In what might be a surprising observation about those whom the king has killed, Kautilya commented that if one must kill a dangerous person, the king must leave his property untouched and "shall not covet the land, property, sons or wives of the slain one." Kautilya had the same insight into human emotions that Machiavelli had nearly eighteen hundred years later. Said Machiavelli, "And when [the prince] is obliged to take the life of any one,... he must abstain from taking the property of others, for men forget more easily the death of their father than the loss of their patrimony." A king becomes hated more readily for taking the property that belongs to a family than for killing the head of the family.

USING SECRET AGENTS, ASSASSINS, DISINFORMATION, AND PROPAGANDA

Kautilya was ready to use almost any means of violence in fighting a war, although he wanted his king to direct his violence toward the leaders of the opposing kingdom and not toward ordinary people. For example, Kautilya discussed at length how to employ poison, but almost always directed its use at key enemy commanders. He advised that when "giving unadulterated wine to the army chiefs, [the secret agent] should give them (wine) mixed with poison when they are in a state of intoxication." Whereas Kautilya did suggest that an army laying siege to a fort try to "defile the water," this measure seems designed to make those in the fort surrender from illness, not to kill everyone in the fort. Mostly, Kautilya addressed the question of how to assassinate a king—by hiding "inside the image of a deity or a hollow wall" and emerging at night, by making something heavy fall on the king, or by using women as secret agents to "drop on him serpents or poisonous fire and smoke." Kautilya was willing to use any possible means to assassinate an enemy king—drown him, burn him with fire, suffocate him with smoke, or even use crocodiles as assassins, not to mention employing women and children as poison-givers. The wonder of assassination, according to Kautilya, is that it is so efficient, "for, an assassin, single-handed, may be able to achieve his end with weapon, poison and fire.

He does the work of a whole army or more." In an unrealistic passage in the *Dharmasutras* that Kautilya most certainly ignored, the authors directed that a king should not "strike with barbed or poisoned weapons"! Aside from assassination, another method used to defeat an enemy without full-scale battle was to arrange for the enemy to quarrel and fight among itself. We have already seen how Kautilya intended to use beautiful women to instigate fights among high officers or officials. If the promise of pleasure can ignite quarrels, so can the promise of power. One should arrange for a secret agent, disguised as an astrologer, to tell a high officer that he has all the marks of a king, and similarly arrange for a female secret agent, the wife of this officer, to complain that the king wants to keep her in his harem. A third secret agent who is a cook or a waiter should lie, saying that the king has ordered him or her to poison the high officer. "Thus with one or two or three means," according to Kautilya, the king "should incite the high officers one by one to fight or desert" the enemy king. In a discussion about sowing dissensions among oligarchies, Kautilya suggested that "assassins should start quarrels by injuring objects, cattle or men at night," "should stir up princelings enjoying low comforts with (a longing for) superior comforts," and "should start quarrels among the followers of the chiefs in the oligarchy by praising the opponents in brothels and taverns." The goals were constantly to "sow discord" and to foment and inflame "mutual hatred, enmity and strife." Much of this advice violated the tacit code of war found in the great Indian epics.

The assassination of envoys and the use of poison were considered to be against the rules of warfare and thus not honorable. Said *The Laws of Manu*, "Fighting in battle, [the king] should not kill his enemies with weapons that are concealed, barbed, or smeared with poison or whose points blaze with fire." Spies were common in Indian history, but not spies who assassinated enemy officials and started quarrels among enemy leaders. An excellent book on warfare in ancient India discusses spies, but does not mention secret agents as assassins. Once more Kautilya judged the means by the result, and the result he sought was the general good of his kingdom. Another military tactic that Kautilya praised was what we now call disinformation or propaganda designed to demoralize or frighten enemy soldiers.

For example, secret agents should appear as messengers to troops saying, "Your fort has been burnt down or captured; a revolt by a member of your family has broken out; or, your enemy or a forest chieftain has risen (against you)." After spreading the rumor that the Regent or a high administrator of the enemy king has announced that the king is in trouble and may not come back alive and thus people should take wealth by force and kill their enemies, secret agents should kill and steal at night, trying to cause civil upheaval: "When the rumour has spread far and wide, assassins should rob citizens at night and slay chiefs, (saying at the time), 'Thus are dealt with [those] who do not obey the Regent.'" Then they should put bloody evidence in the Regent's residence. Again, secret agents should spread rumours, always in a confidential manner, that the king is furious with such and such a leader. Then these agents should assassinate key leaders and say "to those who have not been slain,... 'This is what we had told you; he who wants to remain alive should go away.'" Kautilya was especially fond of the tactic of utilizing disinformation to flatter a second or third son and thus persuade him to try a coup against his own family. Convinced that disinformation could also inspire his own troops, Kautilya wanted agents to announce fabricated victories and fictitious defeats of the enemy: "On the occasion of a night-battle, [secret agents] should strike many drums, fixed beforehand as a signal, and announce, 'We have entered it; the kingdom is won.'" Much of this disinformation made use of religion.

Placed strategically, astrologers "should fill [the king's] side with enthusiasm by proclaiming his omniscience and association with divine agencies, and should fill the enemy's side with terror." Once more the needs of the state are primary, and the king commands religion to serve the state: "He should make (Brahmins) recite blessings invoking victory and securing heaven." Singers and poets should "describe the attainment of heaven by the brave and the absence of heaven for cowards." Secret agents who have infiltrated the enemy side should use animal blood in order to "cause an excessive flow (of blood) from honoured images of deities," and then interpret that as a sure sign of future defeat for the enemy.

Kautilya wanted anyone associated with religion or superstition—"soothsayers, interpreters of omens, astrologers, reciters of *Puranas*" and so on —to proclaim to his own troops and to the enemy the king's "association with divinities" or "his meeting with divinities," creating confidence on his own side and simultaneously terror and misgivings among enemy soldiers. Those priests in charge of interpreting omens must make certain that dreams and other signs are always favorable to the king's efforts and unfavorable to the enemy. Every kind of superstition can be useful. And for Kautilya, religious authorities must be for hire. In addition to brave and well-equipped soldiers, warfare requires deception, and over and again Kautilya advocated the above measures and more for deceiving both his own and the enemy troops.

If caught behind enemy lines, Kautilya outlined ways for one to escape "in the disguise of a heretical monk," "decked out as a corpse," or "wearing a woman's garb." And he was eager to terrify the enemy by such multiple and varied means as by using "machines, by the employment of occult practices, through assassins slaying those engaged in something else, by magical arts, by (a show of) association with divinities, through carts, by frightening with elephants," and so on. A favourite tactic in battle was to pretend to be defeated, retreat in apparent disorder, and then attack a disorganized and unsuspecting enemy. The leader, "feigning a rout with treasonable, alien and forest troops,... should strike at the (pursuing enemy when he has) reached unsuitable ground." At all times, Kautilya wanted his king to use deception, play roles, and create appearances. Why risk heavy losses or even defeat in battle if deception and assassination can weaken or even defeat the enemy? Even if a king is forced to surrender in order to survive, Kautilya wanted him to pretend that his surrender was "an excellent thing" until he was clever or strong enough to fight back. Warfare was violent, but it also called for one who could calmly create false impressions, like a poker player.

Conclusion

To return to Machiavelli's *The Art of War* after reading the military writings of Kautilya is jolting. It becomes readily apparent that Machiavelli is not even trying to tell us something new about warfare, because he believed the ancient Greeks and Romans knew it all—aside from such things as artillery. What did Machiavelli want to resurrect from ancient Rome and transport to Renaissance Florence? He wanted Rome's battalions and legions and cohorts, and maybe Scipio once again arrayed across the plain from Hannibal. And thus compared to Kautilya and Sun Tzu, Machiavelli's writings on warfare are tired and tedious, filled with nostalgia for long-dead legions that once gained glory. He wanted the public battlefield, the grand spectacle, fame for some and cowardice for others. Sun Tzu and Kautilya did not care a whit for glory and fame. They wanted to win at all costs and to keep casualties—on both sides—to a minimum. Said Sun Tzu, "For to win one hundred victories in one hundred battles is not the acme of skill. To subdue the enemy without fighting is the acme of skill." They were also prepared to win in ways Machiavelli would regard as dishonourable and disgraceful—assassination, disinformation, causing quarrels between ministers by bribes or by means of jealousy over a beautiful woman planted as a secret agent, and so on. Machiavelli—who offers no systematic discussion of even guerrilla warfare—would have been easily outmatched by generals reading either Sun Tzu or Kautilya.

STRATEGIC THINKING IN ANCIENT INDIA AND CHINA: KAUTILYA AND SUNZI

This is meant to be only an exploratory comparison between strategic thinking in India and China in ancient times. For one thing, the problem of dating individuals, events and texts in Indian history is a formidable one. In China, on the other hand, it is much less of a problem, although the dates for Sunzi were in dispute for a long time. Interpolations in texts are common in both traditions but the oral tradition in India as opposed to the tradition of writing in China presents greater difficulties in reconstructing Indian texts. But the more serious difficulty in comparing the Indian and Chinese streams of strategic thinking stems from the strong "religious" base of Indian thought. In contrast, Chinese thinking has an unmistakable "secular" base. An off-shoot of the "religious" element in India was the social organisation it produced. Warfare in India was almost exclusively the preserve and even the duty of the *ksatriya varna* (warrior class) which was hereditary, although specific instances of the priestly *brahman varna* can be found thinking about and engaging in warfare. In China, although the shi (scholar-gentlemen) were trained in the military arts among other scholarly subjects, they did not constitute a hereditary group. The absence of a "religious" base in Chinese thinking does not mean that the role of ethics in war was neglected.

The Confucian school, particularly Mencius and Mozi not only emphasized ethical principles in warfare, they were opposed to war as such. But with the rise of the state of Qin and its expansion, the Legalist school of Shang Yang and Han Feizi gradually eclipsed the Confucian opposition to war. And although Legalism was theoretically abandoned when the Qin dynasty was overthrown by the Han (in 207 B.C.), "State Confucianism" as adopted by the Han thinkers did not oppose war in the manner of Mencius. From Western Han onwards, realpolitik dominated Chinese strategic thinking. Whether the Marxist-Leninist base in Chinese strategic thinking in our century marked a partial return to "ethical" principles is a question beyond the scope of this paper. It is probably a comment on the limits of ideology when it comes to applying it to practical matters that despite the strong "religious" base of Indian thinking, a strong school of realpolitik also appeared in India side by side with it.

Thus, ancient Indian thinkers produced two schools of war, diplomacy and interstate relations; the *dharmayuddha* (ethical warfare) school; and the *kutayuddha* (devious warfare) school. The two schools were, however, not mutually exclusive. The practitioners of each school was informed by the principles and methods of the other and practised them. (In China, they were very nearly mutually exclusive). The best example of this is the great *Mahabharata* war in which one can see both schools of thought in operation: in this war the victory went to the practitioners of the *kutayuddha* school although the war itself has always been described as *dharmayuddha*. In the other epic war, the *Ramayana*, although both streams of thought were at work, the victory went to the *dharmayuddha* (righteous/ethical) school. And in the case of the wars fought by Emperor Ashoka, while all of them were presumably won by the methods of *kutayuddha*, after the conquests Ashoka himself turned a complete pacifist. This was the case with an individual (which is what has earned him fame) but in Indian thinking neither school ever completely replaced the other.

At the level of rhetoric, the concept of *dharmayuddha* always reigned supreme. But in practice *kutayuddha* was often the norm. The defeat of Indian kings at the hands of foreign conquerors has been attributed by many to the loss of traditions of war-making, particularly that of *kutayuddha*. This is probably why, at present in modern India, the *kutayuddha* school seems to be in the ascendant, although even there the righteousness of the cause always dominates the rhetoric. In ancient times, India was populated by numerous tribes.

Some indigenous and others who had migrated into the subcontinent. They were culturally and technically unevenly developed and there was constant warfare among them, particularly between the immigrants and the natives, The wars were fought over territory, for lifting cattle (the chief form of wealth), for capturing women (the immigrants arrived with few women of their own), for honour and status, for self-aggrandizement in all spheres and sometimes out of anger, envy, fear or just display of heroism. While such warfare over centuries produced tribal rituals of warfare, codes of chivalry and heroism, technology of warfare and, of course, the all important hereditary group of warriors, the *ksatria varna*, it did not yield any body of thought which can be called strategic thinking which remains the major characteristic of Chinese thinking, particularly since the 4th century BC.

Such thinking started with the establishment of well-recognized kingdoms/states as political entities possessing standing, armies, administrations, laws and social order capable of supporting war. *Shaurya* (heroism) continued to be valued as the virtue of an individual warrior but to this was added the concept of *neeti* (ethical principles) in the conduct of warfare. The belief grew that without neeti, war became merely a display of animal-like ferocity.

For a victory based on principles (*dharmavijaya*), the king and the warriors had to observe certain codes in warfare. These codes were incorporated in the *Dharmashastras* (loosely translated as Books of Law).

Warfare carried out according to the codes was also called *prakashayudha* (illuminated or open warfare). There was nothing secret about it. Preparations for such a war were made openly in the full knowledge of the adversary. There was no element of surprise and there were strict rules about seasons of warfare, the duration of combat was restricted to daylight hours and rigid codes about close combat between warriors were observed.

In all this, there was no room for strategy or tactics; only the numbers of warriors, their skills and the quality of weaponry counted. But, at the same time, diplomacy played an important role in building alliances for war and in making decisions about whether or not to go to war. The Chinese case around the time of Sunzi was quite different; set-piece battles were a thing of the past. Inevitably, in actual warfare, the principles of righteous warfare were often set aside by individual warriors or their commanders.

In fact, such was the sweetness of victory that some kings waged war for reasons of self-aggrandizement. The victory achieved for such selfish reasons came to be classified into two categories *aasurvijaya* in which the enemy's territory was annexed, enemy kings and commanders were booty punished after the war, enemy cities were destroyed and the women were carried away as war booty.

The second category produced *lobhavijaya* or victory out of covetousness or greed. This did not need waging a ruthless war of destruction but one for gain in terms of territory, wealth, women and so forth. Only *kutayuddha* (devious warfare) could produce victories aimed of self-aggrandizement, Although the form was repeatedly denounced by ancient sages, it was nevertheless practised with increasing frequency until by the time of Emperor Ashoka, it came to be accepted as a norm.

From practice, codification of devious warfare was only a short step. Several thinkers like Brihaspati and Shukracharya are known to have done this. But a comprehensive codification was undertaken by Kautilya, the great strategist of the Mauryan period. The term *koota,* in the context of hunting, was used for a trap or snare.

Consequently, in the context of warfare, it came to mean ensnaring or trapping the enemy. This included the use of magic spells and such other occult methods. (Sunzi decidedly rejected that use.) And when it came to weaponry prevalent in those days, it included the use of poisoned arrows, fire arrows and such other unauthorized weapons which could bring about destruction of men and property on a large scale. Other methods included poisoning of the enemy's water sources, attack by stealth, enticing the enemy into an unfavourable position, bribery, assassinations and attacks at night.

Almost every single war described in the epics and the puranas incorporated at least some of these forbidden methods. Sometimes, only one side is said to have done this. In the *Ramayana,* for example, the *raksasa* side is said to have resorted to *koota* methods. In the numerous wars fought between the devas and aasuras the latter are always accused of having used unethical methods. In general, it seems that such methods we attributed to the side which was technologically superior but nevertheless lost the series of wars in the end.

The didactic message of these classics was that righteousness always emerged victorious. A few epics like the *Agni Purana,* however, condoned the use of koota methods by the weak as a last resort. One prominent characteristic of the Hindu reading of reality is that the good is always mixed with or accompanied by the evil.

Human nature is the product of a variety of influences (karma) from the previous births and the present life. So the same human being contains both righteous and unrighteous impulses, even the most ideally righteous person may occasionally commit unethical acts in the interests of larger righteous causes. Thus, in the *Ramayana,* Lord Rama, the most perfect human being known nevertheless kills Vali, a brother of his ally, by deceit.

In the *Mahabharata,* Lord Krishna, himself a major God in the Hindu pantheon, advises and resorts to all kinds of trickery in the service of the weak but righteous side in a dispute over a kingdom. Hindu classics always uphold the rhetoric of righteousness or dharma but condone and often justify lapses from the codes. In this essay, I want to focus on the thinking of two strategic thinkers, Kautilya and Sunzi.

Kautilya (also known as Chanakya and Visnusharman), who comes closest to the thinking of Sunzi as is available to us in his *Art* of *War* (Bingfa)). Like Sunzi, Kautilya also rose as a strategic thinker in a period of constant warfare; both realized the importance of studying war as an important aspect of statecraft. However, Sunzi does not seems to have played any role in helping any particular stale of his time to establish its hegemony over others. Kautilya on the other hand is said to have single-handedly engineered the victory of the Mauryas by destroying the Nanda power and to have put Chandragupta Maurya on the Magadha Ihrone.

Kautilya's thinking on statecraft as a whole is available to us in the great classic Arthashastras (AS hereafter) which may be translated as the "Science of Politics and Administration". Unlike the Bingfa (BF hereafter), it covers a much broader range of subjects. But in this essay, we will discuss only those sections which deal with war and external affairs. The AS recommends that a state should base its defences on the fort *(durg)* and the army.

Of the two, it regards the tort to be more important since it allows the king to survive a siege and practise his diplomacy from that base. The army is, of course, important in defence matters but it can be completely lost on the battlefield leaving the king without any protection. In contrast, the BF totally rules out sieges as being expensive and wasteful. For the defence of the stale against enemies, the AS prescribes al least four bases, one each in every cardinal direction. These should preferably be natural defensive points such as mountains, water, desert, forests and the like.

But in the state capital, a man-made fort is regarded as essential. It should have moats, ramparts and parapets for soldiers to shoot from. Wooden walls are ruled but as a fire-hazard. In the approaches to the fort, traps should be laid for the enemy. Inside it, it should be guarded by four types of formations comprising elephants, chariots, cavalry and infantry, each led by several commanders so that the loss of one or more to the enemy does not leave the formations leaderless. The fort should, of course, be well-stocked to withstand a siege but should have secret escape routes if the situation became desperate. As we shall see, Sunzi's thinking is very different. The troops should, naturally, be from the warrior castes as far as possible.

Lower varna are acceptable but the highest varna, Brahmins, are ruled out because of the peculiar Indian social system. The enemy can put Brahmin troops out of action simply by prostrating before them and prostrating persons, by law, could not be killed. The infantry can be a standing force or it can be raised for the particular war. But other branches, e.g., elephants, cavalry etc., must be standing formations led and trained by specialists. The army of an ally can be used but captured enemy soldiers should be used only with caution. The AS prescribes a detailed hierarchy of officers.

The *Senapati* or Chief-of-Staff is the highest officer, his station is at the rear. The lower commanders (*nayakas*) actually lead the troops in battle. Daily rigorous training must be the norm. Frequent inspections are required to keep the troops fighting fit. As for weapons, there should be a special office for acquiring them and storing them safely.

Each weapon is to be marked with the king's insignia and strict inventories must be maintained to guard against loss. Three main types of weapons are prescribed and seem actually to have been maintained in ordnance depots. The first category consisted of battlefield weapons such as bows and arrows, spears, swords, daggers, shields etc. The second type comprise those for defence of the fort such as stones, catapults and bows and arrows. The third type is meant for attacking enemy fortifications which includes scaling equipment as well as flaming arrows and other incendiary weapons. The AS puts a great deal of faith in magical practices such as casting spells. In Kautilya's time, warfare was limited only to certain seasons.

Generally it was avoided during the rainy season. The AS generally upholds this practice but says that the time for launching a war should also depend cm the terrain which would become the battlefield. It also prescribes that the type of troops to be deployed should be determined not only by the terrain but also by the disposition of enemy troops. The book lays down elaborate rules for establishing camps during the march against an enemy. Although the AS puts a great deal of emphasis on devious warfare (*kutayuddha*), it prescribes that if a king has a clearly superior force and other factors are favorable, he should engage in open and rule-bound warfare *(prakashayudha)*.

Obviously in Kautilya's mind, a certain amount of odium continued to be associated with devious warfare. For it involved among other things attacking the enemy when he was vulnerable, feigning retreat to draw out the enemy into a trap, using elephants to break up closed ranks, attacking one flank and then the other, tiring out the enemy with one's inferior troops first and then attacking with superior ones, laying ambushes, attacking at night to deprive enemy soldiers of their sleep and then attacking them during the day with fresh troops, attacking the enemy troops when they were facing the sun and so forth. All such tactics are routine now but they were regarded as exceptional in Kaulilya's time. The AS, therefore, goes into great detail about the "conventional" warfare of its time.

It prescribes standard battle-arrays (*vyuha*) which have a centre, two flanks and two wings. Each component of the *vyuha* is conceived as being of equal strength containing between 9 and 21 units; each unit in turn, should be based on an elephant or a chariot with five horsemen and 15 infantrymen in front and rear. There are four basic types of battle-arrays: the staff (in-line) array, the serpent *(wavy)* array, the circular array and the loose army. The choice is determined by the terrain and the enemy's troop disposition. Great emphasis is placed on reserves behind every battle-ariay; this is where the king stations himself. The AS shows preference for mountains or forts to station the reserves. With the reserve force, there should be physicians and medicaments to treat the wounded, and field kitchens run by women.

The women are also trusted with the task of "encouraging" the troops. Before the beginning of action, the king should address his troops and emphasize that he is one of them. Next the Chiet-of-Staff *(senapatl)* should also address them and announce rewards for acts of bravery.

Whatever loot the soldiers captured would be theirs but the Chief should also announce gratuities at the end of the war. It was the task of the officers to report acts of bravery by men fighting under their charge. Whatever the form of warfare, the AS is scrupulous about one principle: not to cause harm to the subjects of the enemy king.

So, when laying a siege to the fort, the people inside must be assured of their safety and be allowed to leave the fort for safe places. If territory must be annexed-it was usually not annexed-only the king was forced to become an ally or a vassal-the people are to be won over through all means. Their customs must be respected and their gods must be revered by the new king. After the war, carrying away loot is forbidden.

If the king was reduced to vassalage, he still retained control of the territory and the army and was not obliged to help his sovereign militarily. It needs to be emphasized that the AS does not only speak about making conquests. It also discusses the strategies and tactics for the prevention of conquest by others. This is why a large portion of the book is devoted to statecraft and administration of the state. But whether in conquering others or in preventing conquest, the AS takes conflictual relationship between states as the norm.

So, management of these occupies an important place in Kautilya's thinking. It is almost certain that a large number of ideas he propounds came to him as received wisdom. And after him these ideas were appropriated by different texts as their own. Kautilya's major contribution, in contrast with that of Sunzi. Comes from his sense of political geography. The AS envisages the "international" arena, the mandala, as comprising 12 types of kings/states.

It classifies them as follows: 1. The would-be conqueror, at the centre of the mandala. 2. The enemy whose territory borders on that of the would-be conqueror, i.e., the hostile neighbour. 3. The ally's whose territory lies immediately beyond that of the hostile neighbour. 4. The enemy's ally who is the neighbour of one's won ally. 5. The ally's ally who is territorially distant. 6. The ally of the enemy's ally who is also territorially distant. Types 7 to 10 follow the same sequence but to the rear of the would-be conqueror. The last two types are No. 11, a neutral king/state neighbouring both the would-be conqueror and his/its enemy but is stronger than both. And 12, the king is totally indifferent towards all other kings/states but is more powerful than the would-be conqueror, his enemy and the neutral king/ state. All the advice in the AS is directed to the would-be conqueror (*vijigisu* or one desirous of victory).

The underlying assumption is that neighbours always turn hostile. Another assumption is that a common enemy creates allies. But the categories of enemy and ally are not fixed. Under certain conditions, allies can become friends and vice-versa. The 12 types classified by the AS are possible combinations; they are not to be taken as the permanently existing actual situation in a mandala.

Kautilya assumes that except for the neutral and "indifferent" kings/states, all others in the mandala are of equal strength So, in a concrete situation, the mandala gets divided into two more or less equal blocs, with one blocs-leader seeking to establish hegemony over all the others. The strengths of blocs being equal, diplomacy, strategy and tactics assume great importance attaining hegemony. The AS does emphasize the role of diplomacy but shows no preference for it over war.

This is simply because one important component of the society of his time was the warrior group whose very existence was tied to fighting. Diplomacy, Kantilya was for winning allies, delaying war if one was vulnerable and for making postwar arrangements for a new order. According to the AS, relations with other kings/ states are to be established and carried out through *dutaas* or ambassadors.

It prescribes three types of ambassadors: the plenipotentiary, envoy with limited negotiating powers, and one who is one messenger. It recommends that ambassadors should be stationed in all foreign states on a permanent basis and that they she enjoy what we call "diplomatic immunity" in modern parlance. In contrast to modern diplomatic norms, however, the AS expects the ambassadors to engage in spying, acts of sabotage and most importantly be active in securing defections from the enemy's army. Kautilya distinguished between six major approaches to foreign policy.

The first is a policy of maintaining peace with another state which is based on a treaty detailing the terms and conditions. The second is the policy of hostility which she be followed if one is stronger than the enemy. The third approach is one of inaction: It is most suitable when states are of equal strength. The fourth is outright invasion but this policy is recommended for the very strong. For the very weak is prescribed fifth approach, i.e., seeking shelter with another king and wait for better days, The sixth and the last approach recommend policy of peace with one king/state while maintaining hostility towards another; such a dual policy is possible if help is available from another state to fight the enemy. The AS, naturally realizes that one may become the object of such policies by another king/state.

So the enemy may force peace by a treaty on oneself. If that happens, Kautilya advises that one should drag one's feet in fulfilling the treaty obligations and wait for an opportunity to overthrow the enemy.

If the treaty demands a hostage, for example, one should offer an inferior person. But if the enemy demands one's son as a hostage, the king should offer himself so that the son can plan to overthrow the enemy and rescue the father. The AS describes many kinds of treaties, with or without various stipulations, temporary and long-term ones, sincere and dishonest ones. The aim is always to outsmart the adversary. It also discusses in great detail not only the six broad approaches outlined above but also their combinations. Even the necessity of surrender is not overlooked but it is always for buying time. War-making is only one among the means to attain one's objective of hegemony.

The other means are friendship bribery to be employed against weak kings. Yet another two means to be deployed against the strong are splitting (the enemy's strength and alliances) and coercion (which includes war). The difference between the means and approaches/policies is that the means can be employed against domestic as well as foreign opponents whereas the policies can apply only to other kings/states. By way of broad strategy, the AS recommends that the would be conqueror should first go at the hostile neighbour and with the new power acquired, he should next tackle the neutral king/state.

If he succeeds, he should proceed against the most powerful "indifferent" king. That would complete his hegemony over the mandala as a whole, for the rest would fall in line. If there are no neutral or "indifferent" kings, the conqueror should first tackle his enemies and then secure the allegiance of enemy's allies. In the event there are only two other states, one hostile and the other friendly, the would-be conqueror should crush the neighbouring state regardless of whether it is hostile or friendly and then proceed against the other.

Finally, if there are a number of neighbouring states, they should be tackled one by one gaining strength in the process. It goes without saying that Kautilya underlines all his strategies with the requirement that the would-be conqueror must satisfy himself that he enjoys superiority in such essential aspects as troop morale, war material and above all strategic advice.

At the same time, the king must take precautions against insurrection within his own kingdom while he is away at war. So the AS recommends that a reliable Regent should be appointed and one-third of the army left behind for internal security. The most likely rebel leader should be taken by the king on his expedition. (The AS, as may be expected, also discusses how an insurrection should be planned and executed.) Finally, the AS elaborately discusses how gains and losses from an expedition against others should be estimated beforehand. Kautilya wrote a practical handbook and therefore does not indulge in any theory of a good society, good actions etc. This is why to the modern mind he comes across as a totally amoral and cynical practitioner of strategies of war.

Most Western comment on the AS is therefore negative in the extreme. In India, however, the book has never evoked any such negative response. This seems largely because despite the odium attached to *kutayuddha,* in all epic wars, the righteous side always emerged victorious. *Kutayuddha* always remained a kind of side-show. The second reason, I think, is that the AS was appropriated by other *shastras* and the *puranas* (or epics) in which the moral/ethical side of all human actions was abundantly stressed; so, devious and cynical practices came to be considered secondary, situational and answering only the needs of exigencies. Sunzi was a product of the Warring States period (403-221 BC).

At that time China was divided into numerous states, each with its own standing army. There was constant warfare among them. This allowed a number of "sages" (a) to travel from one state to another to offer advice on military matters to the kings. There is some doubt about whether such a person actually existed or whether what has come down to us as Bingfa (BF) was a compilation of the sayings of several strategists. For the purpose or this essay we will treat the BF as having been authored by Sunzi who may have lived in the 4th century BC.

If BF is to be summarized in one sentence, it would be: The supreme art of war is to subdue the enemy without fighting". Sunzi cautioned the kings and their commanders not to place reliance on sheer military power. He exhorted them to resort to minimum killing and destruction of the enemy. They were to take all intact or as nearly intact as possible.

All this called for very high level skills of diplomacy and devising stratagems of deceit, bribery and extensive use of spies (one's own, from among the enemy's subjects and double spies, i.e., the enemy's spies won over). The army was only an instrument to deliver the *coup de grace* to an enemy previously made vulnerable through other means like subversion and causing a rift between him Andy his allies. Sunzi himself did not believe in magic weapons and asked the kings and commanders not to resort to them.

In contrast, Kautilya favoured their use. Since most kings in Sunzi's time were prone to resort to war to satisfy their whims and greed-they lived unbelievably luxurious lives-Sunzi repeatedly asked them not to resort to military adventures.

War was an important element of statecraft and had to be studied with seriousness. No war should be undertaken without drawing up detailed plans which were tailored to the situation of the enemy. In any case, wars must be short, swift and decisive. There never has been a protracted war which has benefited a country" he said.

He was especially aware of the economic consequence of war, particularly the inflation of currency during and after a war. Sunzi firmly believed that only benevolent and righteous rulers could win wars. Rulers had to have unstinted support of their subjects behind them. By implication, he believed that such benevolent rulers had no fear of internal insurrection, a subject on which Kautilya has much to say. The BF does not convey the impression that Sunzi had any imperial designs in mind for the ruler he was advising.

The BF does use the word *ba* (hegemonic) but it seems to mean a more powerful ruler than others.

In fact, the Legalists (Shang Yang, Han Feizi and Xunzi) who were empire-builders for the Qin state do not seem to have benefited much from Sunzi's teachings, except perhaps for battlefield tactics, When the Qin state ultimately established the first empire, its Emperor ordered that all classics before him (except works on technology) should be burnt. He did not spare the BF. In contrast to AS, the BF has a very limited view of political geography.

Sunzi is aware that the enemy may have allies but he basically speaks of bilateral responses to and initiatives vis-a-vis the enemy. He distinguishes between overall strategy (what should one do about the enemy?) and military strategy (how to win a war if one decides to wage one). He has little to say about the former question but is extremely detailed and meticulous about the second.

Both BF and AS share the importance of the terrain and weather while they differ sharply on the importance of numbers of soldiers and weapons, BF does discuss the use of different kinds of weaponry in some detail but the emphasis is clearly on tactics of mobile warfare China did not then have cavalry, as India did, but AS nowhere speaks of using it for outflanking the enemy. In contrast, BF treats the main *(zheng)* force as a way of intimidating the enemy but actually resorting to the extraordinary (qi) force for attacks on the flanks and the rear of the enemy. The primary target of the attack is the mind of the enemy commander.

Is he rash? Is he quick-tempered? Does he have too delicate a sense of honour? It so, one must plan one's strategy accordingly. Sunzi rules out sieges and frontal attacks except to surprise and cause disarray. He always recommends the "indirect approach." One should attack only when one can win. But one must never hesitate o withdraw to conserve oneself and to entice the enemy to a battlefield favourable to oneself. Given enough rope, Sunzi seems to say, the enemy will hang himself.

The only constant thing about war is constant change of the situation. In fact, a good commander must take the initiative to create change and then to manipulate it. But the foremost method in warfare is deception.

When capable, feign incapacity, when active, feign inactivity, when near the enemy, make it appear to him that you are far away. When you are far away, lead him to believe that you are near. Feign disorder and strike the smug enemy. Pretend inferiority and encourage his arrogance. When the enemy is strong avoid him. As for tactics, when one has ten to the enemy's one, surround him and take him intact: when one has 51 superiority, attack and disperse him.

But if only double his strength, seek to divide him. If equal to the enemy's strength, one can engage him but this requires great skill. If weaker, withdraw. In no case attack his elite troops. If you surround the enemy, leave an escape route; otherwise he will fight desperately. Keep him under strain and wear him down. BF is full of such aphorisms and modern commanders will at once recognize them. Kautilya has also mentioned many of the same tactics. BF is much shorter than AS and does not deal with "international relations" or administration of the state. Unlike AS, BF (despite all known copies having been burnt by Emperor Qin Shihuangdi) was studied and extensively commented upon almost continuously over the next two millennia.

Since late 19th century it has also been used as an important text book in Japanese military academies. There are many scholars and strategists in the West who believe that Mao Zedong's military thinking was based on Sunzi's BF but Mao denied that he had read BF before he came up with his own military doctrines. The two certainly differ on the subject of protracted war although they agree on several tactics. We finally come to an overall comparison between *Bingfa* and the *Arthashastra.*

Both works display great clarity of thought and a strong sense of realism. Neither advocates protracted war or total war although both are convinced that war is a constant reality for the state and therefore must be studied and executed seriously. At the same time, both Sunzi and Kautilya make it abundantly clear that war is much more than just a fight among men: reliance on sheer military power does not assure victory.

What we today call "software" is much more important than the "hardware". Thus strategy and tactics become supremely important elements and they must be practised in tandem with diplomacy. The authors of both works were great practitioners of *realpolitik,* As such they do not indulge in moralizing *or* theorizing about the ends of power. Kautilya does pay lip service to the upholding of a righteous social and political order, but Sunzi does not do that beyond saying that popular and just rulers can mobilize their subjects for victory more successfully than unpopular and unjust ones.

Beyond this concession to righteous principle, both focus their attention on the goal: the achievement of victory over others through any means appropriate for the occasion. These include obtaining accurate information about the enemy's plans and actions to frustrate them. Both strongly advocate measures to break up the enemy's alliances and his internal structure in order to isolate and demoralize him. Both recommend indirect and devious approaches with deception at all levels playing the central role. Oddly enough, despite such single mindedness in achieving victory/hegemony, both Kautilya and Sunzi are.concerned about minimizing the economic costs of war as well as minimizing civilian casualities. A closer comparison will, no doubt, bring out more similarities as well as differences between the two thinkers.

Kautilya, it appears, is far more concerned about preventing conquest by others and far more in acquiring vassals than is Sunzi. Similarly, he also shows more sensitivity about internal security than does Sunzi. Above all, whereas Sunzi focuses somewhat narrowly on war, Kautilya has a much broader set of concerns taking in all aspects of statecraft, of which war is just one. But he applies himself to that one aspect with just as much concentration as Sunzi does. Despite the great similarities — almost identities — between the two, there remains one major difference which has to do with the different social systems of India and China.

As mentioned earlier, SW's thinking may be summed up in one sentence: The victory is one where the enemy is subdued without fighting. Such a sweeping doctrine would have been inconceivable for Kautilya because that would have devalued the entire hereditary warrior *varna*.

For this class, it was a disgrace to die anywhere except on the battlefield. So, a world without war was even theoretically inconceivable so long as one was within the established order. But a world without war was not only conceivable but eminently desirable for those outside the fold i.e., the Buddhists and the Jainas.

Emperor Ashoka established the Magadha empire as a warrior informed by the thinking embodied in the *Arthashastra*, but having done that he saw the futility of it all. That wisdom made it impossible for him to continue as a warrior. And since he ceased to believe in the creed of warriors, his rightful place was outside the "Hindu" fold, in the path of the Buddha. But among the rulers in India, Ashoka was an exception. China did not produce an Ashoka. The Indian rulers after Ashoka, Buddhists and Jaina ones included, waged wars as did the different rulers in China when the empire split up from time to time and they applied the concepts of AS and BE However, in our own century, the Kuomintang in China and the armed forces in India wholly copied the western concepts of warfare almost to the last detail. Mercifully, they ignored one commandment of Clausewitz: "To introduce in the philosophy of war a principle of moderation would be an absurdity. War is an act of violence pushed to its utmost bounds". In our own times neither India, nor Pakistan nor China has resorted to Clausewitz's concept of "total war". Is there a civilizational lesson in this?

6 Principles of War

PRINCIPLES AND WARS

Supporting this claim is experience garnered since the Second World War, including the Vietnam War. During this time frame, some of the traditional Principles of War have not been applied at all, and some that were used proved inappropriate at best and disastrous at worst under certain circumstances. Further, since the end of the Cold War, in conflicts such as those waged in Somalia during the early 1990s, more recently in the Balkans, and in Iraq today, either actual or attempted application of several of the old, 'tried and true' Principles of War has produced results that were at best unsuccessful, and, at worst, constituted military or political blunders.

War in modern times, especially the War on Terrorism, is not waged in the traditional way. The expanded security paradigm has become both cause and effect. War is now fought almost continuously on several very different fronts. The front one most commonly associates with war that is, actual combat 'in the field'is intermittent.

But on such fronts as politics, economics, energy, health and mobility, engagement is necessarily virtually fulltime, especially for state governments. Also, war in its new and fullest sense is more complex and unpredictable than before, because security within a context of globalization and instant communications is always, on all fronts, about both military and civilian concerns. In addition, actions and reactions on all fronts are interdependent, interrelated, or interconnected, meaning that a change in one, suddenly or over time, changes the other. This, of course, intensifies unpredictability.

ARMED FORCES: PRINCIPLES AND WARS

Armed forces know they need better Principles of War, even when they do not articulate that need. This is partially due to the following reasons:

- o Virtually all wars are now limited wars, most engaging both private and public armed organizations.
- o Contemporary conflict is rich in circumstances in which very junior soldiers and civilians from many sectors may, or are required to, take action that provokes strategic consequences.
- o Soldier warriors are morphing, by design, from the soldier scholar, and, by default, the soldiersavior, into soldierdiplomats.
- o Technology no longer is an impartial, undiscriminating tool of the soldier. It has come so far and is moving forward so quickly that it is provoking increasing unevenness in military capabilities and security options. It has magnified the demands for, and on, interoperability in an era when interoperability is a key to success in any war. And, not incidentally, the technology explosion has all but destroyed any reason to hope for broad standardization.
- o War is both art in the minds and hearts and hopes of those warring and science in the weapons, goods, and services at their disposal. Superpower America has learned, again at huge and continuing cost in Iraq, that modern war constitutes much more than just combat, and that security needs encompass much, much more than just technology. New Principles of War have to recognize and embrace the 'art' of war.
- o There is now such a thing as an 'asymmetrical advantage.' A 'failure of imagination' by combatants can erase virtually every advantage provided by conventional power in a war against a committed, conscientious, clever adversary, on any security front.
- o Wars have no end. There is no longer permanent defeat or permanent victory. Life is becoming experiences of 'instances of war' in different places and in various forms,

with diverse results and unpredictable, geographically unlimited consequences.

- o Conscript armies are on the way out. Recognizing that even national service armies, such as that of Singapore, need good fulltime professionals, volunteers are the true foundation of service. Volunteers will expect the principles of their profession to be sensible in the sense that their 'unlimited liability' is at least hedged whenever possible.
- o Contracting for war services has been a longstanding military characteristic. Now renewed and already extensive, the practice may cause a knowledge shift not unlike business outsourcing, such that soldier knowhow, skills, and special capabilities may well weaken, and, in some cases, even vanish from the soldier's repertoire.

CIVILIANS

Civilians, if in different ways due to their nonmilitary cultures and ethos, are increasingly aware of the need for principles with respect to the wars that involve them. The 'homeland security' challenges imposed upon them may not all come as surprises, but they are extremely uncomfortable, since decisions and choices that have previously been made have become infinitely more difficult to do properly, especially in the almost total absence of relevant principles. Such decisions and choices include, but are not limited to:

- o Entry to war: When (time), for what (cause and values), against whom, with whom, and with what?
- o Exit from war: When (time), why (cause and values), how (means), and a notwithstanding consideration.
- o How much national human, monetary, and materiel treasure can be spent, and will be spent?

SOCIETY: PRINCIPLES AND WARS

Further complicating security is the fact that many modern issues engage both civilian and military camps seriously, if not always similarly. The recent emergence of human security expectations, norms, and standards is one such issue. At national and international levels there is now a need for principles to help:

- o Decide the degree of, and manage engagement with, the International Criminal Court (ICC), and
- o Manage compliance with the paradigm of The Responsibility to Protect, the Report of the International Commission on Intervention and State Sovereignty.

A second civil military issue has already been referenced. Much of contemporary conflict is ethnic, religious, ideological, or intrastate, and it focuses intensely on mental and spiritual planes, as well as conventional materiel and technological planes. Consequences of such types of wars are more unpredictable than ever, and they are also more multidimensional than ever. They are also often global in reach.

Therefore, military and civilian personnel have no choice but to be jointly aware of the urgent need for new ways of thinking, planning, operating, and sustaining security. Old, or 'stovepiped' methods are no longer sufficient. Also, more servicepersons and civilians share an understanding that, whereas the fundamental characteristics of fighting a war of violencefire and manoeuvre, death and destructionremain, their features have been changed over time by the wars of the 20th Century and by the contemporary global security paradigm.

'Fire' now often includes actions that create and maintain fear. 'Manoeuvre' now includes a global mobility offering unlimited choice of time, means, and location of target to an attacker. 'Death' no longer is the 'ultimate liability' of predominately soldiers in uniform, but increasingly, it has become the lot of modern mercenaries, and also the fate of even more civiliansinnocent and otherwisecaught up in war. 'Destruction' no longer rains down primarily on the people, goods, and services of the enemy's armed forces, but combinations of funds, technology, and commitment offer the power to threaten and to destroy the symbols, structures, and livelihoods of tens of thousands of military personnel and civilians in an instant.

Also, an adversary's success with any offensive form of fire, manoeuvre, death, or destruction reinforces its reputation and influence, and weakens the confidence of those on the defensive. All the foregoing begs the question: Is it most appropriate to retain the old Principles of War, a set of principles assumed valid for fighting any war, and make changes to them only as and when necessary? Or, should there now be a determined effort to codify truly modern principles of war that begin with a consideration of the relevant subject, namely, modern war in its many forms and contexts? If the former option holds sway, there is clearly an urgent need for changes to some of the old principles, and probably the addition of several new ones.

Whatever a renewed list of principles would consider, it must address more thoroughly the new global security paradigm. Also, these principles, in today's context, could become realistically, and at best, only guides, and not rigid rules. And the same caveat would also apply to any other form of principles adopted. It is suggested that a far better choice would be to construct a set of Principles for War.

These principles could be derived from a selection of war scenarios; scenarios that are plausible, that address context across the range of wars' military and civilian fronts, and that situatepossibly with a form of generative analysismajor consequences. With respect to such scenarios:

- o It should be easier and quicker to design and construct meaningful Principles for War that are not just about aspects of fighting wars.
- o Principles designed purely for warfighting could be based upon, and updated from, a broader foundation of realities and reasonable future conditions, and reflected in the Principles for War themselves.
- o Principles for War should be more broadly and more enthusiastically accepted, having been designed with consideration, not only of experience and of current knowledge and events, but also of what the future may entail. This latter point is extremely important, since it is obviously in the future when any existing principles would be put to the test.

THE PROTEUS FACTOR

How will these scenarios of wars be designed and constructed? They have to be built in ways that recognize a key and fundamental need, namely, the requirement to prepare for and to navigate contexts occurring now and in the future. This concept involves 'getting one's temporal bearings' for peace and conflict (sometimes violent conflict) in the future. This formed the intellectual context for a study on strategic research, completed by the American National Reconnaissance Office (NRO) in 2001. The study was called Proteus, and it spawned a group in 2003 known as the Proteus Consortium. On 30 November 2005, a subset organization, Proteus Canada, was established. The Proteus Consortium then constructed a dynamic strategic vision model.

Initially called Protean Media, its first application was to experiment with a 'manytomany' interaction of eight factions actually existing in contemporary Iraq. The work was based partly upon the referenced study conducted at the NRO, as well as upon research into complex visualization systems at the US Naval Postgraduate School.

The Proteus Consortium has also developed a novel business model that prototypes a technology designed to experience and to apply 'educated intuition' as knowledge 'sensors' and 'weapons' that can be used alongside classic force sensors and weapons, such as those used by the military for contemporary operations. While this technology is new, some results were surprisingly positive, and they portend a rigorous, realtime analytic capability for force application that could lead to a 'navigationofchange' tool for both nonmilitary and military purposes. This business model is a networkcentric acquisition model.

The technical construct is a game that applies a fourdimension knowledge query/acquisition function to a complex environment. The most novel feature of this game is its ability to adapt to the play and to the choices (actions) of the players.

Thus, it does not follow or depend upon a prescribed and set scenario. The temporal bearings construct mentioned earlier is based upon acquiring knowledge while operating with different time scales in an environment consisting of three operational zones for force projection. Those three zones, in which the complex environments carry on simultaneously, are:

- o The source zone: analogous to an image, map, or chart, or a geographical context.

- o The local zone: analogous to the locale on the receiving end of a projected force.

"Old, or 'stovepiped' methods are no longer sufficient." The internal zone: reflecting the human experience at the local zone involving perception, as well as psychological or emotional elements. Projected force is characterized by the classical descriptions of hard, soft, coercive, and persuasive forces.

Force modifiers take many forms, and they reflect key insights grounded in the Proteus Project's research. Game play reveals both effectsbased consequences, and the gaps in knowledge that need to be filled in order to navigate changing situations. Play has also highlighted the weaknesses and incompleteness of the traditional Westphalian Principles of War with respect to modern conflict and as criteria for strategy. This is not surprising, given that:

- o Every threat or target promoted or provoked by the hugely complicated and changing mix of human security, military security, global security, environmental security, state security, democratization security, social security, food security, water security, energy security, and culture security is a moving target.
- o It is either a military's established role, or its new responsibility, or its professional concern, or its fate, to have to be engaged, more or less, with all these security fronts.

New Principles of War must embrace changes in security contexts. Change demands better foresight, analysis of uncertainties, and consequence management. Needed are strategic charting, navigationofchange, and measurement and exploitation of relationships among temporal and positional bearings. Knowledge shifts associated with changing tasks, and even greater changes to traditional 'divisions of labour' have to be better appreciated, as does how and when to apply knowledge and experience to the internal zones, classical forces, and force modifiers within the scenarios we will use to prepare for the future.

PROPOSED PRINCIPLES FOR WAR

The collective experiences of the members of the Proteus Consortium, bolstered by the philosophy of principles expressed in earlier sections of this article, could become the basis for a first set of Principles for War.

They flow from the Proteus insights and they reflect a belief that, for any scenario to be valid, intellectual space must be provided for all security fronts. In effect, the Principles for War that are itemized below are seen as dynamic boundary conditions for military and civilian actors to prepare for, and to make and to manage decisions for, future wars that will materialize, with or without warning. They are:

- o Intelligence in all directions, in time and space, using Proteus scenarios and responding to the capability gaps they expose.
- o Strategy criteria; ways and means, together with their metrics, to influence planning and decisionmaking for security futures.
- o Conciliation; active and patient tolerance for differences as a tool for preventing, when reasonable, or mitigating, when necessary, or bringing closure, when possible, to any form of conflict.
- o Cooperation; to foster interoperability. Cooperation includes 'neutral buyins,' or 'non buyins,' if there is no cost associated with the objective.
- o Arbitration; to recognize the potential for international treaties, laws, norms, and standards as a basis for conciliation. Particularly important issues are property rights and identity rights.
- o Readiness; to acknowledge the causes and effects of factors on all security fronts, as a means to ensure mental, materiel, and monetary readiness of processes and people to fight a necessary or discretionary war.
- o Objective; which is peace, not at any cost, but directed towards a state of affairs in the future more peaceful than that existing at present.
- o Economy; the design and maintenance of interactive overlapping business plans for the funds, manpower, power elements, and time required to stage a necessary or a chosen war.

- o Education; to equip every actor to be a better 'soldier statesman scholar saviour,' by promoting interdisciplinary knowledge and skills, and by fostering an awareness of other players who possess what you do not.
- o Consequence criteria; to conduct impact measurement employing humanrun compatible process technologies.
- o Competence; including, among other components, 'farsight' (all foresight beyond the 'next' target of the Principles), willingness, ability, authority, means, legitimacy, and luck.

PRINCIPLES OF WARFIGHTING

The context for Principles of Warfighting is, not surprisingly, the Principles for War themselves. Relative importance of the elements listed below will depend upon the war being fought.

Also, varying customs and beliefs related to technology, the possession and use of weapons, fighting ethics, the perceived value of life, and 'Just War' considerations will promote different interpretations of the list's elements. The suggested Principles of Warfighting should look very familiar from a traditional vantage point. In no particular order of merit or importance, they are:

- o Security
- o Interoperability
- o Concentration
- o Objective
- o Mobility
- o Economy

TACTICS OR THE THEORY OF COMBAT

War is a combination of many distinct engagements. Such a combination may or may not be reasonable, and success depends very much on this. Yet the engagement itself is for the moment more important. For only a combination of successful engagements can lead to good results. The most important thing in war will always be the art of defeating our opponent in combat. To this matter Your Royal Highness can never turn enough attention and thought. I think the following principles the most important:

General Principles For Defense

1. To keep our troops covered as long as possible. Since we are always open to attack, except when we ourselves are attacking, we must at every instant be on the defensive and thus should place our forces as much under cover as possible.
2. Not to bring all our troops into combat immediately. With such action all wisdom in conducting a battle disappears. It is only with troops left at our disposal that we can turn the tide of battle.
3. To be little or not at all concerned about the extent of our front. This in itself is unimportant, and an extension of the front limits the depth of our formation (that is, the number of units which are lined up one behind the other). Troops which are kept in the rear are always available. We can use them either to renew combat at the same point, or to carry the fight to other neighboring points. This principle is a corollary of the previous one.
4. The enemy, while attacking one section of the front, often seeks to outflank and envelop us at the same time. The units which are kept in the background can meet this attempt and thus make up for the support usually derived from obstacles in the terrain. They are better suited for this than if they were standing in line and extending the front. For in this case the enemy could easily outflank them. This principle again is a closer definition of the second.
5. If we have many troops to hold in reserve, only part of them should stand directly behind the front. The rest we should put obliquely behind. From this position they in turn can attack the flank of the enemy columns which are seeking to envelop us.
6. A fundamental principle is never to remain completely passive, but to attack the enemy frontally and from the flanks, even while he is attacking us. We should, therefore, defend ourselves on a given front merely to induce the enemy to deploy his forces in an attack on this front. Then we in turn attack with those of our troops which we have kept back. The art of entrenchment, as Your Royal Highness

expressed so excellently at one time, shall serve the defender not to defend himself more securely behind a rampart, but to attack the enemy more successfully. This idea should be applied to any passive defense. Such defense is nothing more than a means by which to attack the enemy most advantageously, in a terrain chosen in advance, where we have drawn up our troops and have arranged things to our advantage.

7. This attack from a defensive position can take place the moment the enemy actually attacks, or while he is still on the march. I can also, at the moment the attack is about to be delivered, withdraw my troops, luring the enemy into unknown territory and attacking him from all sides. The formation in depth i.e., the formation in which only twothirds or half or still less of the army is drawnup in front and the rest directly or obliquely behind and hidden, if possibleis very suitable for all these moves. This type of formation is, therefore, of immense importance.
8. If, for example, I had two divisions, I would prefer to keep one in the rear. If I had three, I would keep at least one in the rear, and if four probably two. If I had five, I should hold at least two in reserve and in many cases even three, etc.
9. At those points where we remain passive we must make use of the art of fortification. This should be done with many independent works, completely closed and with very strong profiles.
10. In our plan of battle we must set this great aim: the attack on a large enemy column and its complete destruction. If our aim is low, while that of the enemy is high, we will naturally get the worst of it. We are pennywise and poundfoolish.
11. Having set a high goal in our plan of defense (the annihilation of an enemy column, etc.), we must pursue this goal with the greatest energy and with the last ounce of our strength. In most cases the aggressor will pursue his own aim at some other point. While we fall upon his right wing, for example, he will try to win decisive

advantages with his left. Consequently, if we should slacken before the enemy does, if we should pursue our aim with less energy than he does, he will gain his advantage completely, while we shall only half gain ours. He will thus achieve preponderance of power; the victory will be his, and we shall have to give up even our partly gained advantages. If Your Royal Highness will read with attention the history of the battles of Ratisbon and Wagram, all this will seem true and important. In both these battles the Emperor Napoleon attacked with his right wing and tried to hold out with his left. The Archduke Charles did exactly the same. But, while the former acted with great determination and energy, the latter was wavering and always stopped halfway. That is why the advantages which Charles gained with the victorious part of his army were without consequence, while those which Napoleon gained at the opposite end were decisive.

12. Let me sum up once more the last two principles. Their combination gives us a maxim which should take first place among all causes of victory in the modern art of war: "Pursue one great decisive aim with force and determination."
13. If we follow this and fail, the danger will be even greater, it is true. But to increase caution at the expense of the final goal is no military art. It is the wrong kind of caution, which, is contrary to the nature of war. For great aims we must dare great things. When we are engaged in a daring enterprise, the right caution consists in not neglecting out of laziness, indolence, or carelessness those measures which help us to gain our aim. Such was the case of Napoleon, who never pursued great aims in a timid or halfhearted way out of caution.

If you remember, Most Gracious Master, the few defensive battles that have ever been won, you will find that the best of them have been conducted in the spirit of the principles voiced here. For it is the study of the history of war which has given us these principles. At Minden, Duke Ferdinand suddenly appeared where the enemy did not expect him and took the offensive, while at

Tannhausen he defended himself passively behind earthworks. At Rossbach, Frederick II threw himself against the enemy at an unexpected point and an unexpected moment. At Liegnitz, the Austrians found the King at night in a position very different from that in which they had seen him the previous day.

He fell with his whole army upon one enemy column and defeated it before the others could start fighting. At Hohenlinden, Moreau had five divisions in his front line and four directly behind and on his flanks. He outflanked the enemy and fell upon his right wing before it could attack. At Ratisbon, Marshal Davout defended himself passively, while Napoleon attacked the fifth and sixth armycorps with his right wing and beat them completely. Though the Austrians were the real defenders at Wagram, they did attack the emperor on the second day with the greater part of their forces.

Therefore Napoleon can also be considered a defender. With his right wing he attacked, outflanked and defeated the Austrian left wing. At the same time he paid little attention to his weak left wing (consisting of a single division), which was resting on the Danube. Yet through strong reserves (i.e., formation in depth), he prevented the victory of the Austrian right wing from having any influence on his own victory gained on the Rossbach. He used these reserves to retake Aderklaa. Not all the principles mentioned earlier are clearly contained in each of these battles, but all are examples of active defense. The mobility of the Prussian army under Frederick II was a means towards victory on which we can no longer count, since the other armies are at least as mobile as we are. On the other hand, outflanking was less common at that time and formation in depth, therefore, less imperative.

General Principles For Offense

1. We must select for our attack one point of the enemy's position (i.e., one section of his troops a division, a corps) and attack it with great superiority, leaving the rest of his army in uncertainty but keeping it occupied. This is the only way that we can use an equal or smaller force to fight with advantage and thus with a chance of success. The weaker we are, the fewer troops we should use to keep

the enemy occupied at unimportant points, in order to be as strong as possible at the decisive point. Frederick II doubtlessly won the battle of Leuthen only because he massed his small army together in one place and thus was very concentrated, as compared to the enemy.

2. We should direct our main thrust against an enemy wing by attacking it from the front and from the flank, or by turning it completely and attacking it from the rear. Only when we cut off the enemy's line of retreat are we assured of great success in victory.
3. Even though we are strong, we should still direct our main attack against one point only. In that way we shall gain more strength at this point. For to surround an army completely is possible only in rare cases and requires tremendous physical or moral superiority. It is possible, however, to cut off the enemy's line of retreat at one point of his flank and thereby already gain great success.
4. Generally speaking, the chief aim is the certainty (high probability) of victory, that is, the certainty of driving the enemy from the field of battle. The plan of battle must be directed towards this end. For it is easy to change an indecisive victory into a decisive one through energetic pursuit of the enemy.
5. Let us assume that the enemy has troops enough on one wing to make a front in all directions. Our main force should try to attack the wing concentrically, so his troops find themselves assailed from all sides. Under these circumstances his troops will get discouraged much more quickly; they suffer more, get disorderedin short, we can hope to turn them to flight much more easily.

Principles Governing the Use of Troops

If we cannot dispense with firearms (and if we could, why should we bring them along?), we must use them to open combat. Cavalry must not be used before the enemy has suffered considerably from our infantry and artillery. From this it follows: That we must place the cavalry behind the infantry. That we must not be easily led to use it in opening combat. Only when the enemy's disorder or his rapid retreat offer the hope of success, should we use our cavalry for an audacious attack. Artillery fire is much more effective than that of infantry. A battery of eight sixpounders takes up less than onethird of the front taken up by an infantry battalion; it has less than oneeighth the men of a battalion, and yet its fire is two to three times as effective. On the other hand, artillery has the disadvantage of being less mobile than infantry.

This is true, on the whole, even of the lightest horse artillery, for it cannot, like infantry, be used in any kind of terrain. It is necessary, therefore, to direct the artillery from the start against the most important points, since it cannot, like infantry, concentrate against these points as the battle progresses. A large battery of 20 to 30 pieces usually decides the battle for that section where it is placed. From these and other apparent characteristics the following rules can be drawn for the use of the different arms:

(a) We should begin combat with the larger part of our artillery. Only when we have large masses of troops at our disposal should we keep horse and foot artillery in reserve. We should use artillery in great batteries massed against one point. Twenty to thirty pieces combined into one battery defend the chief part of our line, or shell that part of the enemy position which we plan to attack.

(b) After this we use light infantry either marksmen, riflemen, or fusileers being careful not to put too many forces into play at the beginning. We try first to discover what lies ahead of us (for we can seldom see that clearly in advance), and which way the battle is turning, etc.

If this firing line is sufficient to counteract the enemy's troops, and if there is no need to hurry, we should do wrong to hasten the use of our remaining forces. We must try to exhaust the enemy as much as possible with this preliminary skirmish.

(c) If the enemy should lead so many troops into combat that our firing line is about to fall back, or if for some other reason we should no longer hesitate, we must draw up a full line of infantry. This will deploy between 100 and 200 paces from the enemy and will fire or charge, as matters may be.

(d) This is the main purpose of the infantry. If, at the same time, the battle array is deep enough, leaving us another line of infantry (arranged in columns) as reserve, we shall be sufficiently master of the situation at this sector. This second line of infantry should, if possible, be used only in columns to bring about a decision.

(e) The cavalry should be as close behind the fighting troops during battle as is possible without great loss; that is, it should be out of the enemy's grapeshot or musket fire. On the other hand, it should be close enough to take quick advantage of any favorable turn of battle.

In obeying these rules more or less closely, we should never lose sight of the following principle, which I cannot stress enough: Never bring all our forces into play haphazardly and at one time, thereby losing all means of directing the battle; but fatigue the opponent, if possible, with few forces and conserve a decisive mass for the critical moment. Once this decisive mass has been thrown in, it must be used with the greatest audacity. We should establish one battleorder (the arrangement of troops before and during combat) for the whole campaign or the whole war.

This order will serve in all cases when there is no time for a special disposition of troops. It should, therefore, be calculated primarily for the defensive. The army consists of several such independent corps, which have their own general and staff. They are drawn up in line and behind each other, as described in the general rules for combat. It should be observed at this point that, unless we are very weak in cavalry, we should create a special cavalry reserve, which, of course, is kept in the rear. Its purpose is as follows:

(a) To fall upon the enemy when he is retreating from the field of battle and to attack the cavalry which he uses to cover up his retreat. Should we defeat the enemy's cavalry at this moment, great successes are inevitable, unless the enemy's infantry would perform miracles of bravery. Small detachments of cavalry would not accomplish this purpose.

(b) To pursue the enemy more rapidly, if he should be retreating unbeaten or if he should continue to retreat the day after a lost battle. Cavalry moves faster than infantry and has a more demoralizing effect on the retreating troops. Next to victory, the act of pursuit is most important in war.

(c) To execute a great (strategic) turning move, should we need, because of the detour, a branch of the army which moves more rapidly than the infantry.

In order to make this corps more independent, we should attach a considerable mass of horse artillery; for a combination of several types of arms can only give greater strength. The battleorder of troops described thus far was intended for combat; it was the formation of troops for battle. The order of march is essentially as follows: Each independent corps (whether brigade or division) has its own advancedand rearguard and forms its own column. That, however, does not prevent several corps from marching one behind the other on the same road, and thus, as it were, forming a single column.

The corps march according to their position in the general formation of battle. They march beside or behind each other, just as they would stand on the battlefield. In the corps themselves the following order is invariably observed: the light infantry, with the addition of one regiment of cavalry, forming the advanced and rearguard, then the infantry, the artillery, and last the remaining cavalry. This order stands, whether we are moving against the enemy in which case it is the natural order or parallel with him. In the latter case we should assume that those troops which in the battle formation were behind each other should march side by side. But when we have to draw up the troops for battle, there will always be sufficient time to move the cavalry and the second line of infantry either to the right or left.

STRATEGY

This term means the combination of individual engagements to attain the goal of the campaign or war. If we know how to fight and how to win, little more knowledge is needed. For it is easy to combine fortunate results. It is merely a matter of experienced judgment and does not depend on special knowledge, as does the direction of battle. The few principles, therefore, which come up in this connection, and which depend primarily on the condition of the respective states and armies, can in their essential parts be very briefly summarized:

General Principles

Warfare has three main objects:

(a) To conquer and destroy the armed power of the enemy;

(b) To take possession of his material and other sources of strength, and

(c) To gain public opinion.

To accomplish the first purpose, we should always direct our principal operation against the main body of the enemy army or at least against an important portion of his forces. For only after defeating these can we pursue the other two objects successfully. In order to seize the enemy's material forces we should direct our operations against the places where most of these resources are concentrated: principal cities, storehouses, and large fortresses. On the way to these objectives we shall encounter the enemy's main force or at least a considerable part of it. Public opinion is won through great victories and the occupation of the enemy's capital. The first and most important rule to observe in order to accomplish these purposes, is to use our entire forces with the utmost energy.

Any moderation shown would leave us short of our aim. Even with everything in our favour, we should be unwise not to make the greatest effort in order to make the result perfectly certain. For such effort can never produce negative results.

Suppose the country suffers greatly from this, no lasting disadvantage will arise; for the greater the effort, the sooner the suffering will cease. The moral impression created by these actions is of infinite importance. They make everyone confident of success, which is the best means for suddenly raising the nation's morale. The second rule is to concentrate our power as much as possible against that section where the chief blows are to be delivered and to incur disadvantages elsewhere, so that our chances of success may increase at the decisive point.

This will compensate for all other disadvantages. The third rule is never to waste time. Unless important advantages are to be gained from hesitation, it is necessary to set to work at once. By this speed a hundred enemy measures are nipped in the bud, and public opinion is won most rapidly. Surprise plays a much greater role in strategy than in tactics. It is the most important element of victory. Napoleon, Frederick II, Gustavus Adolphus, Caesar, Hannibal, and Alexander owe the brightest rays of their fame to their swiftness. Finally, the fourth rule is to follow up our successes with the utmost energy. Only pursuit of the beaten enemy gives the fruits of victory.

The first of these rules serves as a basis for the other three. If we have observed it, we can be as daring as possible with the last three, and yet not risk our all. For it provides us with the means of constantly creating new forces in our rear, and with fresh forces any misfortune can be remedied. Therein lies the caution which deserves to be called wise, and not in taking each step forward with timidity. Small states cannot wage wars of conquest in our times.

But in defensive warfare even the means of small states are infinitely great. I am, therefore, firmly convinced that if we spare no effort to reappear again and again with new masses of troops, if we use all possible means of preparation and keep our forces concentrated at the main point, and if we, thus prepared, pursue a great aim with determination and energy, we have done all that can be done on a large scale for the strategic direction of the war. And unless we are very unfortunate in battle we are bound to be victorious to the same extent that our opponent lags behind in effort and energy. In observing these principles little depends on the form in which the operations are carried out. I shall try, nevertheless, to make clear in a few words the most important aspects of this question. In tactics we always seek to envelop that part of the enemy against which we direct our main attack.

We do this partly because our forces are more effective in a concentric than in a parallel attack, and further because we can only thus cut off the enemy from his line of retreat. But if we apply this to the whole theatre of war (and consequently to the enemy's lines of communication), the individual columns and armies, which are to envelop the enemy, are in most cases too far away from each other to participate in one and the same engagement. The opponent will find himself in the middle and will be able to turn against the corps one by one and defeat them all with a single army. Frederick II's campaigns may serve as examples, especially those of 1757 and 1758.

The individual engagement, therefore, remains the principal decisive event. Consequently, if we attack concentrically without having decisive superiority, we shall lose in battle all the advantages, which we expected from our enveloping attack on the enemy. For an attack on the lines of communication takes effect only very slowly, while victory on the field of battle bears fruit immediately. In strategy, therefore, the side that is surrounded by the enemy is better off than the side which surrounds its opponent, especially with equal or even weaker forces. Colonel Jomini was right in this, and if Mr. Von Bulow has demonstrated the opposite with so much semblance of truth, it is only because he attributed too great an importance to the interruption of provisions and carelessly and completely denied the inevitable success of battle. To cut the enemy's line of retreat, however, strategic envelopment or a turning movement is very effective.

But we can achieve this, if necessary, through tactical envelopment. A strategic move is, therefore, advisable only if we are so superior (physically and morally) that we shall be strong enough at the principal point to dispense with the detached corps. The Emperor Napoleon never engaged in strategic envelopment, although he was often, indeed almost always, both physically and morally superior. Frederick II used it only once, in 1757, in his invasion of Bohemia.

To be sure, the result was that the Austrians could not give battle until Prague, and what good was the conquest of Bohemia as far as Prague without a decisive victory? The battle of Kolin forced him to give up all this territory again, which proves that battles decide everything. At the same time he was obviously in danger at Prague of being attacked by the whole Austrian force, before Schwerin arrived. He would not have run this risk had he passed through Saxony with all his forces. In that case the first battle would have been fought perhaps near Budin, on the Eger, and it would have been as decisive as that of Prague. The dislocation of the Prussian army during the winter in Silesia and Saxony undoubtedly caused this concentric maneuver. It is important to notice that circumstances of this kind are generally more influential than the advantages to be gained by the form of attack. For facility of operations increases their speed, and the friction inherent in the tremendous warmachine of an armed power is so great in itself that it should not be increased unnecessarily. Moreover, the principle of concentrating our forces as much as possible on the main point diverts us from the idea of strategic envelopment and the deployment of our forces follows automatically. I was right, therefore, in saying that the form of this deployment is of little consequence. There is, however, one case in which a strategic move against the enemy's flank will lead to great successes similar to those of a battle: if in a poor country the enemy has accumulated with great effort stores of supplies, on whose preservation his operations absolutely depend. In this case it may be advisable not to march our main forces against those of the enemy, but to attack his base of supply. For this, however, two conditions are essential:

(a) The enemy must be so far from his base that our threat will force him into a considerable retreat, and

(b) We must be able to obstruct his advance in the direction followed by his principal force with only a few troops (thanks to natural and artificial obstacles), so that he cannot make conquests somewhere else which will compensate for the loss of his base.

The provisioning of troops is a necessary condition of warfare and thus has great influence on the operations, especially since it permits only a limited concentration of troops and since it helps to determine the theatre of war through the choice of a line of operations. The provisioning of troops is carried on, if a region possibly permits it, through requisitions at the expense of the region. In the modern method of war armies take up considerably more territory than before.

The creation of distinct, independent corps has made this possible, without putting ourselves at a disadvantage before an adversary who follows the old method of concentration at a single point (with from 70,000 to 100,000 men). For an independent corps, organized as they now are, can withstand for some time an enemy two or three times its superior. Then the others will arrive and, even if the first corps has already been beaten, it has not fought in vain, as we have had occasion to remark. Today, therefore, the divisions and corps move into battle independently, marching side by side or behind each other and only close enough to take part in the same battle, if they belong to the same army. This makes possible immediate provisioning without storehouses.

The very organization of the corps with their General Staff and their Commissariat facilitates this. If there are no MORE decisive motives (as for example the location of the enemy's main army), we choose the most fertile provinces for our operations; for facility of provisioning increases the speed of our actions. Only the situation of the enemy's main force which we are seeking out, only the location of his capital and the place of arms which we wish to conquer are more important than provisioning. All other considerations, such as the advantageous disposition of our forces, of which we have already spoken, are as a rule much less important. In spite of these new methods of provisioning, it is quite impossible to do without any depots whatever. Therefore, even when the resources of the region are quite sufficient, a wise military leader does not fail to establish depots in his rear for unexpected emergencies and in order to be able to concentrate his forces at certain points. This precaution is of the sort which are not taken at the expense of the final goal.

Defensive

Politically speaking defensive war is a war which we wage for our independence. Strategically it is the kind of campaign in which we limit ourselves to fighting the enemy in a theatre of war which we have prepared for this purpose. Whether the battles which we wage in this theatre of war are offensive or defensive, makes no difference. We adopt a strategic defensive mainly when the enemy is superior. Fortresses and entrenched camps, which constitute the chief preparations for a theatre of war, afford, of course, great advantages, to which may be added the knowledge of the terrain and the possession of good maps. A smaller army, or an army which is based on a smaller state and more limited resources, will be better able to withstand the enemy WITH these advantages than without them. In addition there are the following two reasons which can lead us to choose a defensive war. First, when the regions surrounding the theatre of war render operations extremely difficult because of lack of provisions.

In this case we avoid a disadvantage which the enemy is forced to undergo. This is the case now (1812) with the Russian army. Second, when the enemy is superior in warfare. In a theatre of war which we have prepared, which we know, and in which all minor conditions are in our favour, war is easier to conduct, and we commit fewer mistakes. When lack of trust in our troops and generals forces us to wage defensive war, we often like to combine tactical with strategic defensive. In that case we fight battles in prepared positions because we are thus again exposed to fewer mistakes. In defensive just as in offensive warfare, it is necessary to pursue a great aim: the destruction of the enemy army, either by battle or by rendering its subsistence extremely difficult. Thus we shall disorganize it and force it into a retreat, during which it will necessarily suffer great losses. Wellington's campaign in 1810 and 1811 is a good example. Defensive warfare, therefore, does not consist of waiting idly for things to happen.

We must wait only if it brings us visible and decisive advantages. That calm before the storm, when the aggressor is gathering new forces for a great blow, is most dangerous for the defender. If the Austrians after the battle of Aspern had increased their forces threefold, as they might have and as the Emperor Napoleon did, then and only then would they have made good use of the lull which lasted until the battle of Wagram. This they did not do, and consequently the time was lost. It would have been wiser to profit from Napoleon's disadvantageous position, and to gather the fruits of the battle of Aspern. The purpose of fortifications is to keep a considerable part of the enemy's army occupied as siege troops, to give us an opportunity to defeat the rest of his army.

Consequently, it is best to fight our battles behind our fortifications and not in front of them. But we must not stand by idly, while they are being conquered, as Bennigsen did during the siege of Danzig. Large rivers, across which it is difficult to throw a bridge (such as the Danube below Vienna and the Lower Rhine), offer a natural line of defense. But we should not distribute our forces evenly along the river bank in order to prevent any crossing whatsoever.

That would be most dangerous. On the contrary, we should watch the river and fall upon the enemy from all sides the minute he crosses, while he has not yet reassembled his forces and is still restricted to a narrow space on the river bank. The battle of Aspern offers a good illustration. At Wagram the Austrians had yielded to the French too much territory without the slightest necessity, so that the disadvantages inherent in a river crossing had disappeared. Mountains are the second obstacle which offers a good line of defense. There are two ways of using them. The first is to leave them in front of us, occupying them only with light troops and considering them, so to speak, a river which the enemy will have to cross. As soon as his separated columns emerge from the passes, we fall upon one of them with all our force. The second is to occupy the mountains ourselves.

In that case we must defend each pass with just a small corps and keep an important part of the army (1/31/2) in reserve, in order to attack with superior forces one of the enemy columns that succeed in breaking through. We must not divide up this large reserve to prevent completely the penetration of any enemy columns, but must plan from the outset to fall only upon those columns which we suppose to be the strongest. If we thus defeat an important part of the attacking army, any other columns which have succeeded in breaking through will withdraw of their own accord. In the midst of most mountain formations we find more or less elevated plains (plateaus) whose slopes are cut by ravines serving as means of access. Mountains, therefore, offer the defender a region in which he can move rapidly to the right or left, while the columns of the aggressor remain separated by steep, inaccessible ridges. Only mountains of this kind are well adapted for defensive warfare. If, on the other hand, their whole interior is rough and inaccessible, leaving the defender dispersed and divided, their defense by the bulk of the army is a dangerous undertaking.

For under these circumstances all advantages are on the side of the aggressor, who can attack certain points with great superiority, and no pass, no isolated point is so strong that it cannot be taken within a day by superior forces. In regard to mountain warfare in general, we should observe that everything depends on the skill of our subordinate officers and still more on the morale of our soldiers. Here it is not a question of skillful maneuvering, but of warlike spirit and wholehearted devotion to the cause; for each man is left more or less to act independently.

That is why national militias are especially suited for mountain warfare. While they lack the ability to maneuver, they possess the other qualities to the highest degree. Finally, it should be observed that the strategic defensive, though it is stronger than the offensive, should serve only to win the first important successes. If these are won and peace does not follow immediately, we can gain further successes only through the offensive. For if we remain continually on the defensive, we run the great risk of always waging war at our own expense. This no state can endure indefinitely. If it submits to the blows of its adversary without ever striking back, it will very likely become exhausted and succumb. We must begin, therefore, using the defensive, so as to end more successfully by the offensive.

Offensive

The strategic offensive pursues the aim of the war directly, aiming straight at the destruction of the enemy's forces, while the strategic defensive seeks to reach this purpose indirectly. The principles of the offensive are therefore already contained in the "General Principles" of strategy. Only two points need be mentioned more fully. The first is constant replacement of troops and arms. This is easier for the defender, because of the proximity of his sources of supply. The aggressor, although he controls in most cases a larger state, must usually gather his forces from a distance and therefore with great difficulty. Lest he find himself short of effectives, he must organize the recruiting of troops and the transport of arms a long time before they are needed. The roads of our lines of operation must be covered constantly with transports of soldiers and supplies. We must establish military stations along these roads to hasten this rapid transport. Even under the most favorable circumstances and with greatest moral and physical superiority, the aggressor should foresee a possibility of great disaster.

He therefore must organize on his lines of operation strong points to which he can retreat with a defeated army. Such are fortresses with fortified camps or simply fortified camps. Large rivers offer the best means of halting the pursuing enemy for a while. We must therefore secure our crossing by means of bridgeheads, surrounded by a number of strong redoubts. We must leave behind us a number of troops for the occupation of these strong points as well as the occupation of the most important cities and fortresses.

Their number depends on how much we have to be afraid of invasions or of the attitude of the inhabitants. These troops, together with reinforcements, form new corps, which, in case of success, follow the advancing army, but in case of misfortune, occupy the fortified points in order to secure our retreat. Napoleon always took great care with these measures for the protection of the rear of his army, and therefore, in his most audacious operations, risked less than was usually apparent.

APPLICATION OF THESE PRINCIPLES IN TIME OF WAR

The principles of the art of war are in themselves extremely simple and quite within the reach of sound common sense. Even though they require more special knowledge in tactics than in strategy, this knowledge is of such small scope, that it does not compare with any other subject in extent and variety. Extensive knowledge and deep learning are by no means necessary, nor are extraordinary intellectual faculties. If, in addition to experienced judgment, a special mental quality is required, it would be, after all that has been said cunning or shrewdness.

For a long time the contrary has been maintained, either because of false veneration for the subject or because of the vanity of the authors who have written about it. Unprejudiced reflection should convince us of this, and experience only makes this conviction stronger. As recently as the Revolutionary War we find many men who proved themselves able military leaders, yes, even military leaders of the first order, without having had any military education. In the case of Condé, Wallenstein, Suvorov, and a multitude of others it is very doubtful whether or not they had the advantage of such education. The conduct of war itself is without doubt very difficult. But the difficulty is not that erudition and great genius are necessary to understand the basic principles of warfare.

These principles are within the reach of any wellorganized mind, which is unprejudiced and not entirely unfamiliar with the subject. Even the application of these principles on maps or on paper presents no difficulty, and to have devised a good plan of operations is no great masterpiece. The great difficulty is this:

To Remain Faithful Throughout To The Principles We Have Laid Down For Ourselves.

The conduct of war resembles the workings of an intricate machine with tremendous friction, so that combinations which are easily planned on paper can be executed only with great effort. The free will and the mind of the military commander, therefore, find themselves constantly hampered, and one needs a remarkable strength of mind and soul to overcome this resistance. Many good ideas have perished because of this friction, and we must carry out more simply and moderately what under a more complicated form would have given greater results. It may be impossible to enumerate exhaustively the causes of this friction; but the main ones are as follows:

1. Generally we are not nearly as well acquainted with the position and measures of the enemy as we assume in our plan of operations. The minute we begin carrying out our decision, a thousand doubts arise about the dangers which might develop if we have been seriously mistaken in our plan. A feeling of uneasiness, which often takes hold of a person about to perform something great, will take possession of us, and from this uneasiness to indecision, and from there to half measures are small, scarcely discernible steps.

2. Not only are we uncertain about the strength of the enemy, but in addition rumor (i.e., all the news which we obtain from outposts, through spies, or by accident) exaggerates

his size. The majority of people are timid by nature, and that is why they constantly exaggerate danger. All influences on the military leader, therefore, combine to give him a false impression of his opponent's strength, and from this arises a new source of indecision.

We cannot take this uncertainty too seriously, and it is important to be prepared for it from the beginning.

After we have thought out everything carefully in advance and have sought and found without prejudice the most plausible plan, we must not be ready to abandon it at the slightest provocation. On the contrary, we must be prepared to submit the reports which reach us to careful criticism, we must compare them with each other, and send out for more. In this way false reports are very often disproved immediately, and the first reports confirmed. In both cases we gain certainty and can make our decision accordingly. Should this certainty be lacking, we must tell ourselves that nothing is accomplished in warfare without daring; that the nature of war certainly does not let us see at all times where we are going; that what is probable will always be probable though at the moment it may not seem so; and finally, that we cannot be readily ruined by a single error, if we have made reasonable preparations.

3. Our uncertainty about the situation at a given moment is not limited to the conditions of the enemy only but of our own army as well. The latter can rarely be kept together to the extent that we are able to survey all its parts at any moment, and if we are inclined to uneasiness, new doubts will arise. We shall want to wait, and a delay of our whole plan will be the inevitable result.

   We must, therefore, be confident that the general measures we have adopted will produce the results we expect. Most important in this connection is the trust which we must have in our lieutenants. Consequently, it is important to choose men on whom we can rely and to put aside all other considerations. If we have made appropriate preparations, taking into account all possible misfortunes, so that we shall not be lost immediately if they occur, we must boldly advance into the shadows of uncertainty.

4. If we wage war with all our strength, our subordinate commanders and even our troops (especially if they are not used to warfare) will frequently encounter difficulties which they declare insurmountable. They find the march too long, the fatigue too great, the provisions impossible. If we lend our ear to all these DIFFICULTIES, we shall soon succumb completely, and instead of acting with force and determination, we shall be reduced to weakness and inactivity.

   To resist all this we must have faith in our own insight and convictions. At the time this often has the appearance of stubbornness. but in reality it is that strength of mind and character which is called firmness.

5. The results on which we count in warfare are never as precise as is imagined by someone who has not carefully observed a war and become used to it.

   Very often we miscalculate the march of a column by several hours, without being able to tell the cause of the delay. Often we encounter obstacles which were impossible to foresee. Often we intend to reach a certain place with our army and fall short of it by several hours. Often a small outpost which we have set up achieves much less than we expected, while an enemy outpost achieves much more. Often the resources of a region do not amount to as much as we expected, etc.

   We can triumph over such obstacles only with very great exertion, and to accomplish this the leader must show a severity bordering on cruelty. Only when he knows that everything possible is always being done, can he be sure that these small difficulties will not have a great influence on his operations. Only then can he be sure that he will not fall too far short of the aim which he could have reached.

6. We may be sure that an army will never be in the condition supposed by someone following its operations from an armchair. If he is sympathetic to the army he will imagine

it from a third to a half stronger and better than it really is. It is quite natural that the military commander will make the same mistake in planning his first operations. Consequently, he will see his army melt away as he never thought it would, and his cavalry and artillery become useless. What appeared possible and easy to the observer and to the commander at the opening of a campaign is often difficult and even impossible to carry out. If the military leader is filled with high ambition and if he pursues his aims with audacity and strength of will, he will reach them in spite of all obstacles; while an ordinary person would have found in the condition of his army a sufficient excuse for giving in.

Masséna proved at Genoa and in Portugal the influence of a strongwilled leader over his troops. At Genoa, the limitless exertion to which his strength of will, not to say his harshness, forced people, was crowned with success. In Portugal he at least retreated later than anyone else would have.

Most of the time the enemy army is in the same position. For example, Wallenstein and Gustavus Adolphus at Nuremberg, and Napoleon and Bennigsen after the battle of Eylau. But while we do not see the condition of the enemy, our own is right before our eyes. The latter, therefore, makes a greater impression on ordinary people than the first, since sensuous impressions are stronger for such people than the language of reason.

7. The provisioning of troops, no matter how it is done, whether through storehouses or requisitions, always presents such difficulty that it must have a decisive influence on the choice of operations. It is often contrary to the most effective combination, and forces us to search for provisions when we would like to pursue victory and brilliant success. This is the main cause for the unwieldiness of the whole war machine which keeps the results so far beneath the flight of our great plans.

A general, who with tyrannical authority demands of his troops the most extreme exertions and the greatest privations, and an army which in the course of long wars has become hardened to such sacrifices will have a tremendous advantage over their adversaries and will reach their aim much faster in spite of all obstacles. With equally good plans, what a difference of result!

8. We cannot stress the following too much: Visual impressions gained during actual combat are more vivid than those gained beforehand by mature reflection. But they give us only the outward appearance of things, which, as we know, rarely corresponds to their essence. We therefore run the risk of sacrificing mature reflection for first impression.

The natural timidity of humans, which sees only one side to everything, makes this first impression incline toward fear and exaggerated caution. Therefore we must fortify ourselves against this impression and have blind faith in the results of our own earlier reflections, in order to strengthen ourselves against the weakening impressions of the moment. These difficulties, therefore, demand confidence and firmness of conviction. That is why the study of military history is so important, for it makes us see things as they are and as they function. The principles which we can learn from theoretical instruction are only suited to facilitate this study and to call our attention to the most important elements in the history of war. Your Royal Highness, therefore, must become acquainted with these principles in order to check them against the history of war, to see whether they are in agreement with it and to discover where they are corrected or even contradicted by the course of events.

In addition, only the study of military history is capable of giving those who have no experience of their own a clear impression of what I have just called the friction of the whole machine. Of course, we must not be satisfied with its main conclusions, and still less with the reasoning of historians, but we must penetrate as deeply as possible into the details. For the aim of historians rarely is to present the absolute truth. Usually they wish to embellish the deeds of their army or to demonstrate the concordance of events with their imaginary rules. They invent history instead of writing it. We need not study much history for the purpose we propose. The detailed knowledge of a few individual engagements is more useful than the general knowledge of a great many campaigns.

Open your heart to such emotion. Be audacious and cunning in your plans, firm and persevering in their execution, determined to find a glorious end, and fate will crown your youthful brow with a shining glory, which is the ornament of princes, and engrave your image in the hearts of your last descendants.

7 The Rules of Warfare and Their Violation

The nations of the world, including our enemies, have at different times signed treaties governing the conduct of war and outlawing certain kinds of behaviour by the forces of the belligerents. The most relevant sources of this written law are (1) the Hague Convention of 1899 relating to the laws and customs of war on land; (2) a revision and extension of this issued in 1907; (3) a convention regulating the treatment of prisoners of war; and (4) a Red Cross convention regarding the treatment of wounded and sick members of armies in the field. The last two were signed in Geneva in 1929. In addition, certain kinds of behaviour are prohibited not only by these international agreements but by the customary or common law of warfare as well.

The provisions of the conventions (written law) and also many of the provisions of the common law of warfare (unwritten law) are embodied in the military manuals of civilized states. For the American Army, the relevant law is contained in FM 27–10, *Rules of Land Warfare*, which summarizes the violations of the laws and customs of warfare most frequently involved, as follows: "Offenses by armed forces.—The principal offenses of this class are: Making use of poisoned and otherwise forbidden arms and ammunition; killing of the wounded; refusal of quarter; treacherous request for quarter;... ill-treatment of prisoners of war;... firing on undefended localities;... misuse of the Red Cross flag and emblem...; bombardment of hospitals and other privileged buildings; improper use of privileged buildings for military purposes; poisoning of wells and streams; pillage and purposeless destruction; ill-treatment of inhabitants in occupied territory." Some of these offenses (for example, refusal of quarter) can only be military crimes, but ill-treatment of inhabitants in occupied territory, if it results in death, can be prosecuted as "murder in violation of the laws and customs of warfare."

OFFENSES AGAINST BELLIGERENTS

German and Japanese troops have violated many if not most of the laws and customs of war. Thousands of such instances have been and are being recorded by the American, Russian, Polish, Dutch, Norwegian, and other governments. Some of these records are already in print, and we shall draw a few typical examples from documents published by the nations concerned. These examples illustrate the scope of the atrocities which the Axis is charged with having committed.

We may usefully begin with some cases relating to the violations of the duties of a belligerent toward enemy troops: The Polish Ministry of Information, in a compilation of Nazi atrocities published in 1942, charges that "After the capitulation of the fortress of Modlin, heroically defended until the moment of the surrender of Warsaw, the Germans in one sector of the front murdered a whole platoon of captured Polish soldiers. They ordered them to kneel down and raise their arms, then shot them all with machine-guns.

Several Polish officers who had been seized, were also shot in the same way. Others were transported to Zakroczym, where they were placed against a wall and shot. On September 2 and 3, 1939, between Rybnik and Wadzim, in Silesia, the Germans captured a detachment of the 12th Infantry Regiment. They took no prisoners, but threw the men to the ground, and drove over their bodies with tanks."

Rules of Land Warfare declare that "prisoners of war are in the power of the enemy power, but not of the individuals or bodies of troops who capture them. They must at all times be treated with humanity and protected, particularly against acts of violence, insults, and public curiosity. Measures of reprisal against them are prohibited." According to the representations of Secretary of State Cordell Hull to the Japanese government, as published in the *Bulletin* of the Department of State, February 12, 1944, the Japanese have savagely disregarded these rights of American and Filipino soldiers.

"Prisoners of war who were marched from Bataan to San Fernando in April 1942 were brutally treated by Japanese guards. The guards clubbed prisoners who tried to get water, and one prisoner was hit on the head with a club for helping a fellow prisoner who had been knocked down by a Japanese army truck. A colonel who pointed to a can of salmon by the side of the road and asked for food for the prisoners was struck on the side of his head with the can by a Japanese officer. The colonel's face was cut open. Another colonel who had found a sympathetic Filipino with a cart was horsewhipped in the face for trying to give transportation to persons unable to walk.... An American Lieutenant Colonel was killed by a Japanese as he broke ranks to get a drink at a stream... Americans were... tortured and shot without trial at Cabanatuan in June or July 1942 because they endeavored to bring food into the camp. After being tied to a fence post inside the camp for two days they were shot."

Rules of Land Warfare provide that "Belligerents shall be bound to take all sanitary measures necessary to assure the cleanliness and healthfulness of camps and to prevent epidemics. Prisoners of war shall have at their disposal, day and night, installations conforming to sanitary rules and constantly maintained in a state of cleanliness." Conditions maintained by the Japanese in the prison camps were a far cry from this humane provision.

"At Camp O'Donnell conditions were so bad that 2,200 Americans and more than 20,000 Filipinos are reliably reported to have died in the first few months of their detention. There is no doubt that a large number of these deaths could have been prevented had the Japanese authorities provided minimum medical care for the prisoners. The so-called hospital there was absolutely inadequate to meet the situation. Prisoners of war lay sick and naked on the floor, receiving no attention and too sick to move from their own excrement. The hospital was so overcrowded that Americans were laid on the ground outside in the heat of the blazing sun. The American doctors in the camp were given no medicine, and even had no water to wash the human waste from the bodies of the patients.

Eventually, when quinine was issued, there was only enough properly to take care of ten cases of malaria, while thousands of prisoners were suffering from the disease.... It is reported that in the autumn of 1943 fifty percent of the American prisoners of war at Davao had a poor chance to live and that the detaining authorities had again cut the prisoners' food ration and had withdrawn all medical attention." The code of warfare among civilized nations prohibits the imposition of "punishments other than those provided for the same acts for soldiers of the national armies... upon prisoners of war by the military authorities and courts of the detaining power." Yet, to quote Secretary Hull again, "American personnel have suffered death and imprisonment for participation in military operations. Death and long-term imprisonment have been imposed for attempts to escape for which the maximum penalty under the Geneva Convention is thirty days arrest."

OFFENSES AGAINST CIVILIANS

The rules governing the treatment of civilians in time of war are as tolerant and forbearing as those relating to belligerents. When a territory is captured, "The authority of the legitimate power having in fact passed into the hands of the occupant, the latter shall take all measures in his power to restore, and insure, as far as possible, public order and safety, while respecting, unless absolutely prevented, the laws in force in the country." This safeguard for the welfare and property of civilians who happen to find themselves in occupied countries has been consistently ignored by the Axis armies. Indeed, it is doubtful whether in the entire history of man's cruelty to man there is anything which surpasses the butcheries of Jews, Poles, Russians, French, Italians, Greeks, and other peoples caught in the Nazi sweep across the European Continent.

The acts of torture, and murder of thousands of men, women, and children in their homes, streets, and barricaded ghettos, in death houses specially constructed for the use of live steam or gas fumes as a lethal weapon, of the forcing of victims to dig their own graves—these acts have been so numerous as to require many volumes to recount them. For example, "In Lublin and the vicinity on the night of March 23 and 24, the Jewish population was simply driven out of their homes, and the sick and the infirm were killed on the spot. In the Jewish orphanage 108 children from the age of two to nine were taken outside the town together with their nurses and murdered. Altogether that night, 2,500 people were massacred and the remaining 2,600 Jews in Lublin were removed to the concentration camps at Bellec, and Trawniki.... Mass murders occurred on such a large scale at Rawa Ruska and Bilgoraj that Jewish communities have ceased to exist.... In Mielec about 1,300 Jews were slaughtered on March 9; in Mir 2,000 Jews were killed; in Nowogródek, 2,500; in Wolozyn, 1,800; in Kajdanów 4,000 were killed. Thirty thousand Jews from Hamburg were deported to Miñsk where they were all murdered."

Since these acts have not the remotest relation to warfare, they constitute ordinary murders in violation of the penal codes of most civilized states. Not only have the Nazis shot people in systematic massacres and boasted of it, as 'in the razing of the Czech town of Lidice, but they have terrorized the inhabitants of occupied countries by seizing-and murdering hostages for the slightest infraction of rules—many of them arbitrary and capricious—which they laid down.

According to *Rules of Land Warfare* "No general penalty, pecuniary or otherwise, shall be inflicted upon the population on account of acts of individuals for which they cannot be regarded as jointly and severally responsible." Yet, as recorded in the *Black Book*, "People were hunted down in the town, on the pretext that an attempt had been made to fire at German soldiers from one of the houses.... About sixty people were seized and shot. One of the houses in the Street of The Blessed Virgin Mary was set on fire by the Germans, after they had thrown hand grenades into it. There were many persons inside.... It was forbidden to bury or to remove the bodies of those who had been shot, the object being to terrorize the inhabitants by the sight of these corpses. They were left unburied until two days later."

"As the German authorities had issued an order the previous day... that all arms were to be surrendered before 8 p.m., there was a general search for arms. In the Institute of the Order of the School Brothers, an old gun and several Scouts' caps were found in the theatre wardrobe. On the false pretext that they had been 'concealing arms,' two of the Friars and the father of another were taken out and shot in the barrack square of the 27th Infantry

Regiment. Their bodies were buried in the barrack garden. Many persons were shot simply because toy pistols had been found in their houses, or old sabres which had been forgotten among the lumber in attics."

Rules of Land Warfare order belligerents to respect "family honour and rights, the lives of persons." The Polish Ministry of Foreign Affairs charges, in the *Polish White Book,* issued in 1942, that "Under pretense of arresting prostitutes, patrols of German soldiers organized regular raids to carry off young women. A patrol of the 228th regiment of German infantry organized such a raid in one of the quarters by the river early in 1940. Soldiers of the 7th anti-aircraft regiment did the same thing twice in the suburb of Mokotow. Women were taken not only in the streets but also from their homes. These young unfortunates were carried off to the barracks of the German soldiers and raped."

Other provisions of *Rules of Land Warfare* order belligerents to respect the "religious convictions and practice" of peoples in occupied territories, as well as to spare, as far as possible, "buildings dedicated to religion, art, science, or charitable purposes, historic monuments," and "places where the sick and wounded are collected, provided that they are not being used at the time for military purposes." Likewise "The property of municipalities, that of institutions dedicated to religion, charity, and education, the arts and sciences, even when State property" should be treated as private property, and all seizures of or destruction to such institutions, historic monuments, and works of art or science are prohibited.

In a volume of *Soviet War Documents,* published in 1943, the Soviet Embassy in Washington states that "Churches in Gzhatsk were turned into stables and warehouses. The Germans set up an abattoir for cattle in Blagoveshchensky Church. The Predtechenskaya Church and Kazan Cathedral were blown up. The wells in the town were poisoned and mined. In Sychevka, of 1,000 dwelling houses 770 were blown up or burned. The museum was burned. Over 5,000 paintings, including works by Repin, Levitan, Perov, Aivazovsky, Korovin and others; sculptures by Antokolsky; and gold, silver and bronze articles by masters of the 17th, 18th and 19th Centuries perished in the fire.... The following were blown up or burned: three secondary and two primary schools, vocational schools... a library, a hospital, a restaurant, two children's homes, the water-pumping tower, the town polyclinic, the telegraph office, the radio station and other buildings."

These are but a few examples of the many atrocities charged against the war criminals. Illustrations could be drawn from every occupied country in Europe and Asia. Who is liable for them? The commissioned officers who issue the orders for pillaging and sacking cities and murdering civilians? The political chieftains who set down the policies that are executed by the military commanders? The rank and file of the Axis armies who pull the triggers of guns that kill hostages, or carry the torches that set fire to buildings, or plant the dynamite that blows up schools, churches, libraries, museums? Is a soldier liable for crimes he is ordered to commit? To try to answer these questions we must first go back and see what happened after the last World War and study the effort made to define war crimes and to punish war criminals.

8 Military Robots and the Laws of War

More than just conventional wisdom, it has become almost a cliché to say that the wars in Afghanistan and Iraq have proved "how technology doesn't have a big place in any doctrine of future war. The American military efforts in those countries (or so the thinking goes) have dispelled the understanding of technology-dominated warfare that was prevalent just a few years ago—the notion that modern armed conflict would be fundamentally changed in the age of computers and networks. It is true that Afghanistan and Iraq have done much to puncture that understanding of war.

The vaunted theory, so beloved in the Rumsfeld-era Pentagon, of a "network-centric" revolution in military affairs can now be seen more clearly as a byproduct of the 1990s dotcom boom. The Internet has certainly affected how people shop, communicate, and date. Amid this ecstatic hype, it is not surprising that many security studies experts, both in and out of the defence establishment, latched onto the notion that linking up all our systems via electronic networks would "lift the fog of war," allow war to be done on the cheap, and even allow the United States to "lock out" competition from the marketplace of war. Nor is it surprising that now analysts are writing off high-tech warfare altogether in the wake of Afghanistan and Iraq. Insurgents armed with crude conventional weapons have proven frequently able to flummox their well-equipped American foes.

Many observers increasingly seem to believe that if irregular warfare is likely to be the future of armed conflict, advanced technologies have no great role. These "all or nothing" attitudes are each incorrect. High technology is not a silver bullet solution to insurgencies, but that doesn't mean that technology doesn't matter in these fights. In fact, far from proving the uselessness of advanced technology in modern warfare, Afghanistan and Iraq have for the first time proved the value of a technology that will truly revolutionize warfare—robotics. When U.S. forces went into Iraq, the original invasion had no robotic systems on the ground.

By the end of 2004, there were 150 robots on the ground in Iraq; a year later there were 2,400; by the end of 2008, there were about 12,000 robots of nearly two dozen varieties operating on the ground in Iraq. As one retired Army officer put it, the "Army of the Grand Robotic" is taking shape. It isn't just on the ground: military robots have been taking to the skies—and the seas and space, too. And the field is rapidly advancing.

The robotic systems now rolling out in prototype stage are far more capable, intelligent, and autonomous than ones already in service in Iraq and Afghanistan. But even *they* are just the start. As one robotics executive put it at a demonstration of new military prototypes a couple of years ago, "The robots you are seeing here today I like to think of as the Model T. These are not what you are going to see when they are actually deployed in the field. We are seeing the very first stages of this technology." And just as the Model T exploded on the scene—selling only 239 cars in its first year and over one million a decade later—the demand for robotic warriors is growing very rapidly. The truly revolutionary part, however, is not robots' increasing numbers, or even their capabilities.

It is the ripple effects that they will have in areas ranging from politics and war to business and ethics. For instance, the difficulties for the existing laws of war that this robotics revolution will provoke are barely beginning to be understood. Technology generally evolves much more quickly than the laws of war. During World War I, for example, all sorts of recent inventions, from airplanes dropping bombs to cannons shooting chemical weapons, were introduced before anyone agreed on the rules for their use—and, as to be expected, the warring sides sometimes took different interpretations on critical questions. While it is far too early to know with any certainty, we can at least start to establish the underlying frameworks as to how robots will reshape the practice and the ethics of warfare.

RISE OF THE ROBOTS

Mechanization and mass production made possible early automatic weapons in the nineteenth century. Military experimentation with machines that were also mobile and unmanned began during World War I—including even radio-controlled airplanes, the very first unmanned aerial vehicles (UAVs). World War II saw the operational use of several unmanned weapons by both the Allied and Axis forces, including remote-controlled bombs; it was also a period of rapid advancement in analog and electronic computing. Military interest in robotics was spotty during the Cold War, with inventors repeatedly finding that what was technically possible mattered less than what was bureaucratically feasible.

Robotic systems were getting better, but the interest, energy, and proven success stories necessary for them to take off just weren't there. The only substantial contract during this long dry spell was one that the Ryan aeronautical firm received in 1962 for $1.1 million to make an unmanned reconnaissance aircraft. The drone that came out of it, the Fire Fly, flew 3,435 missions in Southeast Asia. Overall, though, the Vietnam experience was as bad for robotics as it was for the broader U.S. military. Most of the uses of unmanned systems were classified and thus there was little public knowledge of their relative successes, as well as no field tests or data collection to solve the problems they incurred (16 percent of the Fire Flys crashed). As veteran robotics scientist Robert Finkelstein has pointed out, "It took decades for UAVs to recover from Vietnam misperceptions." The next big U.S. military spending on unmanned planes didn't come until 1979, with the Army's Aquila program.

The Aquila was to be a small propeller-powered drone that could circle over the front lines and send back information on the enemy's numbers and intentions. Soon, though, the Army began to load up the plane with all sorts of new requirements. It now had to carry night vision and laser designators, spot artillery fire, survive against enemy ground fire, and so on. Each new requirement came at a cost. The more you loaded up the drone, the bigger it had to be, meaning it was both heavier than planned and an easier target to shoot down. The more secure you wanted the communications, the lower the quality of the images it beamed back. The program originally planned to spend $560 million for 780 Aquila drones. By 1987, it had spent over $1 billion for just a few prototypes. The program was canceled and the cause of unmanned vehicles was set further back, again more by policy decisions than the technology itself. Work continued, but mainly on testing various drones and ground vehicles, which were usually regular vehicles jury-rigged with remote controls.

During this period, most of the ground systems were designed to be tele-operated—that is, using long fiber-optic wires to link the robot to the controller. Any enemy with a pair of scissors could take them out. One of the few to be built from the ground up to drive on its own was Martin Marietta's eight-wheeled "Autonomous Land Vehicle." Unfortunately, the weapon had a major image problem: It was shaped like an RV, what retirees would use to drive cross-country to see the Grand Canyon. This killed any chance of convincing the generals of its use for warfighting. Another significant program that didn't take off in this period was a 1980 Army plan for a robotic antitank vehicle.

The idea was to take a commercial all-terrain vehicle, rig it for remote control, and load it with missiles. Congress thought that ATVs, while certainly fun for country kids to ride around behind trailer parks, were a bit too small to be taking on Soviet tanks. So the program was canceled. But the military mistakenly came to believe that Congress's real objection was to the weaponization of unmanned systems. "So," as Finkelstein says, "misinterpretation kept weapons off for almost a decade." Despite these setbacks, the American military robotics community didn't waver in its belief in the usefulness of its work. It could point to other nations beginning to successfully deploy unmanned systems, like Israel's successful experience with drones in the 1980s. By the time of the 1991 Persian Gulf War, unmanned systems were gradually making their way into the U.S. military, but in very small numbers. The Army had a handful of M-60 tanks converted into unmanned land-mine clearers, but they were left behind in the famous "left-hook" invasion force that drove across the desert into Iraq. The Air Force flew just one UAV drone. The only notable success story was the Navy's use of the Pioneer drone, an unmanned plane (almost exactly like the planned Aquila) that the Navy had bought secondhand from the Israelis. It flew off of World War II-era U.S. battleships that had been taken out of mothballs in the 1980s and updated for use in pounding ground targets with their massive sixteen-inch guns. The guns fired shells that weighed 2,000 pounds and could leave a crater the size of a football field. The little drones, which the Iraqis took to calling "vultures," would fly over targets and spot where the shells were landing.

"The Iraqis came to learn that when they heard the buzz of a Pioneer overhead, all heck would break loose shortly thereafter because these sixteen-inch rounds would start landing all around them," said Steve Reid, an executive at the Pioneer's maker, AAI. In one case, a group of Iraqi soldiers saw a Pioneer flying overhead and, rather than wait to be blown up, waved white bed sheets and undershirts at the drone—the first time in history that human soldiers surrendered to an unmanned system. Of course, the real stars of the Gulf War were not unmanned systems in the way we think of them now, but new "smart bombs"—that is, cruise missiles and laser-guided bombs. A massive PR campaign was built around the guided weapons as the "heroes" of the hundred-hour war.

The only problem was that they weren't. Only 7 percent of all the bombs dropped were guided; the rest were "dumb." The most influential technology in the Gulf War was not the sexy smart bombs, but the humble desktop computer. By 1990, the U.S. military had bought into the idea of digitizing its forces and was spending some $30 billion a year on applying computers to all its various tasks.

The Gulf War was the first war in history to involve widespread computers, used for everything from organizing the movement of hundreds of thousands of troops to sorting through reams of satellite photos looking for targets for missiles to hit. Calling it a "technology war," the victorious commanding general, "Stormin'" Norman Schwarzkopf, said, "I couldn't have done it all without the computers." Over the rest of the 1990s, as sensors and computer processors improved, unmanned systems became ever more capable.

But the "magic moment," as retired Air Force Colonel Tom Erhard put it, occurred in 1995, when unmanned systems were integrated with the Global Positioning System (GPS). "That's when it really came together." Now widely accessible by devices in automobiles, the GPS is a constellation of military satellites that can provide the location, speed, and direction of a receiver, anywhere on the globe. It allowed unmanned systems (and their human operators) to automatically know where they were at any time. With GPS, as well as the advance of the video game industry (which the controllers began to mimic), the interfaces became accessible to a wider set of users. Drones began to be far more intuitive to fly, while the information they passed on to the generals and troops in the field became ever more detailed. The programs also began to pass some key hurdles of acceptability.

The various military services had long resisted buying any unmanned systems, but slowly they began to accept their use. In 1997, for example, the Air Force Chief of Staff, General Ronald R. Fogleman, instructed his planners that his service could "no longer...spend money the way we have been," and mandated that they consider investing in new technologies such as UAVs. The military advantages of unmanned systems became increasingly clear to observers in the Pentagon. In many situations, robots have faster reaction times and better aim than human beings. They are often ideal for filling roles that people in the field call the "Three Ds": dull, dirty, or dangerous. Unlike humans, who get tired and hungry and lose concentration and effectiveness, robots can perform boring tasks with unstinting accuracy for long periods of time. (As one advertisement for an unmanned plane put it, "Can you keep your eyes open for thirty hours without blinking?") They can operate in dirty environments, such as battle zones filled with biological or chemical weapons, or under other dangerous conditions, such as in space, in rough seas, or in flights with very high gravitational pressures. The rising interest in robots in the late 1990s coincided with changing political winds—a shrinking U.S. military as part of the post-Cold War so-called "peace dividend," and an increasing belief that public tolerance for military risk and casualties had dropped dramatically after the relatively costless victory in the Gulf War.

In 2000, this was the main factor that led Senator John Warner, then chairman of the Armed Services Committee, to mandate in the Pentagon's budget that by 2010, one-third of all the aircraft designed to attack behind enemy lines be unmanned, and that by 2015, one-third of all ground combat vehicles be driverless. And then came September 11, 2001. The annual national defence budget since 9/11 has risen to $515 billion (an increase of 74 percent between 2002 and 2008), not counting the cost of operations in Afghanistan and Iraq. There has been a massive increase in spending on research and development and on procurement, with a particular focus on anything unmanned. "Make 'em as fast as you can" is what one robotics executive recounts being told by his Pentagon buyers after 9/11. Enthusiasm has only grown thanks to successes on the battlefield. With this change in military mentality, money, and use, the groundwork was finally laid for a real military robotics industry. As the *Washington Post* put it, "The undertaking has attracted not only the country's top weapons makers but also dozens of small businesses...all pitching a science-fiction gallery of possible solutions." Robert Finkelstein recalled a time when he personally knew most of the engineers working on military robotics. Today, the Association for Unmanned Vehicle Systems International has fourteen hundred member companies. Almost four thousand people showed up at its last annual meeting.

CLEANING FLOORS AND FIGHTING WARS

During the war in Iraq, improvised explosive devices (IEDs) became the insurgents' primary way of attacking U.S. forces. Often hidden along roadsides and disguised to look like trash or scrap metal, these cheap and easy-to-make bombs can do tremendous damage. At the peak of the Iraq insurgency in 2006, IED attacks were averaging nearly two thousand a month. They have been the leading cause of casualties among American personnel in Iraq, accounting for 40 percent of the troop deaths. On the ground, the military bomb squad hunting for IEDs is called the Explosive Ordnance Disposal (EOD) team. Before Iraq, EOD teams were not much valued by either the troops in the field or their senior leaders. They usually deployed to battlefields only after the fighting was done, to defuse any old weapons caches or unexploded ammunition that might be found.

In Iraq, though, EOD teams went from an afterthought to a critical assignment. In a typical tour in Iraq when the insurgency was at its peak, each team would go on more than six hundred IED calls, defusing or safely exploding about two IEDs a day. Perhaps the best sign of how critical the EOD teams became is that the insurgents began offering a rumored $50,000 bounty for killing an EOD team member. Working alongside many EOD teams have been robots—scouting ahead for IEDs and ambushes, saving soldiers' lives many times over. Most of these unmanned ground vehicles (UGVs) have been made by two Boston-area robotics firms. One of these, iRobot, was founded in 1990 by three M.I.T. computer geeks; it is best known for the Roomba, the disc-shaped automatic vacuum cleaner that the company released in 2002. Roomba actually evolved from Fetch, a robot that the company designed in 1997 for the U.S. Air Force. Fetch cleaned up cluster bomblets from airfields; Roomba cleans up dust bunnies under sofas. The company's other breakout product was PackBot, which came out of a 1998 contract from the Defense Advanced Research Projects Agency (DARPA).

Weighing forty-two pounds and costing just under $150,000, PackBot is about the size of a lawn mower. It is typically operated via remote control, although it can drive itself, including even backtracking to wherever it started its mission. PackBot moves using four "flippers"—essentially tank treads that can rotate on one axis. These allow PackBot not only to roll forward and backward like regular tank tracks, but also to climb stairs, rumble over rocks, squeeze down twisting tunnels, and even swim in under six feet of water. The designers at iRobot view their robots as "platforms." PackBot has eight separate payload bays and hookups that allow its users to swap in whatever they need: mine detector, chemical and biological weapons sensor, or just extra power packs. The EOD version of the PackBots serving in Iraq comes with an extendable arm on top that mounts both a head, containing a high-powered zoom camera, and a claw-like gripper.

Soldiers use these to drive up to IEDs, peer at them closely, and then, using the gripper, disassemble the bomb, all from a safe distance. PackBot made its operational debut on 9/11 when engineers from iRobot drove down to New York City to help in the rescue and recovery efforts at Ground Zero. Soon after, PackBot went to war. As U.S. forces deployed to Afghanistan, troops came across massive cave complexes that had to be scouted out, but were often booby-trapped. The only specialized tool the troops had were flashlights, and they often sent their local Afghan allies to crawl through the caves on hands and knees. "Then we began to run out of Afghans," recounts a soldier. iRobot was then asked by the Pentagon to send help. Just six weeks later, PackBots were first used in a cave complex near the village of Nazaraht, in the heart of Taliban territory. Production and profits for Packbots boomed in the years that followed, culminating in a $286 million Pentagon contract in 2008 to supply as many as three thousand more machines. Meanwhile, iRobot has new and improved versions of the PackBot as well as a host of plans to convert any type of vehicle into a robot, be it a car or ship, using a universal control unit that you plug into the engine and steering wheel.

One new robot that iRobot's designers are especially excited to show off is the Warrior. Weighing about 250 pounds, the Warrior is essentially a PackBot on steroids: it has the same basic design, but is about five times bigger. Warrior can drive at 15 miles per hour for five hours, while carrying one hundred pounds—yet it is agile enough to fit through a doorway and go up stairs. It is really just a mobile platform, with a USB port—a universal connector—on top that can be used to plug in sensors, a gun, and a TV camera for battle, or an iPod and loudspeakers for a mobile rave party. The long-term strategy is for other companies to focus on the plug-in market while iRobot corners the market for the robotic platforms. What Microsoft did for the software industry, iRobot hopes to do for the robotics industry. Just a twenty-minute drive from iRobot's offices are the headquarters of the Foster-Miller company.

Founded in the 1950s—also by M.I.T. grads—Foster-Miller makes the PackBot's primary competitor, the Talon. The Talon, which first hit the market in 2000, looks like a small tank, driven by two treads that run its length. Weighing just over a hundred pounds, it is a bit bigger than the PackBot. It too has a retractable arm with a gripper, but mounts its main sensors on a separate antenna-like "mast" sticking up from the body and carrying a zoom camera. Talon can go up to speeds of about 5.5 miles per hour, the equivalent of a decent jog on a treadmill, a pace it can maintain for five hours. Like the PackBot, the Talon helped sift through the wreckage at Ground Zero and soon after deployed to Afghanistan. And like iRobot, Foster-Miller has boomed, doubling the number of robots it sells every year for the last four years. The company received an initial $65 million in orders for Talons in the first two years of the insurgency in Iraq. By 2008, there were close to two thousand Talons in the field and the firm had won a $400 million contract to supply another two thousand. Under an additional $20 million repair and spare-parts contract, the company also operates a "robot hospital" in Baghdad. Foster-Miller now makes some fifty to sixty Talons a month, and repairs another hundred damaged systems. In technology circles, new products that change the rules of the game, such as what the iPod did to portable music players, are called "killer applications."

Foster-Miller's new product gives this phrase a literal meaning. The Special Weapons Observation Reconnaissance Detection System (SWORDS) is the first armed robot designed to roam the battlefield. SWORDS is basically the Talon's tougher big brother, with its gripping arm replaced by a gun mount that can carry pretty much any weapon that weighs under three hundred pounds, ranging from an M-16 rifle and.50-caliber machine gun to a 40mm grenade launcher or an antitank rocket launcher. In less than a minute, the human soldier flips two levers and locks his favourite weapon into the mount. The SWORDS can't reload itself, but it can carry two hundred rounds of ammunition for the light machine guns, three hundred rounds for the heavy machine guns, six grenades, or four rockets. Unlike the more-automated PackBot, SWORDS has very limited intelligence on its own; it is remote-controlled from afar by either radio or a spooled-out fiber optic wire.

Thanks to the five cameras mounted on the robot, the operator can not only see as if he has.eyes in the back of his head, but farther than had previously been possible when shooting a gun. As one soldier put it, "You can read people's nametags at 300 to 400 meters, whereas the human eye can't pick that up. You can see the expression on his face, what weapons he is carrying. You can even see if his [weapon's] selector lever is on fire or on safe." The cameras can also see in night vision, meaning the enemy can be fired on at any hour and in any climate. And the gun is impressively precise; it is locked in a stable platform, so its aim isn't disrupted by the breathing or heartbeat that human snipers must compensate for, and it doesn't get nervous in a sticky situation. So far, SWORDS has been used for street patrols, reconnaissance, sniping, checkpoint security, and guarding observation posts. It bodes to be especially useful for urban warfare jobs, such as going first into buildings and alleyways where insurgents might hide. SWORDS's inhuman capabilities could well result in even more intrepid missions. For example, the robot can drive through snow and sand, and can even drive underwater down to depths of one hundred feet, meaning it could pop up in quite unexpected places. Likewise, its battery allows it to be hidden somewhere in "sleep" mode for at least seven days and then wake up to shoot away at any foes. Foster-Miller and iRobot feel a keen sense of competition with each other. At iRobot, researchers describe their rivals as thinking, "We hear that robots are trendy, so let's do that."

At Foster-Miller, they retort, "We don't just do robots and we don't suck dirt." (Indeed, thanks to its Roomba vacuum cleaner, iRobot may be the only company that sells at both Pentagon trade shows and Bed Bath & Beyond.) The two companies have even become locked in a bit of a marketing war. If robots were pickup trucks, Foster-Miller represents the Ford model, stressing how the Talon is "Built Tough." Its promotional materials describe the Talon as "The Soldier's Choice." Foster-Miller executives love to recount tales of how the Talon has proven it "can take a punch and stay in the fight." The iRobot team, meanwhile, bristles at the idea that its systems are "agile but fragile." They insist that the PackBot is tough, too, citing various statistics on how it can survive a 400 g-force hit, what they describe as the equivalent of being tossed out of a hovering helicopter onto a concrete floor. They are most proud of the fact that their robots have a 95 percent out-of-the-box reliability rate, higher than any other in the marketplace, meaning that when the soldiers get them in the field, they can trust the robot will work as designed. Beneath all the difference and rancor, the two companies are similar in one telling way. The hallways and cubicles of both of their offices are covered with pictures and thank-you letters from soldiers in the field. A typical note from an EOD soldier reads, "This little guy saved our butts on many occasions."

Future Ground-Bots

Foster-Miller's SWORDS was not the first ground robot to draw blood on the battlefield. That seems to have been the MARCBOT (Multi-Function Agile Remote-Controlled Robot), a commonly-used UGV that looks like a toy truck with a video camera mounted on a tiny antenna-like mast. Costing only $5,000, the tiny bot is used to scout out where the enemy might be and also to drive under cars and search for hidden explosives. One unit of soldiers put Claymore antipersonnel mines on their MARCBOTs. Whenever they thought insurgents were hiding in an alley, they would send a MARCBOT down first, not just to scout out the ambush, but to take them out with the Claymore. Of course, each discovered insurgent meant $5,000 worth of blown-up robot parts, but so far the Army hasn't billed the soldiers. Meanwhile, both iRobot and Foster-Miller are hard at work on the next generation of UGVs.

For testing purposes, iRobot's PackBot has been equipped with a shotgun that can fire a variety of ammunition, including non-lethal rubber bullets, rounds that can blow down a door, and even more powerful "elephant killer" bullets. Another version of PackBot is the Robotic Enhanced Detection Outpost with Lasers (REDOWL), which uses lasers and sound detection equipment to find any sniper who dares to shoot at the robot or accompanying troops, and instantly targets him with an infrared laser beam. Foster-Miller has similar plans to upgrade its current generation of ground robots.

For example, the first version of the armed SWORDS needed the remote human operator to be situated within a mile or two, which can still put the human in danger. The company plans to vastly extend the range of communications so as to get ground robot operators completely off the battlefield. And the SWORDS itself is being replaced by a new version named after the Roman god of war—the MAARS (Modular Advanced Armed Robotic System), which carries a more powerful machine gun, 40mm grenade launchers, and, for non-lethal settings, a green laser "dazzler," tear gas, and a loudspeaker, perfect for warning any insurgents that "Resistance is futile." We will also soon see entirely new armed UGVs hit the battlefield. One such prototype is the Gladiator.

Described as the "world's first multipurpose combat robot," it came out of a partnership between the U.S. Marine Corps and Carnegie Mellon University. About the size of a golf cart, the first version of the vehicle was operated by a soldier wielding a PlayStation video game controller, but software plug-ins will allow it to be upgraded to semiautonomous and then fully autonomous modes. Fully loaded, it costs $400,000 and carries a machine gun with six hundred rounds of ammunition, antitank rockets, and non-lethal weapons. Not all future UGVs, it should be noted, will take on combat roles.

Some are being designed as "medbots," to supplement the work of field medics. The Bloodhound, yet another version of the PackBot, will be able to search on its own for a hurt soldier; it can then be remotely controlled to provide rudimentary treatment. The next step will be specially designed medbots, such as REV and REX. REV, the Robotic Evacuation Vehicle (a robot version of an ambulance), carries REX, the Robotic Extraction Vehicle, a tiny stretcher-bearer that zips out to drag soldiers into the safety of the ambulance. REX has an arm with six joints to drag a soldier to safety, while REV has a life-support pod that even comes with a flat-screen TV facing the wounded soldier's face so that operators can see and communicate with the human on the other end if he is conscious. Ultimately, REV will be configured so that complex surgeries can occur inside the medbot. Coordinating many of the ground robots on the drawing boards is the U.S. Army's $230 billion Future Combat Systems (FCS) program.

It involves everything from replacing tens of thousands of armored vehicles with a new generation of manned and unmanned vehicles to writing the many millions of lines of software code for the new computers that will link them all together. Starting in 2011, the Army plans to start spiraling a few new technologies at a time into the force. By 2015, the Army believes it will be in a position to reorganize its units into new FCS brigades, which will represent a revolutionary new model of how military units are staffed and organized. Each brigade will actually have more unmanned vehicles than manned ones (a planned 330 unmanned to 300 manned). Each brigade will also have its own unmanned air force, with over a hundred drones controlled by the unit's soldiers. They will range in size from a fifteen-pounder that will fit in soldiers' backpacks to a twenty-three-foot-long robotic helicopter.

Up, Up, and Away

Military robots have also taken to the skies. Unmanned aerial vehicles (UAVs), like the now-well-known Predator and Global Hawk, made their debut in the Balkan wars in the 1990s, gathering information on Serb air defenses and refugee flows. These drones are an indispensable part of the U.S. efforts in Afghanistan and Iraq, but commanders' attitudes toward them were very different just a few years ago. Lieutenant General Walter Buchanan, the U.S. Air Force commander in the Middle East, recalled the run-up to the Iraq war in an interview with *Air Force Magazine*: In March of 2002, [during] the mission briefings over Southern Iraq at that time, the mission commander would get up and he'd say, "OK, we're going to have the F-15Cs fly here, the F-16s are going to fly here, the A-6s are going to fly here, tankers are going to be here today."

Then they would say, "And oh by the way, way over here is going to be the Predator." We don't go over there, and he's not going to come over here and bother us.... It was almost like nobody wanted to talk to them. This is far from the case today. The Predator, perhaps the best known UAV, is a twenty-seven-foot-long plane that can spend some twenty-four hours in the air, flying at heights of up to 26,000 feet. Given its price tag—at just $4.5 million, it costs a fraction of what a manned fighter jet costs—the Predator can be used for missions where it might be shot down, such as traveling low and slow over enemy territory. It was originally designed for reconnaissance and surveillance, and about a quarter of the cost of each Predator actually goes into the "Ball," a round mounting under the nose that carries two variable-aperture TV cameras, one for seeing during the day and an infrared one for night, as well as a synthetic-aperture radar that allows the Predator to peer through clouds, smoke, or dust.

The exact capabilities of the system are classified, but soldiers say they can read a license plate from two miles up. Predators don't just watch from afar; they have also been armed to kill. The back-story of how this happened is one of the sad "what ifs?" of what could have been done to prevent the 9/11 attacks. Over the course of 2000 and 2001, Predators operated by the CIA spotted Osama bin Laden in Afghanistan many times, usually when he was driving in a convoy between his training camps. But the unmanned spy planes were toothless and could only watch as bin Laden disappeared. Proposals to arm the drone by mounting laser-guided Hellfire missiles on its wings were not pursued. After 9/11, the gloves were taken off, and the CIA and Air Force armed their Predators.

In the first year, armed Predators took out some 115 targets in Afghanistan on their own. (That's in addition to the thousands of targets that were destroyed by other means after they were laser-designated by Predators.) With that precedent, the Predator also joined the fight in Iraq. Among its first missions was to help take down the Iraqi government's television transmissions, which broadcast the infamous "Baghdad Bob" propaganda. In the days and weeks that followed, the Predator struck at everything from suspected insurgent safe houses to cars being prepped for suicide attacks. The little drone has quickly become perhaps the busiest U.S. asset in the air. From June 2005 to June 2006, Predators carried out 2,073 missions, flew 33,833 hours, surveyed 18,490 targets, and participated in 242 separate raids. Even with this massive effort, there is demand for more. Officers estimate that they get requests for some 300 hours of Predator imagery a day, but that there are only enough Predators in the air to supply a little over 100 hours a day. The result is that the Predator fleet has grown from less than 10 in 2001 to some 180 in 2007, with plans to add another 150 over the next few years. Besides the Predator, there are many other drones that fill the air over Iraq and Afghanistan.

At forty feet long, Global Hawk has been described as looking like "a flying albino whale." Originally conceived as an unmanned replacement for the half-century-old U-2 spy plane, Global Hawk can stay aloft up to thirty-five hours. Powered by a turbofan engine that takes it to sixty-five thousand feet, the stealthy Global Hawk carries synthetic-aperture radar, infrared sensors, and electro-optical cameras. Working in combination, these sensors can do a wide-area search to look at an entire region, or focus in on a single target in high resolution. Like the Predator, the Global Hawk is linked back to humans on the ground, but it mainly operates autonomously rather than being remotely piloted. Using a computer mouse, the operator just clicks to tell it to taxi and take off, and the drone flies off on its own. The plane then carries out its mission, getting directions on where to fly from GPS coordinates downloaded off a satellite. Upon its return, "you basically hit the land button," describes one retired Air Force officer. With such capability, the Global Hawk is not cheap. The plane itself costs some $35 million, but the overall support system runs to over $123 million each. Even so, the U.S. Air Force plans to spend another $6 billion to build up the fleet to fifty-one drones by 2012. The Predators and Global Hawks are mostly directed by personnel in Air Force bases back in the United States, but a veritable menagerie of UAVs now circling above Iraq are controlled by troops on the ground.

Big Army units fly the Shadow, which looks like the radio-controlled planes flown by model plane hobbyists. Just over twelve feet long, it takes off and lands like a regular plane, and its propeller makes it sound like a weed-whacker flying overhead; it can stay in the air for five hours and fly seventy miles. Like its older sibling the Hunter, which is twice as big and can stay in the air twice as long, the Shadow is used on a variety of tactical missions in support of ground forces, including reconnaissance, target acquisition, and battlefield damage assessment. The Raven, the most popular UAV, is just thirty-eight inches long and weighs four pounds; it is launched by tossing it into the air like a javelin.

The Raven then buzzes off, able to fly for ninety minutes at about four hundred feet, carrying three cameras in its nose, including an infrared one. Soldiers love it because they can now peer over the next hill or city block, as well as get their own spy planes to control, rather than having to beg for support from the higher-ups. "You throw the bird up when you want to throw it. You land it when you want to land," says Captain Matt Gill, a UAV company commander with the 82nd Airborne Division. The other part of the appeal is that the pilots of the Raven are just regular soldiers; one cook from the 1st Cavalry Division is actually considered among the best pilots in the entire force. In just the first two years of the Iraq war, the number of Ravens in service jumped from twenty-five to eight hundred.

The small UAVs, like the Raven or the even smaller Wasp, fly just above the rooftops, sending back video images of what's on the other side of the street; Shadow and Hunter circle over entire neighborhoods; the larger Predators roam above entire cities, combining reconnaissance with the ability to shoot; and too high to see, the Global Hawk zooms across an entire country, capturing reams of detailed imagery for intelligence teams to sift through. Added together, by 2008, there were 5,331 drones in the U.S. military's inventory, almost double the number of manned fighter planes. That same year, an Air Force lieutenant general forecast that "given the growth trends, it is not unreasonable to postulate future conflicts involving tens of thousands."

Among the UAVs likely to see action in those future conflicts will be Predators reconfigured for electronic warfare, submarine hunting, and even air-to-air combat; the Reaper, a bigger, smarter, and more powerful successor to the Predator; a variety of planned micro-UAVs, some the size of insects; the Peregrine, a drone designed to find and shoot down other drones; and even an unmanned stealth bomber. And it's not just intelligence and bomber pilots who will be replaced with machines; planning is proceeding on UCAVs, unmanned *combat* aerial vehicles, which will replace fighter jocks, too. Meanwhile, DARPA is working on a VULTURE (Very-high-altitude, Ultra-endurance, Loitering Theatre Unmanned Reconnaissance Element) drone, which the agency hopes will be able to stay aloft for as long as five years.

We may even see the return of blimps to warfare. Lockheed Martin has been given $150 million to design and build a robotic "High Altitude Airship" twenty-five times larger than the Goodyear blimp. Such huge, long-endurance blimps open up a whole new range of roles not normally possible for planes. For example, airships could literally be "parked" in the air, as high as one hundred thousand feet up, for weeks, months, or years, serving as a communications relay, spy satellite, hub for a ballistic missile defense system, floating gas station, or even airstrip for other planes and drones.

The Pentagon has also started work on a number of unmanned systems for potential use in space, although most are still only on the drawing boards. And a broad new set of robots is being introduced for war at sea, too, where the main differentiation is whether they are designed to operate on the surface, like a boat, or underwater, like a submarine. The former are called USVs (unmanned surface vehicles or vessels). They actually have a great deal in common with the simpler land robots, as they both primarily operate in a two-dimensional world, and can be equipped with sensors and guns. The Spartan Scout, one such USV, got its first real-world use in the Iraq war in 2003, inspecting small civilian boats in the Persian Gulf without risking sailors' lives. The boat also mounts a loudspeaker and microphone, so an Arab linguist back on the "mothership" could interrogate any suspicious boats that the Spartan Scout had stopped. As one report put it, "The civilian sailors were somewhat taken aback when they were interrogated by this Arab-speaking boat that had no one aboard." The other type of navybots are UUVs (unmanned underwater vehicles). These are designed for underwater roles such as searching for mines, the cause of most naval combat losses over the last two decades. Many UUVs are biologically inspired, like the "Robo-lobster," which operates in the choppy waters close to shore. But others are mini-submarines or converted torpedoes—like the REMUS (Remote Environmental Monitoring Unit), which was used to clear Iraqi waterways of mines and explosives.

IMPERSONALIZING WAR

The hope that technology will reduce the violence of war is

a venerable one. The poet John Donne told in 1621 how the invention of better cannons would help limit the cruelty and crimes of war, "and the great expence of bloud is avoyed." Richard Gatling hoped his new fast-firing gun would serve to reduce the bloodshed of war, while Alfred Nobel believed the explosives he invented would make war unthinkable. Now, some analysts believe that robot warriors can help reduce the flow of blood and perhaps make war more moral. In some ways, this seems reasonable.

Many wartime atrocities are not the result of deliberate policy, wanton cruelty, or fits of anger; they're just mistakes. They are equivalent to the crime of manslaughter, as compared to murder, in civilian law. Unmanned systems seem to offer several ways of reducing the mistakes and unintended costs of war. They have far better sensors and processing power, which creates a precision superior to what humans could marshal on their own. Such exactness can lessen the number of mistakes made, as well as the number of civilians inadvertently killed. For example, even as recently as the 1999 Kosovo war, NATO pilots spotting for Serbian military targets on the ground had to fly over the suspected enemy position, then put their plane on autopilot while they wrote down the coordinates of the target on their lap with a grease pencil. They would then radio the coordinates back to base, where planners would try to figure out if there were too many civilians nearby. If not, the base would order an attack, usually made by another plane. That new plane, just arriving on the scene, would carry out the attack using the directions of the spotter plane, if it was still there, or the relayed coordinates. Each step was filled with potential for miscommunications and unintended errors. Plus, by the time a decision had been made, the situation on the ground might have changed—the military target might have moved or civilians might have entered the area. Compare this with a UAV today that can fly over the target and send precise GPS coordinates and live video back to the operators; it is easy to see how collateral damage can be greatly reduced by robotic precision. The unmanning of the operation also means that the robot can take risks that a human wouldn't otherwise, risks that might mean fewer mistakes.

During that Kosovo campaign, for example, such a premium was placed on not losing any NATO pilots that planes were restricted from flying below fifteen thousand feet so that enemy fire couldn't hit them. In one case, NATO planes flying at this level bombed a convoy of vehicles, thinking they were Serbian tanks. It turned out to be a convoy of refugee buses. If the planes could have flown lower or had the high-powered video camera of a drone, this tragic mistake might have been avoided. The removal of risk also allows decisions to be made in a more deliberate manner than normally possible. Soldiers describe how one of the toughest aspects of fighting in cities is how you have to burst into a building and, in a matter of milliseconds, figure out who is an enemy and who is a civilian and shoot the ones that are a threat before they shoot you, all the while avoiding hitting any civilians. You can practice again and again, but you can never fully avoid the risk of making a terrible mistake in that split second, in a dark room, in the midst of battle.

By contrast, a robot can enter the room and only shoot at someone who shoots first, without endangering a soldier's life. Many also feel that unmanned systems can remove the anger and emotion from the humans behind them. A remote operator isn't in the midst of combat and isn't watching his buddies die around him as his adrenaline spikes; he can take his time and act deliberately in ways that can lessen the likelihood of civilians being killed. Marc Garlasco of Human Rights Watch told me how "the single most distinguishing weapons I have seen in my career were Israeli UAVs." He described how, unlike jet fighters that had to swoop in fast and make decisions on what targets to bomb in a matter of seconds, the UAVs he observed during the 2006 Lebanon war could loiter over a potential target for minutes or even hours, and pick and choose what to strike or not. In Vietnam, an astounding fifty thousand rounds of ammunition were expended for every enemy killed. Robots, on the other hand, might live up to the sniper motto of "one shot, one kill." As journalist Michael Fumento put it in describing SWORDS, the operator "can coolly pick out targets as if playing a video game." But as journalist Chuck Klosterman put it, a person playing video games is usually "not a benevolent God."

We do things in the virtual world, daring and violent things, that we would never do if we were there in person. Transferred to war, this could mean that the robotic technologies that make war less intimate and more mediated might well reduce the likelihood of anger-fueled rages, but also make some soldiers *too* calm, too unaffected by killing.

Many studies, like Army psychologist Dave Grossman's seminal book *On Killing* (1995), have shown how disconnecting a person, especially via distance, makes killing easier and abuses and atrocities more likely. D. Keith Shurtleff, an Army chaplain and the ethics instructor for the Soldier Support Institute at Fort Jackson in South Carolina, worries that "as war becomes safer and easier, as soldiers are removed from the horrors of war and see the enemy not as humans but as blips on a screen, there is a very real danger of losing the deterrent that such horrors provide." Participation via the virtual world also seems to affect not merely how people look at the target, but also how they look at themselves (which is why people in online communities, for example, take on identities and try out behaviors they never would in real life).

Research shows that this sort of "externalization" allows something called "doubling." Otherwise nice and normal people create psychic doubles that carry out sometimes terrible acts their normal identity never would. One Air Force lieutenant colonel who led a Predator operation noticed how the virtual setting could make it easy for the drone operators to forget that they were not gods from afar and that there are real humans on both ends. "You have guys running the UAV saying, Kill that one, don't kill that one.'" Each new military technology, from the bow and arrow to the bomber plane, has moved soldiers farther and farther from their foes. Yet unmanned systems have a more profound effect on "the impersonalization of battle," as military historian John Keegan has called it. These weapons don't just create greater physical distance, but also a different sort of psychological distance and disconnection. The bomber pilot isn't just above his target, but seven thousand miles away. He doesn't share with his foes even those brief minutes of danger that would give them a bond of mutual risk.

We, Robot

As military robots gain more and more autonomy, the ethical questions involved will become even more complex. The U.S. military bends over backwards to figure out when it is appropriate to engage the enemy and how to limit civilian casualties. Autonomous robots could, in theory, follow the rules of engagement; they could be programmed with a list of criteria for determining appropriate targets and when shooting is permissible. The robot might be programmed to require human input if any civilians were detected. An example of such a list at work might go as follows: "Is the target a Soviet-made T-80 tank? Identification confirmed. Is the target located in an authorized free-fire zone? Location confirmed. Are there any friendly units within a 200-meter radius? No friendlies detected. Are there any civilians within a 200-meter radius? No civilians detected. Weapons release authorized. No human command authority required." Such an "ethical" killing machine, though, may not prove so simple in the reality of war.

Even if a robot has software that follows all the various rules of engagement, and even if it were somehow absolutely free of software bugs and hardware failures (a big assumption), the very question of figuring out who an enemy is in the first place—that is, whether a target should even be considered for the list of screening questions—is extremely complicated in modern war. It essentially is a judgment call. It becomes further complicated as the enemy adapts, changes his conduct, and even hides among civilians. If an enemy is hiding behind a child, is it okay to shoot or not? Or what if an enemy is plotting an attack but has not yet carried it out? Politicians, pundits, and lawyers can fill pages arguing these points. It is unreasonable to expect robots to find them any easier. The legal questions related to autonomous systems are also extremely sticky.

In 2002, for example, an Air National Guard pilot in an F-16 saw flashing lights underneath him while flying over Afghanistan at twenty-three thousand feet and thought he was under fire from insurgents. Without getting required permission from his commanders, he dropped a 500-pound bomb on the lights. They instead turned out to be troops from Canada on a night training mission. Four were killed and eight wounded. In the hearings that followed, the pilot blamed the ubiquitous "fog of war" for his mistake. It didn't matter and he was found guilty of dereliction of duty. Change this scenario to an unmanned system and military lawyers aren't sure what to do. Asks a Navy officer, "If these same Canadian forces had been attacked by an autonomous UCAV, determining who is accountable proves difficult. Would accountability lie with the civilian software programmers who wrote the faulty target identification software, the UCAV squadron's Commanding Officer, or the Combatant Commander who authorized the operational use of the UCAV? Or are they collectively held responsible and accountable?" This is the main reason why military lawyers are so concerned about robots being armed and autonomous.

As long as "man is in the loop," traditional accountability can be ensured. Breaking this restriction opens up all sorts of new and seemingly irresolvable legal questions about accountability. In time, the international community may well decide that armed, autonomous robots are simply too difficult, or even abhorrent, to deal with.

Like chemical weapons, they could be banned in general, for no other reason than the world doesn't want them around. Yet for now, our laws are simply silent on whether autonomous robots can be armed with lethal weapons. Even more worrisome, the concept of keeping human beings in the loop is already being eroded by policymakers and by the technology itself, both of which are rapidly moving toward pushing humans out. We therefore must either enact a ban on such systems soon or start to develop some legal answers for how to deal with them. If we do stay on this path and decide to make and use autonomous robots in war, the systems must still conform with the existing laws of war. These laws suggest a few principles that should guide the development of such systems.

First, since it will be very difficult to guarantee that autonomous robots can, as required by the laws of war, discriminate between civilian and military targets and avoid unnecessary suffering, they should be allowed the autonomous use only of non-lethal weapons. That is, while the very same robot might also carry lethal weapons, it should be programmed such that only a human can authorize their use.

Second, just as any human's right to self-defense is limited, so too should be a robot's. This sounds simple enough, but oddly the Pentagon has already pushed the legal interpretation that our drones have an inherent right to self-defense, including even to preemptively fire on potential threats, such as an anti-aircraft radar system that lights them up. There is a logic to this argument, but it leads down a very dark pathway; self-defense must not be permitted to trump other relevant ethical concerns.

Third, the human creators and operators of autonomous robots must be held accountable for the machines' actions. (Dr. Frankenstein shouldn't get a free pass for his monster's misdeeds.) If a programmer gets an entire village blown up by mistake, he should be criminally prosecuted, not get away scot-free or merely be punished with a monetary fine his employer's insurance company will end up paying. Similarly, if some future commander deploys an autonomous robot and it turns out that the commands or programs he authorized the robot to operate under somehow contributed to a violation of the laws of war, or if his robot were deployed into a situation where a reasonable person could guess that harm would occur, even unintentionally, then it is proper to hold the commander responsible.

To ensure that responsibility falls where it should, there should be clear ways to track the authority in the chain of design, manufacture, ownership, and use of unmanned systems, all the way from the designer and maker to the commanders in the field. This principle of responsibility is not simply intended for us to be able to figure out whom to punish after the fact; by establishing at the start who is ultimately responsible for getting things right, it might add a dose of deterrence into the system before things go wrong. Not merely scientists, but everyone from theologians (who helped create the first laws of war) to the human rights and arms control communities must start looking at where this technological revolution is taking both our weapons and laws. These discussions and debates also need to be global, as the issues of robotics cross national lines (forty-three countries now have military robotics programs). Over time, some sort of consensus might emerge—if not banning the use of all autonomous robots with lethal weapons, then perhaps banning just certain types of robots (such as ones not made of metal, which would be hard to detect and thus of most benefit to terrorist groups).

Some critics will argue against any international discussions or against creating new laws that act to restrict what can be done in war and research. As Steven Metz of the Army War College says, "You have to remember that many consider international law to be a form of asymmetric warfare, limiting our choices, tying us down." Yet history tells us that, time and again, the society that builds an ethical rule of law and stands by its values is the one that ultimately prevails on the battlefield. There is a "bottom line" reason for why we should adhere to the laws of war, explains a U.S. Air Force major general. "The more society adheres to ethical norms, democratic values, and individual rights, the more successful a warfighter that society will be."

9 Law Rather than War on Kashmir

The long running low intensity conflict in Kashmir was bound to escalate. It was only a matter of time. At one level, the current fighting is simply another bloody interlude in a fifty year pattern of India and Pakistan alternately negotiating and fighting over Kashmir. However, things are made more dangerous by both states now having nuclear weapons and policy makers sharing a reckless strategic presumption that their respective nuclear shield protects them from the outbreak of real war or the possibility of defeat. Kashmir is a symptom of a deeper underlying problem, as everyone knows.

Think of the periodic chills and fever that are associated with malaria. More to the point, the disease is serious and given to chronically recurring. So far, at least, the fatal complications common to untreated malaria have not set in. But this is not the occasion to dwell on this infectious disease as a model for nationalism, nor to try identifying the human analogues of the mosquitos who bear this disease from one place to another and across generations, or the parasites who feed of the body politic and are responsible for fever. The need now is to seek help.

The major problem facing any effort to break the impasse between India and Pakistan over Kashmir is that the two states disagree fundamentally on the terms for talking about the issue. Pakistan insists any discussion has to be based on the 1948 and 1949 UN resolutions on Kashmir; coming after the 1947 war, they envisaged the United Nations Commission for India and Pakistan supervising a settlement "in accordance with the will of the people" of the region. India claims primacy lies with the 1972 Simla Agreement; signed after the 1971 India-Pakistan war the treaty commits the two states to settle their disputes "through bilateral negotiations or by any other peaceful means mutually agreed upon between them" and makes no mention of the UN. The Kashmiris are rarely consulted by either state or the international community.

These positions have stalled any effort at a settlement and in fact contribute to the resort to force. Fighting along the Line of Control allows Pakistan to ask for international mediation. For hard-liners here, the more severe the fighting the greater the incitement (they hope) for the international community to talk about Kashmir. Thus Pakistan fans the flames. This however creates pressure for Indian hard-liners to settle the issue directly by force of arms. No Pakistani support for Kashmiris, no problem. There may be a way to break out of this potentially terminal dynamics.

It requires intervention. But not necessarily intervention of the kind that Pakistan has traditionally aimed for, nor India traditionally refused. Rather than a single state or group of states riding to the rescue on Kashmir as if they already knew what the answer to the Kashmir dispute was and imposing it by force, the United Nations General Assembly could take a legal initiative. The General Assembly could choose to ask the International Court of Justice for an advisory opinion on the standing within international law of India and Pakistan's claims over Kashmir, the existing UN resolutions on Kashmir, bilateral treaties and agreements dealing with the dispute, and the right to self-determination of the Kashmiris. The International Court of Justice (otherwise known as the World Court), based at The Hague in Holland, is the highest legal authority within the United Nations system, and thus within the international community.

The UN Charter provides the General Assembly the right to ask the World Court for an "advisory opinion" on "any legal question." This "opinion" is not directly binding on the UN or its member states or even enforceable. It is however understood to be authoritative as a statement of the law. There is precedent for the United Nations General Assembly using it power to ask the World Court for such an "advisory opinion." Most recently the General Assembly asked the World Court whether the threat or use of nuclear weapons was permitted under international law. The World Court ruled in July 1996, declaring the threat or use of nuclear weapons to be generally illegal. The bottom line is that the UN General Assembly simply has to pass a resolution asking the World Court for an "advisory opinion."

It has to be said that the World Court can refuse a request, but only if there "compelling" reasons. It would be hard to see what "compelling" reasons may arise in the case of Kashmir. This is not the place to consider what either India or Pakistan may do, what arguments they may put in front of the Court, or the justifications they may offer for refusing to speak to the Court, or even the possible eventual opinion of the Court. The point here is to offer a suggestion about a process. It offers no shortcut to a solution. The process would seek to clarify what could be a shared basis for the international community for a solution to Kashmir. It could be argued that since the World Court would offer only an "advisory opinion" it would make no difference either to India or Pakistan.

They could choose to ignore it, and the status quo would prevail. However, it is the fact that the UN General Assembly would be taking the action that gives this proposal significance. For want of a better institution, it is the closest thing to a forum for expressing collective aspirations and understanding by the system of states. Once the General Assembly sets out to seek a legal basis for the international community to take a position on Kashmir the context within which India and Pakistan argue their case about Kashmir would change. India and Pakistan would have to decide whether they were prepared to defy the wish of the world community and by so doing jeopardise what international support presently they may have for their position. Depending on the Court's judgment, India or Pakistan (or even both) may well find itself isolated on Kashmir.

This would be a big blow that either would not be able to accept indefinitely, especially if the international community kept insisting that the Court's judgment be used to take some action. The Court's judgment on the general illegality of nuclear weapons has been the basis for resolutions demanding disarmament that now command some 130-150 supporters in the General Assembly, increasingly isolating the nuclear weapons states. If this should start to happen on Kashmir, it would be hard if not impossible for India, or Pakistan, (or both, depending on how the Court decides) could remain defiant for very long. They would be taking on the whole international community backed up by international law. Using the opinion of the Court, whatever it happens to be, the international community could make it clear to both India and Pakistan that there existed a new legal basis for a legitimate solution to the Kashmir dispute and they would have to work within it if they expected any support from the rest of the world.

At the same time, a solution based on an independent interpretation of international law could help politicians in South Asia-if they wanted it to. For the first time there would be an alternative to the long held positions that could be argued to be even more legitimate. Leaders in India and Pakistan would have the opportunity to modify their positions and justify this to their constituencies on the grounds the World Court decision left no alternative. In this, for once, they would be right. There should be no alternative to resolving international disputes except through law.

10 Federal Indian Laws and Policy through the War of 1812

The first federal law regulating Indian affairs was passed in 1790. The fundamental elements of the U. S. Government policy that evolved over the next twenty-five years were six-fold. Laws protected Indian land rights by setting definite boundaries for the Indian country, restricting whites from entering the area (except under certain controls), and removing illegal intruders. Laws controlled the disposition of Indian lands by denying the right of private individuals or local governments to acquire land from the Indians by purchase or any other means. Regulation of the fur trade determined the conditions under which individuals might engage in the trade, prohibiting certain classes of traders, and entering into the trade itself.

Laws attempted to control the liquor traffic by regulating the flow of liquor into Indian Country. Congress provided for the punishment of crimes committed by members of one race against another and compensation for damages suffered by one group at the hands of another. It was hoped to remove the occasions for private retaliation which led to frontier hostilities.

Lastly, civilization and education were to be promoted among the Indians, in the hope they might be absorbed into the mainstream of American society. Although the U. S. government adopted this positive policy, it was extremely difficult to enforce because of inadequate federal troops on the frontier. Difficulties persisted despite efforts by the Indian agencies and the military to enforce these policies equally and fairly. Throughout the late eighteenth and early nineteenth centuries, many new laws were passed to modify or replace previous laws that failed or proved inadequate. A brief chronology of the major federal laws follows.

1787-The newly adopted U. S. Constitution gave the federal government the right "to regulate commerce with foreign powers ... and with the Indian tribes."

1789-The Treaty of Fort Harmar established the policy of acquiring Indian land through purchase rather than conquest. The governor of the Northwest Territory was paid $2000 a year to assume the duties of Superintendant of Indian Affairs, Northern Department, thereby setting the precedent of governors handling Indian affairs.

1790-The first federal Indian law provided for the licensing of the fur traders and establishing penalties for trading without a license. Licenses were to be issued for a period of two years by the superintendent of the department or by someone appointed by the president. Traders had to post a bond of $1000 to guarantee faithful observance of the federal laws and regulations. Issuing agents could recall license and bond if rules were disobeyed. Any apprehended non-licensed trader might forfeit his goods, with half going to the prosecutor and half to the federal government. The new law also declared individual purchases of Indian lands invalid unless made by public treaty with the United States. It included provisions for the punishment of murder and other crimes by whites against Indians. Crimes against Indians in Indian country were to be punished as if the crime took place against any inhabitant in a state or territory.

1793-The President was authorized to give goods and money to the Indian tribes to "promote civilization ... and to secure the continuance of their friendship." Money was set aside to teach the Indians agriculture and induce them to rely on farming rather than hunting for subsistence. A fine of $1000 and twelve-months imprisonment is set for settling illegally on Indian lands or for marking and surveying Indian land. Fur traders could receive a fine of $100 and thirty-five days imprisonment for illegal activities. Superintendents and agents who issue licenses were prohibited from engaging in the trade, with penalties ranging up to twelve-months imprisonment and a fine of $1000. This intercourse act also authorized the President to appoint temporary Indian agents who are under the general supervision of the governors and who report to the War Department. General responsibilities of Indian agents included enforcement of all federal laws concerning the Indians, keeping records of their agency activities, noting the conditions of the local Indians, noting and recording natural history of the area, and noting and recording progress in civilizing the Indians.

1795-Congress introduced government trading factories to promote friendship with the Indians by controlling the fur trade. These government-owned and operated trading posts offered honest dealing and fair prices for furs.

1796-This intercourse act said that U. S. troops, when called upon by civil magistrates, can use military force to remove illegal settlers, apprehend intruders on Indian land, arrest violating fur traders or other offenders, and commit them to safe custody for trial according to civilian law.

The term "Indian country" appeared in statute law, establishing Indian territorial boundaries and denying white claims to unceded lands. New laws forbade whites to cross into Indian country to hunt or to graze animals, with penalties up to six-months imprisonment and fines of $100. Military forts, Indian agencies, trading factories, and roads necessary to reach ceded land were excepted. The death penalty was authorized for a white killing an Indian in Indian country. Indian tribes were to be treated as quasi-sovereign nations with jurisdiction over their own members. In cases of Indians committing crimes against whites, Indians were to turn over tribal offenders to the American authorities. If they did not, military expeditions were to be ordered or hostages taken until the accused tribal members were brought in.

1802-Congress passed a trade and intercourse law that remained in effect until 1834. Major provisions of this law included War Department control of all Indian affairs, restrictions and prohibitions for foreign traders operating on American soil, military force could be used to seize foreign trading goods and furs, and the President was authorized to forbid the sale of alcohol in Indian country.

1806-The Office of Superintendent of Indian Trade was established within the War Department. Its main function was to establish and control government trading factories.

1816-Major provisions of the 1816 trade laws included no trading licenses would be issued to non-Americans (although the President could make exceptions), all trading goods and furs of foreigners could be seized, foreigners traveling in American territory must have a passport, Indian agents were allowed to license certain foreign traders, and traders must submit a bond one-fourth the value of their trading merchandise and a list of all licensed employees. Licenses were not to exceed one year, but could be re-issued by the local Indian agent.

In 1818 by amendment foreign traders were completely excluded without exception. Foreigners who are "odious to our citizens because of activity or cruelty in the last war" were never to be admitted into the trade.

11 Strategy and War Tactics of the Sikhs

Strategy is the plan behind the battle plan; it is the idea of objective that manifests itself in the shape of tactics. The Sikh guerilla leaders, although they were obviously acting upon a systematic military doctrine throughout the course of their struggle, have left behind no account of their designs and deliberations. The contemporary historians, who cared to take notice of their military activities, have merely described what they heard and saw and not what the Sikhs had thought and planned. Consequently, there is little direct evidence available with respect to the strategy of the Sikhs and their battle plans, although there is enough evidence available from which these can be inferred. The strategy of the Sikhs becomes sufficiently obvious if we closely follow the course of their battles and correlate their tactics with their objectives.

While formulating their strategy they seem to have taken into account the obvious factors, such as, their own objectives and those of their enemies, as also the character and composition of the enemy forces and the real source of his strength. India has, since times immemorial, been victim of three types of invaders from the northwest. One type were the early invaders who came to this country to make it their abode or made it their home once they were secure in their new possessions. They defeated and drove away the original inhabitants only to settle down in their place. This marked the beginning of their undoings and their eventual absorption into the life of the land.

They influenced and got influenced, and once a working synthesis was achieved they merged themselves into that vast stream of religions and cultures called Hinduism. Such were the

Aryans who are said to have come to India in 2000 B.C., and the Parthians, the Scythians, the Huns, the Gurjars and various other tribes who invaded India between 500 B.C. and A.D. 500. The second type of invaders were the robber-kings who had little territorial or political objectives in India and marched upon this country primarily for the sake of plunder.

They came with enormous hordes of hungry tribesmen, lured to their standards by the prospects of plunder, and carried sword and fire to every place they visited. They fought and defeated the Indian Kings, burnt and plundered the towns and villages, sacked and slew the local population, and went back with enormous booty of gold and grain, gems and girls. They swept the capitals bare of their wealth, took away the crowns, and whilst returning restored the empty throne to its previous occupant or bestowed it upon their slaves to rule if they could. However, quite often they showed little concern as to who ruled after them and how. The more notorious among them were Mahmud Gazni and Mohammed Ghori who invaded India in the eleventh century, and Nadir Shah and Ahmad Shah Abdali who came in the eighteenth century. The third type of invaders were the military commanders who came to this country to occupy it and to rule over it. They also plundered as they conquered but this, they considered, a part of warfare.

They defeated and dethroned the native Kings and set themselves up as new monarchs. Many of them were great empire builders and followed a systematic policy of expansion. They squeezed the people and invested the resources of this country in raising mercenary forces with which they conquered more territories and subjugated more people. They invested as they earned, and expanded as they invested. Their armies were the source of their treasury and their treasury was the source of their military might. Together, these two generated the power with which they forcibly maintained themselves over the people until they were ousted by a more powerful contender. Such were the men who created the Slave, the Khilji, the Tughlak, the Lodhi and the Mughal Empires in India. Although the Sikh records do not speak of any such historical interpretation in clear terms, the two different strategies formulated by the Sikh guerilla leaders in their struggle against the Mughals and Ahmad Shah Abdali do show that they were conscious of this interpretation and fully realised as to what type of invaders their two enemies were. As there was considerable difference between the character and composition of the Mughal and Afghan armies, and as they were pursuing two different objectives, the Sikhs were obliged to formulate two different strategies which we propose to discuss in sufficient detail in the following pages.

STRATEGY AGAINST THE MUGHALS

The Mughals, as has been said earlier, were imperialist-expansionist type of invaders who had continuously been expanding their empire in India during the past 200 years through squeezing the people and investing their revenues in raising mercenary forces. The real strength of the Mughal empire lay not in its army but in the vast resources of Hindustan. The Sikhs seem to have realised this. They, accordingly, devised such a strategy as aimed at denying them these resources. To begin with, the Sikhs persuaded the peasants to withhold payment of land revenue to the Mughals. Where persuasion failed, as it failed more often than it succeeded in initial stages, they resorted to calculated terrorism in the countryside. They raided the villages and plundered the landlords, the moneylenders, the revenue officers and the hostile Peasantry, Conse quently the land revenue collection went down. Rattan Singh, whose Panth Parkash is based on contemporary oral evidence, has thus summed up the military implications of this economic warfare of the Sikhs: "Land revenue the Mughals could collect none as the peasants refused to pay any on the ground that they had already been robbed of their produce by the Sikhs. The Mughals, as they could not collect enough taxes, had little money to pay to their soldiers who consequently deserted them. And tell me if anyone can collect revenue from the peasants without being able to enforce recovery?" None could, not at least in those days.

The Sikhs also infested the trade-routes and plundered the merchants on the move. They frequently raided the Sarais or the inns and the ferry sites. Within a few years they were thus able to close the highways to trade and traffic. Merchants avoided the

Panjab plains and preferred to take their goods through the hill states of Jammu and Kangra. This resulted in sizeable loss of income to the state from customs and transit duties. The third target of the Sikhs were the escorts carrying state revenues from the parganahs or the revenue estates to the districts and thence to Lahore and Delhi. They ambushed the escorts, raided their camping sites and plundered them in everyway. Thus they strove to block the flow of wealth to the capital, a centre where it generated power. This economic warfare waged by the Sikhs had far-reaching political and military implications. The Mughal economic system, primitive as it was, was not capable of bearing the burden of a disruptionist war of attrition. Consequently, it broke down under strain, and with it collapsed the Mansabdari and Jagirdari systems which were the backbone of the Mughal military system. These barons, the Mansabdars and the Jagirdars, when they failed to collect the revenues assigned to them, also failed to raise and furnish stipulated contingents for the royal army.

The Sikhs further combined their economic strategy with the political and evolved a system of taking control of the population through the Rakhi system. Those were the days when confusion and anarchy reigned in the Panjab. There was virtually no government and the law of the jungle prevailed. People had become an easy prey to anyone who chose to oppress them. The common man lived in constant dread of the invading hordes of the Afghan robber-soldiers, the professional robbers, the Sikhs, and worse-than-robber type of revenue collectors. "Revenue administration there was none; the cultivator followed the plough with a sword in his hand, the Collector came at the head of a regiment, and if he fared well, another soon followed him to pick up the crumbs." "Society lived in a sort of trustless truce broken from time to time by treacherous murders and thievish forays." In such times the Sikhs offered to protect the people on payment of a nominal 'protection fee', the Rakhi. In return they were not only to refrain themselves; they were also to restrain others and to protect the people from all types of marauders. In the areas thus brought under the Rakhis system raids were prevented, disputes settled and justice (rough and ready) meted out. In this way the Sikhs took over all the police functions of the state, and these were the only functions of the state in those days. Thus the people get relief and respite and the Sikhs got an opportunity to prove that they meant to rule. Politically, the Rakhi system made them saviours of the people; economically it assured them of regular legal income; and militarily, it put their organisation on sound footing. In terms of guerilla strategy, it meant an onslaught on the stable image of the Mughal empire and the staying power of the Afghan occupation forces.

In terms of pure military strategy, the Sikhs made the mercenary spirit of the Mughal soldiers, their principal target. The so-called Mughal army of the Panjab Governors of those days was mainly composed of the Irani, Turani and other Central Asian mercenaries. Individually though, these soldiers were brave and reckless, their weakness lay in their mercenary spirit and their lack of loyalty to their Prince and the country of their employer. They had no direct stake in the ontcome of the battle and consequently had little interest in serious fighting.

They frequently changed sides and often made off on the slightest pretext of reverse. Even in the midst of an offensive they were actually on the defensive because they were always keen to save their horses, the loss of which ruined them irretrievably: If they lost their animal they also lost the trooper's extra allowance. The Sikhs were different. Soldiering was not their livelihood. It was a political necessity and a religious duty for them. The Sikhs believed in a war of mutual extermination; for them capitulation was ruled out. They were thus able to turn the contest of arms into a clash of wills, and such was their success that "fifty of them were enough to keep at bay the whole battalion of the King's forces".

STRATEGY AGAINST AHMAD SHAH ABDALI

Ahmad Shah Abdali, except that he wanted to annex the Panjab to his Afghan empire, had little political ambitions in India. After his fourth invasion (1756-1757), when the Mughal empire lay prostrate at his feet, he made no effort to capture it even though Shatba (the prayer for the new King) was read in his name. He merely plundered in and around Delhi and while returning, he restored the throne to the vanquished Mughal

Emperor, Ahmad Shah. Even in the Panjab he tried to establish his direct rule only once (May 1757-April 1758) and frequently plundered it although it was his province ever since 1752. To Ahmad Shah war did not mean an extension of politics; it meant, at best, a means of extortion through politics. And, to his Baluch-Afghan hordes, it simply meant an organised plunder, a trade by arms. The main objective of the repeated invasions of Ahmad Shah Abdali was to plunder the wealth of India and to carry it to Afghanistan. It was so apparent from his conduct that every Panjabi understood it, as is clear from their common saying: Those born in Kabul are our regular guests. The Sikhs, although they were not the first people to understand the true object of the repeated invasions of Ahmad Shahs were certainly the only ones who decided to frustrate it.

Their technique was simple: they robbed the robber. Initially they concentrated on plundering raids involving little fighting and subsequently, they combined serious fighting with plundering. They hung loosely around the Afghan army making use of every opportunity of plunder that fell in their way. Whenever it suited them to take the part of assailants, they fell upon the Afghan baggage train and on their convoys relieving the Afghans of much of their booty. Further, they hovered round the Afghan camp cutting off stragglers and intercepting supplies. They also ambushed the foraging parties and plundering detachments which ventured to go away from the main Afghan force. As their strength increased, their raids grew both in frequency and ferocity. They made frontal attacks on the Afghan vanguard and towards the close of their struggle they did not spare even the main Afghan force. The Sikhs thus frequently aimed their blow at the robber instinct of the Afghan soldiers and hit his mind and morale through his belly. Over a period of time the Sikhs were thus able to convince the Afghans that while it was easy to plunder in India, it was difficult and risky to convey the booty through the Panjab. This way, they made the Afghan trade by arms unprofitable.

The diminished chances of plunder were one of the reasons of desertions in the Afghan army during the last invasion of Ahmad Shah Abdali. The military strategy of the Sikhs was elusive-offensive in nature and aggressive in content. They always strove to retain initiative, and this was necessary. Ahmad Shah Abdali, unlike the Mughals, fought a highly mobile and aggressive type of war. Against an enemy on the defensive there was nothing that could stand between him and the victory. The Sikhs had known it all along and further learnt it at their own cost in the holocaust of 1762, though they were then entrapped much against their wishes. Consequently, they never permitted themselves to be manouvered into a pitched battle of sufficiently long duration, not even till the end. They would only offer him a battle when Abdali was not in a position to accept it, either due to the urgency of returning home or because his soldiers were already exhausted. Defensively, the plan best adopted by them was to offer nothing tangible to the enemy to attack. They never tried to impede the advance of Ahmad Shah except on few occasions in which they suffered heavy losses. They appeared where he was not, threatening his base camp or the advance guard, and disappeared as soon as the main Afghan force arrived on the scene. This way they exhausted and demoralised the Afghan soldiers and then, as usual, confronted them with battle when they were eager to return home. Although the Sikhs could never achieve a decisive victory over Ahmad Shah in this manner, but ultimately he lost. "Guerrillas never win wars but their adversaries often lose them."

TACTICS AND COMBAT METHOD

The tactics of the Sikhs were not static and were usually worked out by the men on the spot. Rattan Singh whose account is based on contemporary oral evidence, was told by a former veteran that one basic tactic of the Sikhs was: "Hit the enemy hard enough to kill, run, turn back and hit him again; run again, hit and run till you exasperate the enemy, and then, melt away." Their entire theory of war is summed up in the word Dhai Phat or two and a half injuries. They considered approach, and all that goes into the making of it when element of surprise is to be secured, as one secret of success. This they called one Phat or injury and regarded it 40 per cent of their battle activity. The half Phat was the sudden swift Shock action which put the enemy off his balance. Then they suddenly withdrew before the enemy could strike back and disappeared to where he could not chase them. They considered speedy and orderly withdrawal to be the second secret of success or the other complete Phat. Qazi Nur Mohammed who fought against the Sikhs, sums up their science of war as follows: To face the enemy like a hero and then to get safely out of action.

They practised all types of harassing tactics such as ambush, dusk and dawn raids, but their favourite was to lead the enemy into baited traps. Unable to destroy the whole Afghan force and unwilling to let it remain intact, they devised a method of killing it bit by bit. With this object in view they would lure a section of the enemy to clsase them, and when it was cut off from the main force they would wheel round and encircle it. When facing the main Afghan force, a party of them would gallop forward and come to a sudden stop to discharge its muskets. Then they would wheel round making room for the others, and thus they kept up uninterrupted fire and smashed the enemy lines. Forster says that their mode of attack was different from that of any other cavalry in Asia. In those days when retreat meant rout and dispersal meant defeat, the Sikhs successfully dispersed to operate and returned to renew the attack. These were entirely new elements which the Sikhs introduced in the north Indian warfare of the period under review

12 The Politics of Total War II: Rise and Fall of the Military-Democratic State

The first phase of total war produced situations in which a classical model of socialist revolution would briefly flourish: the second generated, as social historians of war have frequently demonstrated, the conditions for a particular model of social reform. Both variants of socialism were, of course, available as strategies long before the full unfolding of the total war-society relationship. Each was presented, in the classical debates over 'reform and revolution', as dependent on socio-economic relationships. And yet the processes of total war were necessary to bring variants of first the revolutionary, and then the reformist model into being. This is hardly a good advertisement for the explanatory powers of socialist theory, which in none of its early forms really began to grasp the forces which would prove most powerful in shaping socialism in the twentieth century just as the war-society relationships which produced proletarian revolutions in the first phase of total war were to further transform revolutionary politics in the second phase, so the decisive experiences of social reform in this phase were anticipated in very significant ways by earlier developments.

Parliamentary democracy itself, with mass political parties-as opposed to parliamentary systems with limited suffrage based on property-only developed in a number of Western societies towards the end of the nineteenth century. This development is widely recognised as reflecting the impact of the industrial working class, and the recognition by capitalist political forces of the need to incorporate it into the political system.

The period was one in which mass trade unionism, on the one hand, and a mass circulation press, on the other, first appeared.

The development of parliamentary democracy is more often related to these pressures than to preparations for total war. And yet the development of a disciplined mass industrial workforce also, from the point of view of the state, made potentially possible the creation of disciplined mass armies. The development of state bureaucracy to administer a more complex industrial society was also the creation of an infrastructure for mass military mobilisation. The growth of press and parties, viewed as new means of mass social control, was also the growth of new means of patriotic, militaristic ideological diffusion. It is not necessary to argue that mass parliamentary democracy was a product of mass militarism.

The point is rather that since industrial capitalism developed within a framework of competing states, it inevitably had profound effects on the prospects for war. Virtually every aspect of the development of capitalism, from the rapid advance of technology, transport and communications to the evolution of new class forces and the political and ideological responses to them, had a major military significance. To adopt the traditional sociological terminology, social changes had both the socio-economic functions which were 'manifest' to contemporaries and social theorists, and military functions which were much more 'latent'. Mass militarism can be seen, as it was for example by Karl Liebknecht in 1907, as the form of warfare appropriate to capitalism.

But there is also a sense in which industrial capitalism and parliamentary democracy were the social and political forms required by a new form of state militarism. In the late nineteenth and early twentieth centuries it was clear that both political nationalism and direct military needs would have social implications. Imperialism begat social reform; the inadequacy of the labour supplied to the armed forces (for example, in Britain during the South African war) stimulated concern at the health and diet of the working class.

Warfare had always had implications for welfare, but at the beginning of the twentieth century it was a recognisable motor for change. The First World War greatly accelerated this change, particularly by expanding expectations among working people themselves-expectations which were to be disappointed in the aftermath of the war.

'PARTICIPATION' IN TOTAL WAR

It is tempting to see the period 1914-45, as a period of 'citizen wars' characterised by a dialectic of wartime participation and the expansion of citizenship (with the decades before 1914 as the social preparation for this military process). As is always the case, however, wide-ranging international experience cannot easily be encompassed by a single category. The actual processes were complex-and contradictory. The First World War did not, directly, produce the extinction of democracy which most revolutionary Marxists predicted at the time. Despite wartime repression, parliamentary democracy became fuller and more widespread in the aftermath of the war. More states were republics; more had universal or quasi-universal suffrage (if only for men and restricted groups of women). The social demands provoked by the war continued to be fought over in post-war politics.

Yet the extension of democracy, both in political and social terms, was extremely precarious. The chief reason for this was of course economic instability: vast social needs could not be met in a world market system whose inadequacies had been deepened rather than overcome by the results of the war. The socio-political potential of mass militarism was, as we have seen, as much revolutionary as reformist. The war generated a dialectic of revolution and counter-revolution; parliamentary democracy in crucial states, notably Italy and Germany, was a fragile compromise imposed on the initial defeat of social revolution, and sooner or later to be overturned in a fuller victory of the counter-revolution. Any virtuous dialectic of citizen rights and warfare was largely overtaken by a much more vicious relationship between totalitarianism and remilitarisation. True, Hitler and Stalin could boast full employment and some forms of welfare, and in Germany living standards were maintained; but these rulers did not offer citizenship, only (at best) the perks awarded to obedient slaves.

The social changes resulting from wartime participation thus varied markedly, within both world wars, as Marwick's comparative study suggests. War unleashed not one but several conflicting sets of social and political processes. To explain these really requires analysis on two levels: the general processes of the mode of warfare and the specific forms which they produced in national societies. The mode of warfare envelops a large number of states: to the extent that they are fighting, or preparing to fight, each other, they are governed by common imperatives of technology, strategy and military organisation, and also of economic and political mobilisation. But each state brings to these relationships its own particular economic strength, geopolitical interests, political system and military tradition. The national experiences result from the interaction of these national state characteristics with the mode of warfare: competition influences the competitors, not least in the actual experience of war by both armies and societies.

Although we are accustomed to thinking of the two world wars as two experiences of total war, the mode of warfare was undergoing rapid development both within and between the two wars. Some of the changes we have already discussed: the expansion of state mobilisation capacities from the ad hoc constructions of 1914-18 to the better planned and more comprehensive activities of 1939-45; and the politicisation of total war as a result of the revolutionary and counter-revolutionary developments which issued from the First World War. Equally important and interacting with these political-economic changes were, however, the specific military-technological and strategic changes. These were just as much the product of the experience of the first war. The land stalemate of the trenches had, after all, stimulated the two technological developments-the tank and the bomber-which were to dominate the course of the Second World War. Combined with the advance of statisation and the politicisation of warfare, these produce the main characteristics of the second phase of total war.

Technology and Strategy

Since we have discussed at some length the political-economic processes, it is important to comment on the role of the technical dynamic. The industrialisation of warfare is, in a sense, the most fundamental of all the processes of total war: the development of the military' forces of production'. And yet its role depends on the 'social relations' of militarism, and changes over time. Industrialisation is the most obvious military development of the nineteenth century, and has been well described by writers such as McNeill and Pearton. And yet the most striking product of military industrialisation, the modem warship-on which the greatest economic resources were lavished before 1914-ultimately proved less crucial to warfare than other less impressive and costly developments. The First World War was dominated by labour-intensive mass militarism, by millions of soldiers armed with guns and shells produced by millions of munitions workers. No matter that the form of warfare they produced resulted in the appalling stalemate of the Western Front: neither battleships, nor the gas, planes and tanks which were introduced during the war could shift the dominance of a more simple, perhaps essentially nineteenth century, kind of war.

If the First World War remained to the end a war of attrition between millions, and the Second World War could not dispense with similar millions of foot soldiers, nevertheless the balance shifted sharply between the two. Although one of the main technical developments-chemical and biological warfare-lurked in the background and was never widely used, tanks and bombers were, as we have seen, central to the war's methods. The Second World War saw rapid improvements in guns, tanks, planes and submarines, and depended much more on the technical changes which were being made and the strategic uses to which they were put. During the war, of course, the most important single military research project ever was carried out, producing the atomic bomb for the Americans in 1945.

The role of technical development depended, we have suggested, on its social context: both broadly socio-economic and more narrowly military-political. No single set of processes within total war, however dynamic, can be seen as decisive in isolation. It is the interaction of technology with strategy, politics and economics which counts. Nevertheless, military technology has proved an increasingly critical instrument. The ability to mass produce guns and shells, means of transportation, and later tanks and planes, was what enabled states to maintain massive armies in the field. Once this was possible, it was inevitable, in any serious war, that it would be done: and so, with the development of the means of total war, there followed its social and economic organisation. Once, then, societies and economies became incorporated into the supply side of war., it was strategically rational-however socially or morally dangerous-to break down the distinction between combatants and civilians, and to seek to attack the socio-economic infrastructure of the enemy. Again, however, the means (primarily aerial bombardment) had to be developed to accomplish this transition.

There were, of course, crucial political and ideological processes involved in this evolution of warfare. It is arguable that some of them were already well set long before the industrialisation of war. Even in the Middle Ages, civilians were frequently regarded as part of the enemy, and later the ideology of the nation had provided a modem basis for this idea. Yet it is not difficult to see that modem arms and methods of military organisation facilitated the abandonment of long compromised 'standards' of warfare. In the First World War, national ideologies easily allowed civilian deaths to be seen as legitimate-even if enemy civilians were not so widely or deliberately attacked as in 1939-45. Total conflict of states and peoples and increasingly absolute means of killing produced such slaughter, in 1914-18, that indiscriminate death came to seem normal. The disenchantment with war, as a result of this experience, might have produced a decisive reaction. But the war also gave rise to totally opposed political systems, and so provided renewed justification for war, even with what was then known of its consequences.

It is characteristic of the second phase of total war, therefore, that while the technical dynamic was greatly accelerated, political polarisation also reached an extreme. The relationship between these two processes is central to understanding both the general features of this phase and the different national experiences. At a general level, the combination of politics and military technology meant that attacking civilian population centres, not merely as economic targets but because of their significance for political morale, became a 'normal' feature of warfare. The escalation of this strategy, initiated by Germany, became a central feature of Allied activity. It culminated in Europe in the fire-bombing of Dresden, which was of neither major military nor economic significance, only months before the final defeat of Hitler. This development explains why the atomic bomb, with its enormous enhancement of the capability for indiscriminate killing, could so easily be used against Japan. The strategic choices which undermined possible moral objections had already been made at lower levels of weaponry. The awesome new atomic technology simply carried forward the strategic and political lines already established. Only after the bomb was dropped did the new issues which it raised slowly begin to be perceived.

Absolute political polarisation permitted the large-scale indiscriminate killing of civilians, which military technology made possible, in the Second World War. For governments and peoples, there was little possible qualification of the politics of the struggle; whatever was militarily necessary-and strategic, even atomic bombing could certainly be presented as necessary, however much we may argue with hindsight-was politically justifiable. This same combination of total politics and murderous technology was involved in the Nazis' extermination policies. The difference was that killing, here, was the direct realisation of a political goal, not a sordid military means to an altogether more-praiseworthy politics. The distinction is there, but it is not always as clear in practice as it appears in theory and apologia. Certainly the exterminist politics of Nazism adapted the increasingly exterminist military means of total war to its particular ends. But the bureaucratic efficiency of the extermination process belonged to the methodology of modem total war. As we have already suggested, it is not easy to explain it outside the context of the Second World War.

NATIONAL EXPERIENCES OF THE SECOND WORLD WAR

The second phase of total war differed from the first in that mass politics increasingly displaced more traditional definitions of state interests, and that qualitative changes in military technology and strategy started to displace sheer quantities of men and munitions as critical factors. The transition can be seen as one from labour-intensive, nationalistic mass militarism to technologically and politically enhanced mass militarism. During the Second World War, we were still in the epoch of mass armies, but rapid technological (as well as political) changes had taken place which produced a quite different war. The second phase has much more in common with the first than with the coming third (nuclear) phase, but there are clear fines of development within it which anticipate the more radical transformation of the years after 1945.

National experience of the phases of total war is enormously varied. Most fundamentally, it depends on economic development: no state can participate in modern warfare without at least some of the necessary elements of population, industry, state organisation, etc. And yet there is nothing like a one-toone correspondence between economic strength, or level of economic development, and military capacity. The Tsar mobilised his peasants in 1914, only 50 years out of serfdom, to compete with the armies of industrialised Western Europe. The Chinese Communists mobilised their peasants against the industrial might of Imperial Japan. Both struggles reflected their economic base: Tsarist Russia eventually broke under the strain, while the Chinese alone could not defeat the Japanese. In both world wars too, the industrial might of the USA ultimately played a decisive role; and Soviet industrialisation, for all its costs, was a necessary foundation for the Soviet Union's historic role in defeating Nazism. It was at least very unlikely that the Axis powers could ever have withstood the combined weight of the Allied economies in a prolonged war. This, after all, was why Hitler tried to rely on *Blitzkrieg*.

While economic strength is the foundation of military capacity, it is no more than this, and everything depends on how it is used. The state which makes its military commitments a higher priority may be the military equal of an economically stronger state; and, in any case, major wars are intersecting contests of a group of alliances rather than individual states. The actual outcome of war, moreover, can hardly be read off from the disposition of military-still less economic-forces at its outset. In military terms, as strategists have indicated, the interaction of policy, strategy and supply is crucial. In the end there is no substitute for understanding the processes of war itself, culminating, as Clausewitz argued, in the experience of battle. But battle, in total war, is no longer something which takes place apart from society, involving only professional armed forces. The armed forces are drawn, through conscription, from the entire society; society experiences war both indirectly, through economic and political mobilisation, and directly, as centres of population are systematically fought over on land and in the air.

Battle in total war takes many forms, some of which-at sea, in deserts and remote jungles, etc.-are in isolated 'battlefields' but many of which-aerial bombardment and some tank advances, for example-are actually concentrated on civilian centres. The transition from the first to the second phase of total war is crucial here. The 'home front', which in 1914-18 was largely an economic and political arena, became in 1939-45 much more of a real military 'front'. On the one hand this was because, especially in continental Europe, the shifting land battlefield engulfed successive societies and regions. On the other hand, it was because the major combatants' hinterlands, the true 'home fronts' inaccessible to land attack, became aerial targets. Here is the real convergence of the social and military logic of total war.

National experiences of total war have largely been encompassed by sociologists and social historians under the rubric of the 'Military Participation Ratio' (MPR) thesis. First advanced by Andreski as part of an ambitious comparative sociology of military organisation, it suggests that a crucial factor in the effect of war on society is the proportion of a society's members who are mobilised in its armed forces. In the more grounded historical work of Marwick, this formula is modified to suggest that 'wartime' rather than, in the strict sense, 'military' participation is the key.

Although Marwick's comparative study shows a full awareness of the varied forms of civilian participation and their social effects in different national contexts, his earlier popular study of Britain helped to crystallise a particular sense of wartime participation. In line with other studies of Britain in the Second World War, the society is seen as one in which the active participation of citizens in wartime struggle resulted in a major process of social reform. Mann has gone further, seeing this as a general tendency of 'the period of citizen wars' (1914-45). Such wars, he argues, while characterised by great attrition, destruction means to the stated ends' are nevertheless 'rational as a contribution to citizen well-being'.

One general concept of civilian 'participation' requires some discussion before we look at the British case in comparative perspective. The term 'participation' is open to weak (neutral) and strong (positively evaluated) meanings. The population always participates in total war in the sense that it is mobilised, used, forced to work, fight and die for the state. It does not always participate in the sense of being able to influence the aims and conduct of the war, or of enhancing its post-war influence on social and economic organisation or its post-war social rights. Total war is at its very best a two-way process, in which the state coerces the population but the population endorses its own coercion and thereby improves its position in and influence on the state. At its worst, as in the cases of Nazi Germany, Imperial Japan and Stalinist Russia-whatever their popular appeal or temporary economic benefits they offered-all significant rights are denied, and only coercion remains.

It seems wrong to see these negative cases, as exceptions in this period of militarism. On the contrary, they are organic products of the second phase of total war, with its political polarisation, and represent major models of mass militarism. While, on the assumption that the USA was bound to enter the war, it may be argued that the Western democracies were bound to be victorious, this smacks of the complacency of hindsight.

The totalitarian models of war-mobilisation could have been successful, and if they had, the outcome of the Second World War would have been unprecedented darkness. Orwell, after all, saw 1984 coming despite the victory of the democracies, and he was fight to the extent that the subsequent decades have seen a continuing problem of authoritarianism in Western democratic states.

With a different outcome in 1945, he would neither have needed, nor been able, to write the book: a close approximation to his nightmare would already have been reality. Such a world would doubtless have contained its own contradictions, economic as well as political and military, but it would have been a very different conclusion to the period of total war.

The post-1945 economic and political systems were therefore the result of the victory of particular military forces, representing particular forms of wartime mobilisation. The main victors were the United States, Britain and their allies, which were able to assist forces favouring parliamentary democratic states to restore or create such institutions, and with them pro-American governments, in Japan and most Western European societies. The secondary victor was the Soviet Union, which was able to manoeuvre to bring about Soviet-type states in all the Eastern European countries it occupied. Local victors such as the Yugoslav, Albanian and Chinese Communists were able to create states according to their own models (the Chinese only after further revolutionary struggle).

The dialectic of wartime participation and post-war change was muffled in most of the occupied countries by the role of the new occupiers, the victorious Allies. In Western Europe, local resistance forces who had fought against Nazi occupation did have some part in the post-war order, but radical leftwing movements were either defeated by force of arms (as in Greece) or inhibited from pressing their claims by Stalin's agreement with the US and Britain (as in Italy and France). By the late 1940s, left-wing parties were manoeuvred out of government even in countries where the Resistance had been strong. The forces which survived to dominate the state were those sections of the Right not tainted by collaboration with fascism, such as Gaullists and Christian Democrats. The Communist parties consolidated their right to be the main forces of opposition in Italy and France. In the defeated countries, especially Germany and Japan, the post-war order was erected within the firm constraints imposed by the occupying Allies, and handed over to leaders of whom they approved.

In Eastern Europe, moreover, the dialectic of resistance and post-war change was even weaker. The Soviet Union was careful not to rest its control on leaders who had a national base. In Poland, for example, the Red Army had not entered the capital until after the defeat of the Warsaw Uprising, thus ensuring that it did not have to share power with the heroes of a national revolt. Where the Communist Party had some real support, notably in Czechoslovakia, the Soviet Union ensured that the party leaders relied for their positions on Moscow rather than the working class. There, as elsewhere, it was Moscow Communists rather than those with a local base who inherited the post-war state and eliminated their non-Communist rivals.

The consolidation of parliamentary democracy in most Western states rested more, then, on the international balance of military, political and economic power than on the strength of popular forces. The extension of democratic rights to include social rights, and the subsequent development of a welfare apparatus in most countries, were the result of a number of factors other than the wartime participation of the population. Important among these were the central role necessarily taken by states in the immediate post-war reconstruction; the ideology of planning and intervention which had been strengthened by wartime experience; and the elimination of much of the traditional right because of its associations with fascism.

Most crucial of all, though, was probably the development of new economic conditions. Reconstruction generated a boom, boosted by Korean War rearmament in the US, Britain and elsewhere, which created seemingly permanent full employment. Social reform in most Western countries was not therefore, as in Britain, an immediate consequence of war. On the contrary, the early post-war years in most of continental Europe and Japan were years of great hardship and desperate reconstruction measures. Social reform only developed in conditions of full employment in the 1950s: instead of being implemented by left-wing parties, it was often carried through by the new moderate forces of the Right which benefited from the boom.

The character of post-war states certainly depended in large part on societies' experience of war: but not according to a single pattern of wartime participation and social reform. At this point it is important to stress the variety of national experiences in the Second World War. Of course, the condition in which societies entered the war is also important. Economically, they ranged from the advanced capitalisms of North America, Western Europe and Australasia; through the less industrially developed societies of Japan, the Soviet Union and Southern and Eastern Europe; to the largely peasant societies of China, India and the rest of Asia and the Middle East. Politically, they were sharply divided between parliamentary democracies, fascist, Stalinist and other authoritarian regimes. Actual war experience interacted with the different bases provided by socio-economic relations and political institutions.

National war-experiences in 1939-45 offer an immense range. Although this was a 'world war', some parts of the world were not directly involved. Most of Latin America was neutral, and it has been argued that important economic and political developments stemmed from its relative isolation; much of Africa, belonging to the colonial empires of the European combatants, was only indirectly involved, although the war stimulated movements for national independence.

In Asia, the war was fought with murderous intensity from China south to the East Indies, and from India eastwards to the Pacific. In countries occupied by Japan, Communist and other nationalist resistance forces flourished and after the war eventually brought about the liquidation of the colonial states. In India, which stood in a similar relation to the war in Asia as did Britain to the war in Europe, the war effort of the Raj gave a new impetus to the Congress's drive to independence.

Its eventual, but qualified, success-and the almost uniquely long-lived parliamentary system which resulted from it-are testimony to something like the 'wartime participation' effect which can be seen in Britain. Elsewhere in Asia, however, where the war more directly ravaged society, post-war political developments took more drastic forms: from the successful revolutionary struggles of the Chinese and (after 30 years' further war against France and the US) the Vietnamese Communists; to various authoritarian nationalisms such as those of Malaysia, Indonesia and Burma.

In the industrialised and semi-industrialised states of North America, Europe, Japan, Australasia and South Africa, the range of war experience was, if anything, even wider. At one extreme the United States (after the trauma of Pearl Harbor), Canada, Australia, New Zealand and South Africa experienced little or nothing that resembled direct attack on their societies. North

America in particular was never in much danger of invasion: its people participated in a war that was comfortably across the oceans. The main cost was the loss of American lives in far-flung theatres of war.

For the people at home, the Second World War brought an unprecedented economic boom. War expenditure abolished unemployment, drove forward economic growth, and saw a rapid increase in real living standards. The American Left, which had prospered in the New Deal period and the labour struggles of the 1930s, advanced further during the war and its immediate aftermath. But overall the left was still marginal, and there was relatively weak pressure for social reform in a society where private affluence had grown so markedly. The Cold War and Senator McCarthy put paid to the modest momentum for social advances which resulted from the war years.

There is an overwhelming contrast between the European and North American experiences. Most of continental Europe was fought over and much of it was devastated. Nevertheless, the experiences involved were extremely varied. For the Jews of Eastern Europe, 'wartime participation' ultimately meant their systematic extermination.

The Poles, Russians, Ukrainians, and other peoples of the western Soviet Union, despite contrasting political positions with regard to the war, shared a common pattern of appalling misery, brutal occupation, and massive loss of life. By comparison, the peoples of Western Europe suffered much milder forms of occupation-the Nazis followed their racial theories to prefer Western Europeans, especially Aryans, to Slavs and Jews. There was great hardship and repression, but the death toll was very modest by comparison with the East.

The Germans stood, of course, at the centre of these contrasting experiences-at the height of their success, commanding an empire of huge extremes. As the German people prospered in the early part of the war, with the Reich victorious and only modest inroads into their relatively comfortable living standards, so of course they suffered from the mass bombing and eventual disintegration of their economy in the later years. The Nazis' war first offered real advantages to many Germans (although, even more than the ultimately victorious Americans, the conquering Germans had to lose enormous numbers of soldiers). But in the end it left their society devastated. A similar pattern was followed in Japan.

In the range of war experiences, from the unprecedented slaughter of civilians in Eastern Europe to the war boom in the US, Britain's experience stands out as unique. Britain stood, in terms of the intensity of civilian deaths, danger and hardship as well as in its geographical position, between occupied Western Europe and secure North America. Unlike most of Europe, Britain was never occupied or defeated. Unlike the other major European protagonists, Britain experienced mass mobilisation under a parliamentary democracy rather than fascist or Stalinist totalitarianism. But unlike (for the most part) the white dominions and the US, Britain's democratic mobilisation occurred under conditions of real hardship and direct physical threat.

The uniqueness of British war experience lies in the combination of a real but unrealised threat of invasion, real but relatively limited civilian casualties and hardship, and a process of democratic mobilisation. British society was threatened, and suffered, enough to have radicalising social effects; but not so much as to lead to invasion, defeat or the sort of devastation and killing which left the people of Eastern and Central Europe (and much of Asia) so desperate in 1945. Post-war British democracy was forged as a result of a severe test of state and society, in which the state directly mobilised society and society was in turn able to secure (within a short period after the end of the war) major reforms in the state. But there was continuity in the state, in the maintenance of modestly adequate living standards, and in the working-class movement. The British post-war 'settlement' was an adaptation of existing parliamentary institutions to the demands for social reform generated in the population as a result of the war effort. The post-war Labour government was headed by Attlee, who had been Deputy Prime Minister in charge of the 'home front' for five years: this symbolised not just the social democratic bias of the settlement, but the continuity with the framework of social policy and participation generated by the war.

Britain is therefore an *exceptionally* strong case of what Mann calls 'the dialectic of development of civic and military participation'. Everywhere, in the aftermath of the Second World War, the state's role was greatly enhanced: the wartime accumulation of powers led directly into the mammoth task of post-war reconstruction.

In every industrialised state that fell under the control of the Western democracies, some form of parliamentary democracy was established. Equally, in an era of planning and reconstruction, the state everywhere concerned itself more than ever before with the health, education, welfare and economic security of its citizens. (This was also true of Eastern Europe, where political rights, although legally established, had little practical meaning.) Although the role of the resistance in many countries ensured that the state form was not simply imposed by the Allies and the ruling groups which they fostered, only in Britain were democratic forms extended as a direct consequence of wartime participation.

This meant, first, that Britain had a formally more complete 'welfare state' than most other countries: only Australia and New Zealand (whose war experience is most closely analogous to Britain's) and the Scandinavian countries provide rough comparisons. But, more crucially than that, although some other countries might match Britain's welfare system (and in terms of standards, many eventually surpassed it), it meant that in Britain the 'welfare state' rested on exceptional, unique wartime foundations.

Most post-war parliamentary democracies combined considerable political and socio-economic democratisation with a concentration of military, political and ideological power in state structures defined by emerging international alignments. In a few, traditional non-alignment or post-war geopolitics meant formal neutrality in the new conflict between the two parts of a divided continent: such states have paid their respects to the realities of power, and have maintained their own very considerable armaments. In most states, however, post-war conflicts have meant military and political incorporation into the Atlantic Alliance. State institutions have been formed around these fundamental commitments, involving generally very substantial military forces and expenditures. The realities of East-West conflict have meant that military institutions have retained a major weight in most states, despite the extension of democracy.

In this sense, all post-1945 democracies can be described as 'military-democratic' states. In the United States, where the most striking period of welfare state advance was in the 1930s, the post-war years are most notable for the build-up of military power. C. Wright Mills suggested that the military had become one of the three constituents of the US power elite. The precise weight to be assigned to the military, compared to the political and economic elites, may be controversial. What is undoubtedly true, regardless of whether it is the political or military elite which exercises power, is that military issues and decisions have become central to it. As the US has become dominant in the world order, and as nuclear weapons have centralised military decision-making, so a higher level of power has undoubtedly crystallised to which only a few have access.

In Western European states, which have lost their global direction from that of the US. Compared to the uncertain democracy of the inter-war years, the democratic gains have been real, both in political and socio-economic terms. But, as suggested above, the defining character of international military realities makes the military commitments of states dominate all social goals. In this sense, European states can still usefully be described as military-democratic. The importance of this dual description is that it indicates an ongoing source of tensions in the state, between its external commitments and the social forces which may be active in its internal democratic pace.

Among Western military-democratic states, Britain is one in which both sides of the modern state form are exceptionally developed. On the one hand, Britain is, in consequence of its junior partnership in the victory of 1945, a member of NATO with military importance disproportionate to its declining economic and political roles. Britain has had military expenditure at a consistently higher level than any other European NATO state (or Japan); indeed this is one explanation put forward for Britain's economic decline. On the other hand, British democracy has not only a long history, uninterrupted—invasion or dictatorship; it has been almost uniquely reinforced by the social consequences of war participation. But this over-determination of the military-democratic state in Britain also means that it has become unusually vulnerable the conflicts inherent in its structure.

The argument that the framework of post-war democracy is limited and contradictory has been widely advanced: as Stuart Hall has put it, the Keynesian Welfare State 'is a contradictory structure, a "historic compromise", which both achieved something in a reformist direction for the working class and became an instrument for disciplining it'.What has largely been missed in discussions of this contradiction is how far it as the product of wartime mobilisation. 'Democracy' in wartime issued from above: the government, and 'experts' such as Keynes and Beveridge whose ideas and reports helped I shape the desired better society, were the sources of initiatives.

They responded to what they perceived as the demands of the people, and to feedback from them, but there was very limited scope for direct popular initiatives. Participation-the ambiguity of the term has already been noted-did. not mean direct democracy from the bottom. The state, which was centralised for war, remained centralised for the peace. Indeed, social reform was largely a matter of converting the wartime planning machine to the problems of peace. Democracy consisted in the expectations of, and support for, this development which undoubtedly existed in the majority of the population, rather than in direct mass involvement.

The post-war Labour government was noted for its centralist, bureaucratic methods. These have often been ascribed to the statist ideology of Fabianism, or Labourism, but ideology alone cannot explain them. The working-class movement had, after all, other ideological traditions. The 'selection' of a statist ideology reflected the general advance of the state in society between-and even more during-the wars.

The centralism of welfare-state social democracy, with its concepts of nationalisation and bureaucratic planning, issued from the centralism of the war-state and war-economy. Its contradictions were the contradictions of Second World War democratic militarism: between the imperatives of control and mass manipulation by a secretive centralised state, and the democratic, reform-based input of mass participation.

The tension was largely controlled, during the actual war years and the immediate aftermath, although popular expectations did sometimes run ahead of state action. It gradually became fully apparent, and finally developed into a fundamental cleavage, in the late post-war period. The war-state has become a target for both grassroots democratisers on the left and economic libertarians on the right.

The context of military participation has widely been seen as fundamental to the social changes of the war and immediate post-war period. They are well served by social and political historians such as Calder and Addison, as well as by the more sociologically explicit work of Marwick.

The problem arises with the main post-war period (that contemporary Britain is still, 40 years later, defined in relation to wartime experience says much about its centrality). Here the military context becomes, necessarily, less total and less visible, and tends to be almost wholly replaced by the socio-economic issues which are, obviously, at the front of the stage. Social historians of military participation have not carried their analyses seriously into the longer post-war term: even a writer such as Middlemas, who recognises the centrality of war in earlier periods, neglects the military context in his account of socio-economic change. Similarly sociologists concerned with the problems of political power and the decline of consensus, as a sample of otherwise excellent recent British textbooks shows, define these almost completely without reference to the context of military power. Here social theory clearly lags behind social consciousness, for since 1979 international and military issues have been central to the problems of the state in Britain and other Western societies.

What is proposed here, then, is a double revision of existing historical and sociological interpretations. On the one hand, the social theory of military participation, which has been qualified as a general theory of wartime experience, should nevertheless be extended so that we may examine its relevance to the post-war period. On the other hand, it is suggested that almost all historical and sociological writing, not least Marxist-influenced writing, has neglected a fundamental dimension of the processes of socio-economic and political change in Britain since 1945. Unless we see Britain at that point as something like a 'mflitary-democratic' state, we cannot chart its subsequent mutation.

It is not difficult to see the early post-war reforms as belonging essentially to the period of wartime mobilisation. This is not to deny the political role of Labour reformism which, as Morgan has emphasised, took the wartime coalition's welfare proposals significantly further. But Labour's dominance was itself a product of the wartime period. In political terms, the war-mobilisation period can be seen as lasting until about 1947, by which time most of Labour's main reforms had either been achieved, or at least launched. The year 1947 was one of crisis for the government, and was marked internationally by the onset of the Cold War.

The decade after 1947 can be seen as one of transition from the politics of war mobilisation to the politics of the nuclear age. In this decade, despite military and economic demobilisation from the unprecedented levels of 1939-45, Britain remained within the mould cast for it by the war. Economically, it retained the appearance of a major power, while most of Western Europe and Japan were concerned with fundamental reconstruction. Politically, Britain was still undisputably one of the great powers, a major actor in the Cold War era-even if its inferiority to the superpowers was there for all to see.

Militarily, early 1947 also saw the beginnings of Britain's atomic bomb, the ultimate expression of the Labour government's belief in Britain's status. But this programme-which remained secret until after Churchill returned to power in 1951-was at this stage only an addition to Britain's military capabilities, which were still based on a Second World War kind of militarism. The Korean War saw massive conventional rearmament; the armed forces remained based on conscription (for the first time outside war); and a comprehensive system of civil defence stayed in place.

The period from about 1947 to 1957 was marked, then, by a modified version (obviously much less intense outside actual total war) of the Second World War model of military participation. Presided over by its wartime leaders (Attlee, Churchill, Eden), there was a continuation of the wartime consensus on two fundamental bases. The first of these was the widely recognised economic and social 'settlement' of the welfare state, full employment and economic intervention. The second, less often acknowledged by recent writers but equally essential, was the political-military framework of the Atlantic Alliance-Britain's world role and continuing national mobilisation. Where 'democracy versus fascism' had once provided the ideological cement, it was now 'democracy versus Communism'. This was the era of Cold War conformity, as stifling in Britain as it was threatening in the US.

Korea marked the high point of this phase, and also the point at which it was clearest that the Cold War polarisation blocked off further social advance. Suez was its denouement, showing that it was no longer possible for Britain to continue as a great power in the old way. The following year, under Macmillan, came a fundamental reassessment of Britain's military policies, recognising the supremacy of nuclear weapons and marking the beginning of the end for the 193945 model of military participation. Conscription was to be mded, defence spending reduced, and instead there was a reliance on the 'independent nuclear deterrent'. This was Followed by moves to demobilise civil defence, and in 1968 by its virtual disbandment.

The changing basis of 'defence' marked the beginning of he end for Britain's 'military-democratic' state. From 1957 onwards, the military establishment became more and more separate, and ultimately almost invisible, from the people. The state recognised that it would dispense with the people in ~ future nuclear war; it had largely dispensed with the pretence of involving them in war-preparation, too. The secret, capital-intensive part of the state's military power was c) be developed; the people were not expected to discuss or decide, but merely to give their passive consent. The new policies were not, however, the abandonment of Britain's great power pretensions, but a recognition that they were either politically viable nor financially affordable on the old basis. The state was opting for the cheaper, symbolic assertion f Britain's continuing military pretensions, rather than the older model of large armies and global reach. 'East of Suez' as finally abandoned, after a further crisis, under the Labour wernment in the mid-1960s; but the logic had been anticipated a decade earlier.

The explicit recognition of the nuclear age at first provoked an opposition movement. The young who were roused by the Suez fiasco were not likely to embrace a nuclear defence policy. The Campaign for Nuclear Disarmament (CND) brought about the first popular cleavage in the post-war 'consensus'. (Rumblings of opposition to Korean war rearmament, German rearmament and earlier nuclear tests had occurred within the Labour movement, or in small and marginal protest groups.) The first steps to break up the 'military-democratic' consensus were, therefore, met with a mass movement. But this was worn down, defused, and eventually marginalised: after 1964, the issues of nucleai weapons and defence policy were absent from popular radical politics, indeed from national politics generally except in that elite corridors of the defence establishment. The state enjoyed 15 years of virtually complete popular indifference to its military preparations, ended only by the cruise missile debate at the very end of 1979.

CND laid the foundation for a succession of radica campaigns and protest movements which often focused or international or domestic issues touching defence or nuclear policy. But despite this continuing radical presence the central contradictions of the nuclear age appeared (before the 1980s) to be socio-economic. It seemed that the economic growth of the post-war boom had opened up a new phase o class conflict, exacerbated by the onset of recession in the 1970s.

Wages and trade union rights, and later inflation unemployment and the welfare state, were the central issue: of British politics. Debates about Britain's military role in general, especially its nuclear-armed core, were so marginal between 1964 and 1979 that it is difficult to credit the idea that military participation can tell us anything significant about the overall trajectory of the British state.

It must be argued, however, that the decline and near disappearance of a crucial social cement, holding together the post-war social order and the state, is as important as its earlier centrality. Hand in hand with military participation had gone economic and social participation; along with military duty had come economic and social rights.

The connection of the two had been central to their general acceptance-in particular to the support of the political right in the Conservative Party for reforms which it had previously considered dangerously left-wing. Wartime participation was, in this sense, essential to the post-war consensus. Even if economic and social participation, as values, achieved a centrality of heir own-the core of the consensus coming to be located in state intervention, full employment and the welfare state-hey were more easily jettisoned when their underpinning in military participation was gone. The decline of military participation was a necessary, if not a sufficient, condition for the break-up of the consensus.

The disappearance of militarism from public consciousness was not of course its disappearance from society, but a separation of militarism from the sources of social democracy n the broad sense. So long as 'defence' remained a purely elite issue, the consensus on defence could survive, when the socio-economic consensus was already under strain. The final rupture, in 1980-81, was therefore quite dramatic, as soon as a popular challenge to defence policies re-emerged.

In May 1979 a Labour government left office, having secretly modernised Polaris, authorised NATO's 3 per cent real increase at a time of welfare cuts, begun negotiations about Trident, and participated in NATO policy discussions on cruise missiles. By January 1981, at its Wembley conference, Labour (in response to the peace movement and the influence of unilateralists in the trade unions) was moving towards a non-nuclear defence policy. In response to this movement, and also to constitutional changes, a section of its right-wing formed the Social Democratic Party. To understand how such fundamental developments could take place so rapidly, we must recognise that the Atlanticist, nuclear consensus of the main parties had long since lost the active basis of ideological support, let alone the real military participation, of its origins. It rested on a passive, at best routine, acquiescence of the population in the military preparations of the state.

The British state has moved, therefore, from a military-democratic to a nuclear relationship with society. Nuclear weapons have, centralised military-political power and reduced democratic politics to the lower rungs of power. Even the ideological dimensions of nuclear rivalry stayed passive in Britain, as in most Western societies, so long as the arms race remained more of a technical than a political conflict. But a regime which is dispensing with much of the consensus socio-economic legitimation of state power needs to emphasise older, more fundamental legitimations: 'law and order' and 'defence'.

The re-creation of an ideology of defence in Britain has relied considerably on the basic concept of 'deterrence', deployed against CND a quarter of a century ago, despite all its inherent contradictions and subsequent strategic mutations.

In Britain especially, in contrast to other countries in Western Europe, the political argument has often been remarkably crude and unreconstructed.

In part this has to do with the simple party and electoral systems within which British politics are conducted. War brought no constitutional reform, only the consolidation of a Labour-Tory two-party system.

Equally, however, the crudeness of the argument reflects the weak popular appeal of nuclear defence, and the difficulty of popularising new weapon systems. A good deal of ideological weight has therefore been given, not to Reaganesque pictures of 'evil empires' which would have limited appeal in the British case, but to a military analogy with the situation before the Second World War.

The analogy is inevitably extremely simple, since Gorbachev is manifestly not Hitler, and no serious comparison could be drawn between the strategic interests and policies of the Soviet Union today and Nazi Germany. But the Thatcher government clearly needs to appeal to that part of the ideological foundation of the 'military-democratic' state which is available to it; even as it dismantles and disowns the socio-economic content of the post-war settlement.

The ideological residues of military participation were most effectively, if ultimately incongruously, exploited by Thatcher in the Falklands war. The ideological framework of post-war British politics can be traced back to the marriage of Tory-imperialist patriotism and Labourist social reform in the wartime coalition government. 'Churchillism': the shared ideology of the political elite. Its echoes in the Falklands war were, however, hollow and deformed: myths and symbols lacking in their original substance.

The shrill version of national leadership offered by Thatcher lacked the wide base of Churchill's; 'Argy-bashing', while reminiscent of Cold War 'Red-baiting', lacked the foundations of real hatred which were felt for Nazism in the Second World War. Ultimately the explanation for this is the decline of military participation: the Falklands were not an exception, but confirmed the trend. Although the symbols of the Second World War could be applied, as Barnett notes, their practical meaning was fundamentally changed.

The Falklands War vindicated small, professional armed forces, acting on behalf of the nation but needing no real mass participation to carry out their tasks. British civilian involvement was little more than that of the tiny Falklands population itself. For the vast majority, it was limited to the utterly passive, vicarious consumption of exceptionally closely filtered news, and the expression of support in the opinion polls.

Far from the Falklands representing a renewal of the Second World War type of participation, the war was a perfect demonstration of Mann's division between the 'deterrence science' militarism of the professional elite and the 'spectator sport' militarism of the mass. Tens of millions of people in Britain were glued to their TV sets for scanty news of the few thousands tossing in the South Atlantic on their behalf-as clear a picture as one could want of this divide.

Britain is therefore, in the late 1980s, a society in which the contradictions of the military-democratic state have been further exposed than in any other-by the development of nuclear militarism.

In Britain, above all, it is important that any perspective for social change should be based on understanding the changed character of warfare.

Society and state have moved beyond the forms which classical total war created; so, as we contemplate the form which radicalism can take in Britain, we must clearly move beyond the politics of total war.

13 Military Industrialism and the Phases of Total War

There is an emerging consensus that the old debate over whether capitalist industrialism is 'inherently' pacific or militarist is simply beside the point. It is neither, but there exists a contingent historical association between capitalism and war: simply because of its technical progress, capitalism has vastly increased the dangers of war.

Although the mode of warfare should be seen as distinct from capitalism, the tension between the two is crucial. E.P. Thompson goes so far as to suggest that the application of industrial technology to warfare has ultimately produced a new social form, dominated by a nuclear arms race which is leading to total annihilation. The problem, it seems, is not whether to transcend the traditional sociological and Marxist debate, but how, precisely, to take the argument further. Part of the answer may be provided by the rethinking of the theory of the state which has been going on both sides of the Atlantic.

In the 1980s, however, both the theoretical assumptions and the abstract methodology have come under sustained attack from a new group of 'institutional' theorists committed to historical-sociological research. Interestingly, a key text of this new wave, Theda Skocpol's States and Social Revolutions, introduced war as a key context of state-formation and revolutionary crisis. The subsequent development of the position, however, has not taken this particular aspect any further, concentrating on establishing a state-centred social theory without any special attention to war.

A state-centred social theory, especially when it makes use of war to explain state development, obviously takes us closer to a theory of war and society than a mode of production-centred theory. But it is not the same thing as a social theory of war, since it will not necessarily explain how warfare has become a central determinant of social and political relations. In fact, what we need is a war-centred social theory. The aim of this chapter is to begin to supply some of the concepts which are necessary for this.

The most useful sources are not the debates in social theory, but the more theoretically aware historical analyses of war that have been produced in recent years. Although clearly war held a central place in many preindustrial societies, industrialism is both so different from previous forms, and so widely seen as not inherently militaristic, that we need to start by asking how war has become central to this particular sort of society.

Even to pose the question in this way could be said to accept, too easily, the assumption that the two can originally be separated, and beg the question of how real this separation ever was.

It can be argued that the emergence of a competitive state-system, with frequent inter-state warfare, helped to stimulate capitalism in Europe, while the lack of both inhibited such development in other civilisations. It can also be argued, more specifically, that industrialisation was speeded up and its direction shaped by war-and, in particular, that the Napoleonic Wars had this effect on the classical 'Industrial Revolution' in Britain.

The autonomy of industrial capitalism from warfare (we need to reverse the usual formula) was therefore quite relative even in its formative period. What is true, however, is that, by comparison with later historical developments, the early effects of industrialisation on warfare were minimal at this stage, and that the impact of warfare on society, although considerable, was of a different order from that which industrialised warfare was later to make. It is the great expansion of the role of war with which this chapter is concerned.

INDUSTRIALISED WARFARE AND POLITICISED ECONOMIES

The origins of total war are, earlier than 1840. The Revolutionary and Napoleonic wars represent a primitive model:

a political, ideological and military-organisational form, although without the technical and economic basis of industrialised warfare. Population growth, resulting from agricultural improvements and the beginnings of industrialisation, supplied the demographic basis for mass armies: the French Revolution provided the more important elements of mass participation, citizenship, and nationalist fervour.

The levie en masse which produced the revolutionary army of 1793 was 'an attempt to mobilise not just a mass army in a hurry but, behind it, a whole politicised population'. Revolutionary nationalism motivated what was at first a people's army, although later the ideology was adapted to Napoleon's imperial ambitions.

The Republic from 1793-4 was a 'society taken totally to war, with, for a while, price-controls and the requisitioning of labour, products and property, to a degree unprecedented and unmatched until the Second World War'. Although at a primitive, labour-intensive level, Republican France under the Terror was a war-economy of a recognisably modem kind, a 'military State... to such an extent that its turning into a military dictatorship marked the end of a logical road'.

This model of 'total war'-whose revolutionary origins are of no small interest-impressed the Prussian professional soldiers who were pitted against it, and left its mark on military theory in the work of Clausewitz. But, for a century after 1814, there was no large-scale repetition of the experience, at least not in Europe, and warfare seemed once again to resemble the more limited rivalry of the eighteenth century.

The most important exception was the American Civil War, in which once again mass armies were pitted against each other in years of battle, with the societies of North and South mobilised behind them. In the half-century after the close of the Napoleonic Wars, however, industrial technology had been applied to weapons, transport and communications. Mass production of guns, railways as means of moving large numbers of men, telegraphic communications: these made the Civil War 'the first full-fledged example of an industrialised war', even if this A-as only rccognised in Europe in the bitter light of 1914-18.'

Industrialisation of warfare proceeded apace from the midnineteenth century until the full demonstration of its potential in the First World War. Technical change in land armaments, although 'radical enough measured against older standards, was modest only by comparison to the galloping transformation in naval armaments'.

Massive warship building programmes, beginning in Britain and France in the 1880s, were emulated in Germany and the United States in the 1890s. The scale and complexity of the new ships-and even more of entire ship-building programmes-altered the relationship between the producers and the procurers of arms. What McNeill calls 'command technology', in which market relations were replaced by the design of new weaponry to order, became dominant in the 30 years before 1914.

Growing 'like a cancer within the tissues of the world's market economy', naval construction created a new sector within first the British and then other leading national economies. The big arms firms were closely tied to their naval and political patrons, and 'quickly evolved into vast bureaucratic structures of quasi-public character'. They were often seen by liberal and Marxist critics as private profit-seekers whose greed was responsible for the proliferation of arms. In reality, a sector of capital was growing because of its dependence on state militarism and the ambitions of both civil and military bureaucracies.

As perceptive a military writer as Engels could see the state as loser in the naval arms race and make the amazingly optimistic comment that 'the warship is being developed to a pitch of perfection which is making it both outrageously costly and unusable in war'. This description illustrates the inadequacy of social theory which treats war-preparation, and even more war itself, according to 'ordinary' (i.e. market-derived, capitalist) economic criteria.

Although there must always be a compromise between military and non-military forms of economic activity, and even more of state expenditure, the rise of large-scale military industry is the rise of an economic sector which is autonomous from the market and the logic of capital. The profits of private arms firms are ultimately dependent on the state's military purposes and on how its bureaucracies perceive its needs. In war, the state's purposes transcend ordinary accounting: in the twentieth century, it has become quite normal for states to risk not only their most costly military investments, but their whole economies and peoples.

The development of the military-industrial sector thus introduced an alternative principle-the military requirements of the state-into the capitalist market economy. From the start, this affected crucial heavy industrial areas of national economies: engineering, shipbuilding, etc.

But the implications of this development were barely foreseen before 1914. If it was apparent that technology and economy had become vital to warfare, it was less obvious that a major European conflict would turn into an all-out, protracted war which would be 'total' in an entirely new sense. And yet, once war had broken out, and a settlement had not been reached within months (as so many expected), the combatant states were obliged to mobilise their whole national economies for the struggle. The military principle of economic organisation, previously affecting only special sectors, now embraced the entire economic life of major societies.

WAR ECONOMIES AND TOTAL WAR

All authorities emphasise that the development of war economies was *ad hoc* and unprepared. 'All the belligerents', writes Bond, 'displayed an understandable reluctance to abandon the policy of "business as usual" in favour of a strictly controlled and regulated war economy.' Or, as the official British historians of the Second World War put it, looking back at the unplanned effort of 1914-18: 'The political economy of war came into existence as fact before it was conceived as an idea.' Nevertheless, major, unprecedented extensions of state economic regulation took place in all the main combatant states.

Nationalisation, control, planning, rationing, direction of labour, appeared in various forms and at different paces in all countries. Economic controls were more haphazard and incomplete than they became in the Second World War, and they limited the market economy rather than replacing it. Some balance was maintained between military requirements and civilian consumption: the relative failure of Germany, and even more of Russia, to maintain this 'balance' has been seen as a major weakness of their war efforts.

But a war economy came into existence in the sense that supplying the war effort became the overt, dominant aim of all economic activity, the framework within which the market economy functioned and civilian needs were satisfied. War economies in 1914-18 have to be seen within a particular phase or model of total war.

While the main technological thrust and investment of the previous three decades was in naval warfare, the war itself was dominated by the stalemated and armies in Continental Europe. World War I was a labour-intensive war: the main effort went into deploying and maintaining the massive armies which Continental powers had been building up since the mid-nineteenth century, and which were now augmented by general conscription. Economically, the main business was mass-producing the guns, shells and vehicles needed for the front, a task which drew millions of workers (often women) into the munitions factories.

Technologically, the main advances of the actual war period (typically in modern war, these greatly speeded up the technological innovation of the pre-war years) were designed to overcome the stalemate on the ground: chemical warfare, tanks, and aerial bombing.

War economy in this period therefore completed the basic model of 'total war' which dates back to the Napoleonic period, adding economic mobilisation for munitions production to the pattern of military conscription plus political mobilisation. It is important, however, to examine the stage in the 'totalisation' of warfare which had been reached.

In this basic model, civilian populations were incorporated into the supply side of war, and in Clausewitzian terms the problems of mobilising them can be seen as forms of 'friction' limiting the destructiveness of battle. These problems included not only those of administration and economic organisation, on which military and economic historians have tended to dwell, but also those of war-resistance-war-evasion in the trenches, and working-class resistance to the direction of labour, dilution, etc.-which have concerned social and political history.

Increasingly, too, the economic strength of the enemy, and the 'morale' of its civilian population, came to be seen as military factors. Attacks on economic targets-not only merchant shipping but, with the development of aerial warfare, factories and dockyards-were legitimate; civilian deaths and hardship, if not actively promoted in the manner of the Second World War, could be seen as contributing to strategic goals. Civilian deaths, although still small in relation to those of combatants, were on an unprecedented scale, and many resulted directly from more indiscriminate forms of warfare by submarine, artillery and air attacks.

Taken overall, therefore, there was still a distinction between civilian and military participation in war, but it was beginning to break down. Society was incorporated into war on the supply side, as a distinct 'home front' concerned with economic and political problems rather than as a military battlefield.

Especially for Britain and (in its brief participation) the USA, which were not invaded or fought over, this distinction was fairly clear, although the social effects of the human damage in the trenches were far-reaching.

Equally, the distinction between civil and war economies, although far from clear in practice in the war period, in general remained, and wartime controls were seen as 'abnormal'. Attempts to adapt the war model of economic organisation to the social problems of peace were too weak to withstand the post-war re-emergence of the inherent problems of the capitalist market economy.

Nevertheless, neither states nor societies reverted to their pre-1914 condition. The world before the war vanished-indeed one side of it (the life of the upper and middle classes) was to be romanticised forever as a golden age of lost innocence. Nor were class relations all that were fundamentally altered: states, too, learned how to 'intervene' and organise economic life. Everywhere, although war economies were quickly dismantled, the threshold of state economic power was higher, and the model of a war economy remained. Elements of this model were developed in the 'command economies' of the Soviet Union and Nazi Germany in the 1930s, while a more limited form of state intervention developed in 'New Deal' America under Roosevelt. (It was this triple experience of extending state power, rather than mere changes in ownership and control, which prompted James Burnham's famous 1940 critique of Marxism, *The Managerial Revolution*.) Even where, as in Britain, the politics of non-intervention remained dominant, the state had learned many of the lessons of 1914-18 and was planning for war. The 'leisurely essay writing' of the Committee of Imperial Defence was replaced after 1935 with systematic planning for conscription, food control, a wartime restructuring of ministries, and building up war industries. Of course, 'believing that "industry ought not to be interfered with", the Government was attempting to impose rearmament upon recovery within an uncontrolled economy.'

There is some historical debate about how far Germany had developed a war economy before 1939. The traditional view is that Germany had been on a war footing since 1935 or so: it has been pointed out that by 1938 Germany was devoting 25 per cent of its national income to military expenditure, Britain only 7 per cent. Milward, however, argues that in Germany rearmament went hand in hand with economic recovery and that a great deal of state expenditure after 1933-for example, the *Autobhan* programme-had a dual civil and military purpose. Nazi economics before 1939 was based on guns *and* butter: civilian consumption was not seriously reduced for some while even after war broke out. German war planning was based on the concept of *Blitzkrieg*, and hoped by this means to avoid being overwhelmed by the superior economic strength of its potential adversaries. It was also 'a method of avoiding the total economic commitment of "total war"'. According to Milward, 'in September 1939 Germany had not yet ventured on the basic reorganisation of her economy which the war would eventually entail, whereas Britain had.' Only the invasion of the Soviet Union finally exposed the weakness of the *Blitzkrieg* economy, creating severe strains which led from the winter of 1941-42 to more drastic reorganisation, restriction of consumer goods, etc. Yet, argues Milward, 'even in 1944 when German armaments production was so high, the economy could not be called a full war economy as a high production of consumer goods was maintained.

Certainly, what this argument suggests is that there is no simple model of a 'war economy' which is switched over to at the outbreak of war. The nature of each war economy depends on the conception of war, economy and state which are dominant in the states themselves.

These vary, not only according to the general character of the regime, but according to its specific policies (e.g. there were vast differences between the wartime economies of Germany itself, the occupied countries of Western Europe, and the enslaved areas to the East). They also vary according to the specific requirements of the war at different stages, although they may be far from expressing a 'rational' military-economic response (c.f. the Nazis' diversion of scarce resources to the extermination of Jews at the period of their greatest military weakness).

The Second World War was a total war in an even fuller sense than the First World War, therefore, not simply because its economic organisation was far more planned-although it was-but because of the unfolding demands of the conflict. In so many ways, however, the course of the Second World War was determined by the legacy of the First: not only because of state control and economic planning for war, but by the national-political ideologies which drove popular mobilisation, and in the military strategies and technologies involved. Indeed it was partly because of the way in which the military-technological threat to civilian populations reinforced national solidarities and ideologies that the war could not be stopped short at a Blitzkrieg, but developed into all-out struggle lasting for six years.

In the sense that the war was a war of mass armies, based on mass production of weapons, vehicles and supplies of all sorts, the Second World War continued the mode of warfare of the First. But politics and economics, strategy and technology combined to create a new phase of total war. States' controls voer economy and society were everywhere more thorough and complete, bearing strong resemblances to each other, but the ideologies of mobilisation reflected real differences in political systems. Fascism, Stalinist state socialism and Western democracy appeared as contrasting models of war mobilisation, offering different models of society after the war. Strategy and weaponry underwent similar changes on all sides, the innovations of 1914-18 becoming commonplace in 1939-45. Land warfare, avoiding the trenches, was dominated by the tank; aerial warfare was widely seen, both before and during the war, as crucial. Civilian populations as such, as well as the economic installations around which they lived, were now seen as legitimate targets. All the evidence, from Britain and Germany, that bombing reinforced rather than undermined civilian support for the war, instead of leading to its abandonment, only produced more blanket attacks on cities. Dresden, not an economic or military target, was destroyed in a firestorm in the closing months of the war in Europe. Hiroshima and Nagasaki testified to the war's greatest technical 'progress' when single atomic devices accomplished a scale of killing previously requiring thousands of bombs.

The interaction of military and political logic is evident. War required-as 1914-18 had already shown-the total mobilisation of the people. Political and ideological support was essential for economic and military achievement. Since this was true on both sides, the strategy of each had to be based on attacking the people as well as the army of the other. Such attacks in turn intensified the identification of the people with the state, its form of national ideology, and the political system. The Second World War not only seemed to be, but was, in a real sense, a war of political systems (although it was much else besides). This is what made it much harder for citizens to refuse their support for it than either the First World War (in which the politicisation of the conflict was far less complete) or, for reasons which will become apparent later, the preparations for the Third World War.

NUCLEAR WAR-ECONOMY

It has been argued above that total war is not a single mode of war, but a developing relationship between war and society. Within this relationship it is possible to distinguish various main strands-economic, political, strategic, technical-each of which develops according to its own logic, while affecting other sides of the process and contributing to the overall result. Each element can be seen as reinforcing the others in determining the overall direction of the movement towards the 'totalisation' of war. War can be said to become 'total' in at least two main senses: on the one hand, in the sense most used by social scientists, that it more and more completely incorporates the whole of social life; and on the other, in the military sense, that it increasingly becomes an 'absolute' struggle of life and death for states and peoples.

In reality, these are but two sides of the same process. The political-economic totalisation of war both facilitates and requires the military-technological totalisation. This is why the atomic bomb on Hiroshima, which obliterated a city and threatened an era of war as total annihilation, represents a logical conclusion to a century of industrialised warfare. If 1945 represents a crucial turning-point in processes which can be traced back to the 1840s, if not beyond, it presents us with a conclusion which is not yet final. In that sense, although an end-point to total war was now clear, a new phase of total war opened up.

The end of the Second World War would, in any case, even without the emerging technological climax of atomic weaponry, have ushered in such a phase. After 1945 it was much more evident than after 1918 that the end of a war was not the end of war as a dominant social reality; or, to be more precise, not the end of the developing process of total war. The Third World War is widely held to have begun even before the Second World War ended. The rivalry of the United States and the Soviet Union was clear enough in the final stages of that war, and was one of the factors influencing the use of the atomic bomb on Japan. By the late 1940s this new conflict was clearly institutionalised and becoming known as the 'Cold War', to signify a deep opposition and the full potential for open war. By the early 1950s the Cold

War had become 'hot' in the limited theatre of Kom but stopped short of any escalation to global conflict. Ultether the entire East-West conflict, which has been contianotis since 1945, should be called the 'Cold War', or whether this term should be reserved for particularly frosty periods (late 1940s/early 1950s and, more problematically, the 1980s), is largely a semantic debate.

What is important is that the East-West conflict has been a crucial, defining reality for all economic, social and political change since 1945, and that it is necessary to see the entire period as a phase of total war. Only when this is clearly recognised does it become possible to discuss changes within the period. It could clearly be seen, even in 1945, that the use of the munic bomb marked not just the end of the Second World War but a turning point in war itself, but it took a decade or more for a real change in the mode of warfare to develop. Since at first only the US possessed atomic weapons, and in it sufficient quantities for all-out war, the early period of East-West conflict was characterised by a continuation of the 1939-45 type of war-preparations while demobilising from wartime levels.

So, although war economies were rapidly converted to the purposes of reconstruction, historically high levels of 'peacetime' military expenditure were maintained-and military demobilisation was soon halted by the Korean War. Mass armed forces based on conscription remained universal, although large resources were directed into research for an atomic arms race. Everywhere, too, in the period of reconstruction and the early Cold War, states retained the sort of economic supremacy which total war had given them.

Only states-and to a large extent, only the USA, which alone was greatly strengthened by the war-could rebuild the many economies which were shattered. Both those states which emerged victorious and those which were rebuilt by the victors assumed central economic roles in national societies. The requirements of the new Cold War and of reconstruction combined to ensure this. The wartime experience of state economic direction, superimposed on the failure of private capitalism between the wars, gave credence to interventionist economics, reinforced by the political strength of the left in the immediate aftermath of the war.

The first decade after 1945 gave relatively little indication, therefore, of the fundamental change in the total war 'system' of war-society relationships in the nuclear age. The invention of atomic weapons was, however, a qualitative leap in the industrialisation of warfare. From now on, a very few weapons, which could be produced and operated by very few people, could decide the whole outcome of a major war. Such weapons have not, of course, replaced what are now known as 'conventional' weapons-these have continued to be required for secondary wars as well as to provide less destructive or supplementary fire power in a major war. Indeed the victory of technology involved much more than the development of the atomic bomb: constant technical innovation and refinement have become a major concern of military and political establishments at all levels of weaponry.

In an obvious sense the ultimate destructive potential of nuclear weapons had been created by the late 1950s or early 1960s. The superpowers had acquired 'overkill'-the capacity to totally destroy each other, and indeed human civilisation as a whole, recognised in the strategic doctrine of 'Mutually Assured Destruction'. But both despite and because of the strategic impasse which this represented, military-scientific innovation has continued to escalate well beyond this interim climax. The search has long been on for the technical 'fix' which will allow escape from the nuclear stalemate, whether in 'lower' levels of weaponry such as battlefield nuclear weapons or high-technology conventional armaments, or in the lofty, even fantastic realms of 'Star Wars'.

A great deal has been written about the links between the post-war arms race and the economy. On the one hand, it has been suggested that the alliance of the military and the industrial sectors dependent on them constitutes a military industrial complex, which dominates and directs American society in particular. C. Wright Mills's 1956 study of *The Power Elite* gave great weight to military-industrial linkages within a system of power which as a whole had increasingly been centralised by military conflict and nuclear technology. Thompson argues, even more radically, that modem societies 'do not have military-industrial complexes-they are military industrial complexes'. For him, 'exterminism' is the driving force of the entire social system. On the other hand, more specifically economic analyses were put forward to suggest that Western (and, by implication, Eastern) systems were arms economies', in which arms production provided the central dynamic of the economic system as a whole. Originally developed during the Second World War and its immediate aftermath, especially Korea, as a theory of a Permanent War Economy, this was subsequently modified as it was recognised that nuclear weapons could inhibit major wars while stimulating military expenditure which had a fundamental economic effect. So the arms economy was presented as an explanation of the post-war boom.

It is clear in retrospect that much of this analysis reflected a moment of transition in post-war militarism: the point at which the labour-intensive militarism of classical 'total war' was still strong, but the central significance of nuclear weapons was already clear. Theories of an arms economy, in particular, tended to amalgamate these two realities, seeing the nuclear arms race as the apex of an entire system of military expenditure. In one sense of course this was, and remains, true: even the most technologically advanced military force still comes down to soldiers with mass-produced weapons. But the trend has been to substitute machines-large-scale, highly complex and sophisticated machines-for men. Instead of soldiers with weapons, there are weapons systems with their operators, as many of them concerned with maintenance as with actual use. (Today research is underway to replace soldiers with robots in some battlefield situations.)

The warships which consumed such phenomenal sums in the naval arms race at the turn of the century were the precursors of modem armaments of all types, land and aerial as well as naval. The atomic bomb symbolises a new sort of militarism, scientifically and technologically based, and capital-intensive. While real spending on military purposes has soared, armies have become smaller and more professional. Although Britain remains an exception in having completely abandoned conscription, the relative importance of soldiers (especially conscripts) has generally declined.

The political economy of modern militarism necessarily differs from its mid-twentieth century predecessor. A large, immensely well-funded military sector in all major economies turns out equipment of a size, complexity and sophistication hardly matched in many civil industries. The gap is perhaps most notorious in the Soviet Union, which has sacrificed investment in civilian production to 'keep up' in the military field. But, American military technology-the world leader-is itself increasingly baroque: if not unusable, then difficult to use. This is true both in a strategic sense, since technological refinement is increasingly cut off from viable military theory (a technical expression of the strategic impasse), and practically, since complex machines take a colossal effort to keep serviceable.

Military technology in the first half of the twentieth century required large workforces to produce its weapons, and large quantities of basic raw materials to make them with. Weapons and military vehicles were often similar in kind to non-military commodities (hence conversion from peace to war and war to peace was easier). Now, at the end of the twentieth century, military industries have become capital-intensive, use highly specialised materials and are often producing items of a kind which have little affinity with civilian production. Military industry may still affect the civilian economy, but often by producing distorted reflections of its own requirements rather than creating employment (as in earlier periods).

The relationship between nuclear weapons production with its raw material, plutonium, and the civilian nuclear industry is a major case in point: the nuclear industry came into existence is a by-product of nuclear weapons and has been maintained by states for military and political as much as energy-policy reasons. The nuclear industry is a sector of the civil economy which mirrors the military and the military-industrial sector in its high-technology, low-employment base, its skilled workforce and its security requirements.

A major paradox of the mid-century phase of total war was the association of warfare with welfare: even Nazi rearmament, we have noted, was based on guns and butter, and remained so until the war itself became a desperate struggle or the state's survival. The states which emerged from the Second World War all adopted historically advanced social policies, leading to rapidly expanding social expenditure simultaneous with high military spending. At the margin, the two forms of state activity competed for resources, but taking he early post-war period as a whole, both were vastly expanded compared to the inter-war years. The post-war boom, however, was a triumph of private capitalism, emerging from its subordination in the war to take advantage of the post-war reconstruction. Military-industrial sectors played a leading economic role in the 1950s, but as the boom became self-sustaining, the proportion of military expenditure in most national incomes declined. Consumer goods industries were central to the boom, and the leading roles belonged to those countries which had relatively low military expenditures, notably Japan and West Germany. At the height of the boom, in the mid-1960s, and in the early stages of economic crisis, in he early 1970s, military expenditures were declining relative lot only to national incomes, but also to state social expenditures.

Only in the late 1970s, with the coincidence of deepening economic crises and East-West tensions, did military expenditure begin to rise in relation to total production. This time, however, there was no apparently benign association of warfare and welfare: on the contrary, military expenditures were increased in a period of profound crisis for state spending as a whole, and grew at the expense of, rather than in conjunction with, various forms of social expenditure. Indeed, the paradox of the current phase is that military statism has been taken furthest by those Western governments that are most actively anti-statist in ideology. Instead of going in hand with welfare-statism, the new militarism is linked to hightechnology, aggressive private-enterprise capitalism.

Social theory has been none too successful in unravelling such paradoxes. On the one hand, a major recent textbook by three Marxist writers, despite an informative aecount of the role of war, states and reconstruction in the origins of the post-war boom, treats the actual boom and its crisis in exclusively economic terms, making militarism once again a purely extraneous if not irrelevant factor. On the other, Thompson offers his nightmare of a society which is, as a whole, 'exterminist': dominated by a military technology which is leading to its destruction. The polarisation of viewpoints reflects the difficulties of grappling with the present phase of the total war/society relationship. In the earlier phases, this relationship was manifestly central: militarism meant social mobilisation, and war carried this to an extreme. In the modem phase, militarism consumes massive resources but does not mobilise society.

Total war becomes less total in the sense of direct social participation at the very point at which it becomes greatly more total, indeed potentially absolute, in the military sense. Thus while in one sense it is utterly correct to see the entire global social system as conditioned by total war-in exterminist terms-much of social reality apparently contradicts this insight. The economic, social, even political and ideological links between the arms race and most social life become less direct, the more sophisticated and lethally accurate nuclear weaponry becomes. The nuclear arms race has largely been conducted out of sight of society, with states deliberately eschewing even ideological, let alone practical, mobilisation. Even in the United States, by far the most obviously militarist of Western societies, militarism and related political and nationalist ideologies are far less unequivocally dominant than they were in the 'Cold War' of the first decade after 1945. This has a great deal to do with the fact that the function of actual war has radically altered. War cannot be recognised unequivocally even as a possible outcome of war-preparation; and war, if it came, would not heighten social mobilisation as in all previous phases, but result in the most extreme demobitisation-physical destruction of the majority of-society's members.

Here then we have an explanation for the paradox of modem militarism. As the strand of technological rivalry becomes dominant within the total war, society becomes simultaneously both more and less dominated by warfare. On the one hand, any major war would be so utterly decisive for society, that military preparations have an enormous priority over other social and political aims of states. They are not the only claimants on states' resources, and when military pressures recede, other interests are more effective: but in periods of active military-political tension, like the early 1980s, very impressive military-economic commitments are made. The Reagan administration could launch a military spending boom financed by budget deficits; the Soviet

Union would attempt to match US military efforts, despite its weaker economy, thus continuing to spend roughly double the US proportion of its national income on 'defence'; even Britain under Thatcher could increase real military spending by 30 per cent between 1979 and 1985, in a period of economic stagnation and within a general policy of reducing state spending.

On the other hand, all this can be accomplished without increasing the size of armies, extending or reintroducing conscnption, or employing more people in defence industries. Ideologically, the nuclear arms race, even with the excesses of Reagan's America, is muted compared to the jingoism of the pre-1914 period or the fervour of the early Cold War: it has more limited need of popular support. Of course, there is a major difference between the superpowers and the other industrialised states which are, for the most part, allied to them. Military preparations and the ideologies of militarism are both more important in the USA and the USSR than they are in Western or Eastern Europe or Japan. But even where militarism is stronger, its character has changed. The dominance of technology leads to a bifurcation between what Michael Mann has called the 'deterrence-science' militarism of the elite, and the 'spectator-sport' militarism of the mass. If the majority of society continues to participate in militarism, it is in a passive, vicarious manner, since war-preparation requires only their tacit ideological consent, no longer their practical involvement. Short of all-out East-West war, most forms of militarism emanating from advanced industrial states-whether in the nuclear arms race or more actively in limited wars in the Third World (archetypally, in the Falklands/Malvinas war, which will be discussed later)-require an extremely limited, controlled response from the majority of society. This circumstance utterly transforms the politics of total war, and should lead us to question the main forms of response to war which emerged earlier in this century and are still dominant today.

14 Critique of Sociology and Military Theory

The fear of war hangs over society. This is almost literally true, for it is not the invader in the streets but the warhead exploding on us which dominates our nightmares. The descent of the intercontinental missile is a symbol of the external character of war: a danger which appears from completely outside the everyday social relations in which most people live, confronting them with absolute obliteration. This sort of war seems far removed from society, even from the activities of the considerable part of society professionally concerned with war, that is the armed forces and armaments workers.

They are too reassuringly human, sharing as individuals the mundane economic troubles and social anxieties of their fellow citizens, to fully represent the awfulness of the threat to life on earth. Yet the existence of these social groups reminds us that war is something which is prepared within society. Just as an immense concentration of human activity in the Soviet Union produces the missiles which could destroy us, so a comparable social organisation here produces similar missiles aimed at them. Western democratic societies, especially in Europe, may be among the least overtly militaristic which civilisation has produced, but we harbour the most murderous weapons ever created, and we devote the greatest resources ever provided by any society, outside actual war, to producing and maintaining them. The isolation of missile bases in the countryside, away from centres of population, is another physical symbol of the disjunction of nuclear militarism from our urban-industrial world. But it is a disjunction which is more apparent than real, since the nuclear weapons-systems originate in that society and, if they are used, will return to it with a most terrible vengeance. Nevertheless the role of war, and war-preparation, in the modem world presents us with an essential paradox.

How is it that a society which has created such potential for human liberation-in technology, human cooperation, and ideas-can produce at the same time and with the same means such appalling danger? The conflict of these two sides of our society must ultimately be resolved, in practice as well as in theory. However obvious this point is from a simple human point of view, it has not proved easy for thinkers to grapple with, any more than it has been easy to overcome the conflict in the real social and political world. Most thinkers about society have not been able to grasp the huge problem which war poses for our understanding of society in general: they have marginalised it, treated it as exceptional, abnormal, etc. Most thinkers about war, on the other hand, have tended to treat it as if it were a self-contained process, certainly depending on society for its resources, but ultimately operating according to its own laws. Although the more intelligent of them have recognised the implications of modern warfare for society, they have generally dealt with them much too obliquely, for fear perhaps that these implications would simply topple the whole edifice of military thought and practice.

The problem of war and society can therefore be seen as a dilemma, the horns of which have been tackled separately by social and military theory, but the heart of which has rarely been exposed. The aim of this book is to confront this dual problem, of how society has changed war and how war has changed society, as a unity. One writes 'has changed' because it is important to understand the problem historically, to see the processes which have created the present situation. But it is this problem, the danger of nuclear war in our time and the social institutions which sustain that danger while being distorted by it, which gives the argument its coherence and direction.

This book takes its premises from both social and strategic thought, while criticising both. On the one hand, it argues, with such social theory as has considered war, that war must be seen as a social activity related to the whole complex of social life and organisation. On the other, it agrees with strategic writing that war must be seen as a very unique social activity, with its own character and logic which cannot be reduced to any ordinary social dynamic. The relationship of war and society is portrayed as one of constant tension. It is argued that there are dialectics of war and society which, while they grow out of other social contradictions, fundamentally alter the social process as a whole. The dialectics of war not only threaten to displace the dialectic of social change which has been considered by a whole tradition of social analysis: they posit the danger of a fundamentally different end to human history. If we are to avoid this end, we need to understand the processes which are producing it, and to grasp the contradictions which offer some rational basis for optimism about the outcome.

This chapter is devoted to exploring this theoretical issue: first by a discussion of how social science has failed to grapple with the nature of war itself, and second by a critique of strategic theory, which is more interesting in its treatment of this problem, but has generally abstracted it too much from its socio-historical context. In conclusion, a proposal will be made as to how the relationships between war and society should be understood in general terms.

THE FAILURE OF SOCIAL THEORY

For virtually all schools of social thought, wars are exceptional phases of social life, abnormal phenomena which interrupt the fundamental social patterns. On this point there is no serious disagreement between, say, a functionalist sociologist like Talcott Parsons, for whom society is essentially consensual and harmonious, and a Marxist theorist of modes of exploitation and class struggle. War is as much a disturbance of the ordinary pattern of capitalist development and class conflict as it is of the self-equilibriating social system. Warfare is recogniscd as a social activity.

Most social theorists would accept the anthropological arguments that war, while near-universal, is nonetheless a social rather than a biological or psychological product. Some sorts of warmaking in 'primitive' societies are indeed so ritualised and minimally violent that they are readily accommodated under the rubric of routine social life. Ritualisation, routinisation and regulation are also recognised to be part of the process of war-preparation and even of war-fighting right up to the present day. The rituals of tribal warfare are echoed in the medieval codes of chivalry and even in the arcane pursuit of war-limitation by nuclear strategists. Routinisation is evident in the bureaucratisation of warfare: military institutions are models or reflections, according to one's analysis, of the general form of social organisation in our time. Regulation, although woefully inadequate to the goals of preventing or controlling war, is subscribed to in principle by all states. It is evident in the plethora of international laws, conventions and institutions, although these are of dubious practical value.

Despite a wide acceptance of the social character of war, it is equally widely excluded from the basic models of modem society which are on offer in social science. The concept of 'industrial society' which has informed mainstream sociology from Saint-Simon, Comte and Durkheim onwards was defined by contrast with the military hierarchy of feudal agrarian society. A rational, scientific social organisation of labour-the basic sense of 'industry'-must imply peace.

It has long since been proven that this optimism was utterly misplaced: but the concept of 'industrial society' has survived, minus the assertion of pacificism, as a *de facto* model of a warless society. Sample any sociological textbook and you will look in vain for a discussion of war among the institutions of industrialism. Where early nineteenth-century theory explained war away (with superficial historical justification, as it turned out, since the end of the Napoleonic Wars ushered in a century without general conflicts), late twentieth-century theory, which ought to confront a war-ridden century, largely ignores the uncomfortable facts.

The model of 'capitalism' derived from Marx offers no more direct, basic recognition of war than that of 'industrial society'. Marx too assumed-indeed articulated-the nineteenth-century separation of civil society and the state. The Marxist theoretical edifice was built on the autonomy of the mode of production from the state: everything to do with the state, international relations, even international trade, was abstracted from Marx's basic model. Capitalism was the 'pure' mode of production par excellence:

however sullied by the historical survival of less pure modes, it was tending towards a direct social conflict between labour and capital. Change would arise from the dialectic of class struggle, springing from the contradictions of forces and relations of production in the capitalist mode. War was seen by Marx as very much a secondary phenomenon, determined perhaps by the economic base (in ways which we shall discuss later), but providing little more than an external influence on social development. Later Marxism confronted the twentieth century experience of war by adapting the model, to theorise about the state, imperialism and nationalism. These code words have entered the wider sociological parlance, generally permitting their users to skirt round the problem of war by examining the wider economic, political and ideological relations: rarely the social process of war itself. The classical Marxist tradition on this point has been reconstructed in a narrowly orthodox way. Lenin's theoretical conservatism, which separated imperialism and the state, has become the focal point of subsequent debate, rather than Bukharin's more radical model which saw these as fused under the impact of world war.

Where the main body of social science recognises the problem of war, it invariably translates it into one of 'militarism'. The distinction between war, the actual conflict, and militarism, the preparation and ideology of war, is a crucial one, without which there can be no understanding of the relationship between the two. War-preparation is, in appearance, an 'ordinary' social activity, integrated institutionally into all the structures of society-economic, political and cultural. It can, it seems, be analysed in these terms, without reference to its ultimate ends. War itself, on the other hand, is a wholly exceptional, abnormal affair, at best an intrusion into the social structure which may temporarily suspend its usual workings. Seen in this way, it is no surprise that while social science has had some thoughts on militarism, which can be linked to capitalism, imperialism, nationalism and the state, it has had all too few on war. It has been reluctant to admit that at the heart of the social institutions of contemporary capitalism lurks a destructive potential of the kind which modem warfare represents. It is as if a principle alien to social scientific thinking threatens to distort the whole development of society: not just at some future date when the whole structure is vaporised, but now as the processes of war preparation insinuate themselves into social life.

The heart of this problem is the premise of rationality. Mainstream social science has been built on an axiom that people will seek to fit means to ends: what does not satisfy this model is a residue of the traditional, the sentimental, in the end the 'irrational'. This idea dominates economics, politics and sociology. When formulated, as for example by Max Weber, it has been criticised in a number of ways: the irrationality of the choice of ends; the effect of irrational factors on the choice of means; and (relevant to our discussion) the irrational effects of conflicts between opposing 'rational' actions. But the criticisms have hardly upset the persistence of the basic assumption, which has simply been qualified or redefined, for example by Marxists for whom the agents of rational action are primarily classes, and its ends determined by class interests.

The problem is that war is seen by social science as a means, governed by ends which are determined in economic, social and political life. But war, as a means, has unique characteristics, which are becoming more and more contradictory to the ends for which it might be waged; and it has its own logic and rationality which can impose themselves on society. War appears not only to be escaping from the control of rational social interests, but to be taking society with it. The attempt to treat war, or the preparation for it within society, under the rubric of social rationality reaches a point where it breaks down under the recognition of what war has really become.

The Limits of Strategic Thought

Strategic thought might appear to be dominated by the same assumption of rationality. After all, it was Clausewitz who wrote: 'War is nothing but the continuation of policy by other means'- an idea which endeared him to Lenin and others in the Marxist tradition. Certainly, modem strategic thought is based on the belief that armed force can be an effective instrument of political policy, and fears, above all, the argument that this is no longer true in the nuclear age. Clausewitz himself provides us with the basis for criticising this notion.

War's function as an instrument of policy was only one element, alongside primordial violence and the play of chance: together these composed the 'remarkable trinity' in his definition. The essence of war as a means was the actual process of fighting, and all the other activities of war – the business of war-preparation, which has become such an industry in our day-were devoted to this end. In fighting, the destruction of the enemy's force was the primary goal, best achieved in a single great battle or 'slaughter'. Clausewitz was at great pains to emphasise this 'destructive principle' of warfare.

It constituted his view of the very nature of war: it was 'an act of force', and 'there is *no logical limit to an act of force*'. The resort to force-or, more precisely, to violence, or indeed to killing, the ultimate destructive action of human beings against each other-was a total commitment. Once two powers were set in violent motion against each other, there was no limit until one had destroyed the other's capacity for resistance, and subordinated it to its will. War was, of its nature, total and absolute: this was Clausewitz's crucial insight, which has caused so many problems for modern strategic theory. True, it was greatly qualified, and rightly so. Clausewitz stands out in strategic thinking partly for the acuteness of his social and historical awareness. He wished to highlight how it was that the involvement of the people, as a result of the French Revolution, had intensified military conflicts, compared to the much more limited affairs of the eighteenth century. He emphasised, on the other hand, that war was never a self-contained activity, and that it was restricted by the circumstances in which it was fought. In his famous concept of 'friction' he crystallised the idea that, while war might tend towards the total, there were in practice all sorts of constraints on this tendency (geographical, technical, logistic). Real war always fell short of the 'ideal' of a total contest of force.

Friction, as much as the totalising tendency of force, was something inherent in war itself. But it clearly depended greatly on the general socioeconomic, technological and political conditions of warfare. This is something we can see all the more clearly now that technology has overcome so many of the sources of friction in previous wars. Clausewitz prophetically envisaged a situation in which friction was eliminated:

> If war consisted of one decisive act, or a set of simultaneous decisions, preparations would tend towards totality, because no omission could ever be rectified. The sole criterion for preparations which the world of reality would provide would be the measures taken by the adversary, so far as they are known; the rest would once more be reduced to abstract calculations.

Howard rightly comments that this is 'a depressingly accurate description of contemporary nuclear strategy... all [the] traditional constraints on "absolute war" have been removed and its complete realisation has for the first time become a practical possibility'.

Clearly, immense social changes lie behind this achievement of the potential for absolute war. The development of modem industrial capitalism, state systems, technology: these are the preconditions. But such sociological explanation should not detract from the central point. War has reached in theory, if not yet in practice, the inner limit which Clausewitz so brilliantly defined for it: the total and instantaneous destruction of the 'enemy' (which becomes, of course, mutual destruction). In reaching this limit, war also negates itself. If there are no longer internal constraints, and war becomes absolute destruction, it becomes invalid as a means of policy. Discriminating ends require discriminating means.

Modem strategic thought clearly recognises the dangers that, as war approaches this inner limit, military force becomes unusable. Much of modem strategy can be seen as an attempt to avoid redundancy. Essentially it has taken two forms: the attempt to rehabilitate strategy first as a means of war avoidance rather than war-fighting and, second, by envisaging limited wars short of total nuclear war. Both these responses recognise the theoretical limit of all-out nuclear war: the first by accepting it, and hence displacing the goal of military preparation from war itself to 'deterrence'; the second by recoiling from it to levels at which policy goals and friction become meaningful again. Both these responses, which in practice tend to overlap, are in the end evasions of, rather than solutions to, the crisis of war.

This is most obvious in the case of the 'deterrence' response. On one level, of course, deterrence *is* rational: states are indeed inhibited by the awesome destructive power with which they face each other. For so long as this is the case, deterrence may 'work'. But on another level, the concept is patent nonsense, and at its worst sheer political sophistry. There can be no general distinction between deterrence and warfighting, since the enemy is only deterred if it believes in our willingness to use our weapons. The credibility of the 'deterrent' is as much a matter of will as of technical capacity, as the development of strategy and weaponry has shown in the past. The crisis of the crude deterrence of 'mutually assured destruction' was precisely that because of the undoubted destructive capacity of strategic missiles, willingness to use them was dubious. The logic of deterrence demanded more limited weaponry, because it was more credible that this would be used. This development — the US strategy of 'flexible response' and the corresponding gradations of strategic, intermediate and battlefield nuclear weapons — was not a transition from 'deterrence' to 'warfighting'. It was, rather, a demonstration that warfighting was always inherent in deterrence: that they are two sides of the same 'strategy'. It was also a demonstration that the business of strategy cannot seriously be redefined as one of war-avoidance.

Concepts of 'limited war' are sometimes advanced as part of a 'deterrence' posture, but also — more honestly — with some indication of a belief that such wars can actually be fought. In one sense this is obviously true: there is still considerable scope for conventional wars in the Third World, both between local states and between such states and the Northern powers. But this 'space' for war expresses the relative backwardness of the Third World, and its incomplete incorporation into the superpower conflict. And while militarisation is in one sense increasing the scope for war, in a more general perspective the limits of war are appearing: first because of the nuclearisation of the Third World, and secondly because of the linkages between local and superpower conflict. Although local conflicts may be fought, and *may* in fact remain limited, it is becoming less possible to say categorically that they will be. The risks are rapidly increasing.

The real argument about limited war concerns direct conflict between the superpowers. Two sorts of limitation can be envisaged, by geography and weaponry, although in practice the limitations are likely to coincide. In either case, limitation will depend not just on arbitrary attempts to restrict the 'damage' of war, but on an understanding or convention of war as a form of conflict resolution. No such understanding has been successfully proposed, still less agreed, between the superpowers. It seems preposterous to think that it could be: that given the immense destructiveness of even a conventional war in Europe, let alone a limited nuclear exchange, such a war could be restricted to preconceived levels of response by rational political decision. It is historically true that even the wars that were most obviously limited, by political circumstances and goals as well as weaponry, have tended to surpass the limits initially foreseen for them. It is impossible to believe that such a global confrontation between over-armed powers, into the avoidance of which so much has been invested, could ever be restricted if it should take place. Even if theoretically conceivable, this would be unlikely in practice, especially now that nuclear technology has created the conditions — and hence also the necessity — for a 'disarming first strike'. Éscalation, which is virtually a law of war, would very probably turn out to be instantaneous, not gradual.

THE SOCIAL DIALECTICS OF WAR

Neither the deterrent nor the limited-war versions of strategic theory can divert attention from the main issue: that the *means of war have outstripped any rational use for them.* The problem with strategic theory, however, is that even when this conclusion is reached, it can offer us no way out except to prove the finality of the outcome in the actual use of nuclear weapons. The dialectic of war, considered in isolation, simply comes to a self-negating full stop. War can only be abolished, in these purely military terms, when nuclear immolation removes the means and agents of war from the face of the earth. And there must remain the suspicion that even this will not be final: that in the twilight world of the 'aftermath', the brutalised survivors will mock strategic theory with an internecine struggle for survival. To pose the matter at all constructively we must re-intcgrate military theory with social thought.

As the more historically minded strategic writers have understood-but the nuclear planners must needs forget-war has developed in the context of society, as one social activity among many. War can only be understood in the context of the totality of social relations. The idealised dialectic of military theory, which has expressed the active (in reality, destructive) inner character of war, needs to be transformed by a materialist social history which can show how war has arisen from and returns to society. Strategic theory, even at its most sociological, has generally seen these relations-society-war-society-in terms that are too linear.

In explaining that war expresses social purposes, and necessarily affects society, the strategist may too easily conclude that society must be incorporated into the battlefield. Indeed this doctrine is sometimes advanced by revolutionaries, who wish war to be a social struggle rather than a narrowly professional military activity. When formulated as a general proposition, however, the notion that war must involve (an invasion of the fabric of the opponent's social order' (as one recent academic strategist has suggested) assumes frightening overtones in the nuclear age. If society is indeed the battlefield, then society may simply be destroyed when technology makes this feasible. A sociological 'translation' of strategic theory is not enough: its only virtue is to clarify the social consequences of military concepts.

What is required is an altogether more dialectical concept of the relations between war and society, which understands the contradictory nature of this relationship, as of society itself. War does not express the common purposes of 'society' as a whole, but arises out of particular relationships and institutions in society. Warfare has been, almost continuously in known history, a major part of the development of social conflict and contradictions. Anthropologists suggest that war is a main cause (and effect) — if not the only one — of the formation of social classes and states. In large scale historical civilisations, warmaking has invariably been a core function of privileged social groups and state institutions. A dialectic of military expansion and the constant need for slaves governed the rise and fall of the Roman Empire. The feudal social hierarchy of medieval Europe was closely defined by military obligations. In most pre-modern societies, the linkages of warfare and the socio-economic order are clearly defined, expressed in the dominant ideology and immediately recognised by the historian.

Only in early industrial capitalist societies is there an apparent separation, not just of warmaking, but of the entire range of state activities and institutions, from the mode of economic life. Production, as Marx argued, was initially freed from the extra-economic constraints of feudal society. For the first time, it became relatively pure commodity production, production of exchange values rather than (directly) of use values. Warfare was no longer one of the purposes of socio-economic activity, but a purpose of the highly distinct sphere of political life. The 'optimistic theory of industrial capitalism' incorrectly concluded from this institutional separation that warfare was a historical residue, unlikely to coexist for long with industrialism. The Marxist theory, more realistically, drew attention to the social linkages between the differentiated spheres of production and the state. Marxist theorists have argued that the class which owns the means of production thereby rules politically as well; or, in a more sophisticated version, that the nature of competitive capitals concerned with production of exchange values *implies* that the capitalists must constitute themselves as a class in a distinct political sphere, in order to carry out those necessary social tasks which they cannot carry out as individual capitals. Warfare is, of course, one such task, although why it remained 'necessary' in industrial capitalist society is a question which Marxist theory has hardly answered. In general, it has seen war as an extension of the competitive struggle between capitals: but the question of why the struggle between capitals takes the form of war between states requires an analysis of the system of territorial states. This system pre-dated capitalism, although of course it has been modified by it.

The territorial aspect of the state, so fundamental to its very constitution, as non-Marxist definitions have suggested, is often neglected in the attempt to link the state to the internal class division of national societies. This external side of the state's functioning, connected to its role in an international system of states, is an essential feature in any attempt to link industrial capitalism and warfare. It is not possible to argue simply that capitalism itself requires warfare. It is possible to argue that capitalism historically has presupposed a system of nation-states, in which warfare is the ultimate form of conflict. Capitalism has greatly altered both the state system and warfare; and, at the same time, that the workings of the state system, and especially warfare, have fundamentally affected the nature, workings and forms of capitalism. Whether capitalism, considered from the standpoint of pure theory, requires either a state-system or war, is in this sense irrelevant: 'capitalism' is a historical abstraction from a world society structured by a system of states and warfare.

We can analyse the 'mode of warfare' in society as something analogous, but never reducible, to the mode of production. Warfare is a social activity which may have a role in terms of the socio-economic and political systems, but which has its own specific character and ends. The 'mode of warfare' should be distinguished from the 'role of warfare'. Using Clausewitz's suggestion-which appealed to Marx and Engels-that battle is to war what cash payment is to commodity exchange, warfare as a rational, goal-oriented social activity loosely comparable to the system of production for profit. The comparison is limited, however, in quite crucial ways. First, battle — actual war as opposed to war-preparation — occurs so much less frequently than cash payment. Commodity values are realised thousands of times per second: military values may be untested for decades. This leads to considerable distortion of the mode of warfare, above all in the nuclear age when the use of weapons becomes self-defeating. Secondly, the mode of warfare can never reproduce itself, but is always parasitic on the mode of production.

However much war and war-preparation may be carried on for their own ends, they depend on the mode of production for their resources. 'Because armaments do not re-enter the production process, the entire cost of armaments — cost of production plus mark-up — represents a deduction from surplus-value earned elsewhere in the economy'. War is therefore an 'a priori burden on and potential interruption to the process of capitalist accumulation. This tension between warfare and capitalism explodes periodically in war.'

By contrast, then, with Marxists, who see warfare as necessary— almost 'functional' — for capitalism, its distinct logic as a problem for capitalist accumulation. The enormous demands of the mode of warfare, in the context of a permanent arms race, distort the economy and accentuate crisis. The absence of actual war makes the mode of warfare ever more artificial, overblown and rigid, which increases the pressure for war simply to test the military plans: and yet war as a means is so obviously self-defeating. No sectors of capital can actually have a rational interest in nuclear war: some may pursue war-avoidance to the point of becoming allies of peace movements suggests Kaldor, although she still seems uncertain of this.

The dialectic of war is therefore seen, at its simplest, as leading to an opposition between war and society. War grows out of society, feeds upon the enormous growth of productive resources brought about by industrial capitalism, and will ultimately destroy not only that particular system but every form of human society. But as I have already suggested, the simple terms, 'war and society', or even 'war and capitalism' must be broken down. Each term in these pairs is highly complex: the very concept of an opposition between the two terms is increasingly misleading. While war appears to be a relatively discrete social activity, apart from society, imposing its requirements on the socio-economic system, in reality the two are closely integrated. To theorise about the 'mode of warfare' as distinct from the 'mode of production' may be necessary, in order to establish the specific requirements of warfare by contrast with those of commodity production. But to take this analytical distinction for a separation in reality is mistaken. There is no more than a partial disjunction between the two, since society (and specifically production) has been incorporated into warfare, and correspondingly warfare into society (and production). However much the requirements of warfare may appear to conflict with those of production , in reality the tension.

The dialectic of war and society should not therefore be seen in terms of such a simple opposition. The integration of the two means that we must modify the terms: we are talking about the role of socialised warfare in a militarised economy and society.

We can no more understand the contradictions of society outside its military frame than we can those of warfare apart from its insertion in society. The integration is neither perfect nor complete, but it is fundamental to both.

The solution to the dilemmas of military theory is only to be found when this is recognised. The theoretical limit of nuclear war cannot be evaded with the deterrent or limited-war options; but neither can we wait for nuclear weapons to achieve the self-negation of warfare. The answer to the problems is to recognise that 'friction', virtually eliminated from the actual fighting of wars by the achievement of the capability for instantaneous total immolation, has been transferred back into war-preparation. The very elimination of friction from warfighting increases the friction affecting war preparation. This is true in two senses. First, the unlimitedness of nuclear war inhibits governments both directly-in that they recognise the self-defeating nature of it-and indirectly, in that the catastrophic outcome for society creates popular pressure against war. Secondly, the nature of the economic and technical resources required for the arms race at its limit creates a new form of friction. A tension with the requirements of civilian production inhibits all but the most powerful states from full participation in it, and creates economic contradictions in the military efforts of all states, even the superpowers.

Of course, these constraints on war-preparation, and on the conversion of war-preparation into warfighting, are not absolute. Understood only in the military sense, as 'friction', they offer no solutions, only a delay. It is only if forces exist in society which are capable of understanding the limits to war, and of acting to prevent it, that answers can be found. There is no solution in continuing to ask: How can wars continue to be fought? but only in asking: How can we create the conditions in which they will never be fought again?

At this point, it is obvious that military theory must give way to social theory, but only to a social theory which has recognised the immense impact of the military problem in society. Simply to identify the 'ordinary' socio-economic contradictions is not enough: we must examine how war and militarism have permeated the structure and processes of society, including the forces and movements often seen as offering solutions. The integration of warmaking and socio-economic development has long since passed the point at which war can be considered an 'extraneous' factor. Unless we arc able to understand how war has moulded society in the twentieth century, we shall be unable even to glimpse the possibility of a solution to the problem which war now poses.

In this century, the spectre of military totalitarianism has frequently haunted society. The prospect of a ruthless, totally manipulative regime, bent externally on military expansion and internally on political repression, has seemed the greatest danger and evil of our time. Because Western-and even Communist-states are some way from this model (and they manifestly are), because 1984 was not realised in 1984, the real role of militarism in our society has often been underemphasised. The absence of the most overt forms of militarism belies the role of a subtler form. It can be shown, I believe, that there are general and long-term tendencies transforming industrial society as a consequence of its mode of warfare. The nature of these tendencies and the different forms they take is the subject of the greater part of this book; but first it is necessary to discuss how warfare itself was transformed by industrial capitalism.

15 Beyond the Politics of Total War

We have seen in previous chapters that each of the phases of total war has seen the development of specific radical political forms. The first phase of labour-intensive mass militarism generated revolutionary contradictions, and led to the first successful socialist revolution in Russia. The second phase, in which politicisation and technological development transformed total war, created the conditions in which social reformism could succeed, above all in Britain. These political forms had different relationships to militarism.

Social revolution grew out of the contradictions of mass militarism, and involved revolutionary anti-militarism. The Russian Revolution, as we have seen, can be considered in large part a revolution against militarism, although for the revolutionary leaders this was a conditional stance. Revolutionary anti-militarism gave way to revolutionary militarism as counter-revolution threatened. Social reform, on the other hand, grew out of the bonding together of society and state: it was not anti-militarist in any except the vague sense of wishing see a peaceful world after the conclusion of the war. Social revolution and social reform grew, moreover, out of conditions which only developed fully with war itself.

Far more radical changes occurred when war was superimposed on social conflict, than in the period of 'peace' or war-preparation. Mass mobilisation created huge social forces, more concentrated than had ever been seen in 'peacetime' capitalism, with a potential for revolt. In Russia in 1917, the soldiers at the front combined with the workers in heavy industry and the munitions factories to create a revolution, with the peasants, too, rising against the sufferings the war imposed. Elsewhere the revolt was more restrained, but it existed: even in Britain, workers organised against the effects of war, while at the front British soldiers were involved in extensive war-avoidance and even in mutinies. None of this led to social revolution, but revolutionary anti-militarist politics developed on the British left during the First World War. Social reform in the Second World War resulted partly from an awareness of the revolt generated in the first war, the disillusionment at the failure of social reform after it, and the need to overcome the resentments of the depression.

Only a much closer socio-political linking of society and state could achieve the mobilisation needed to defeat Nazism. Despite the reform potential of the wartime coalition in Britain, class conflict remained, erupting into industrial struggles towards the end of the war. Nothing like the political anti-militarism of 1914-18 developed, however, since the left, after 1941 at least, was almost united in support of the war. The third phase of total war utterly transforms the relationship between radical politics and war-resistance.

In the first place, social contradictions will hardly play the same sort of role in a nuclear war. If, as seems likely, the war is instantaneously absolute (even NATO scenarios envisage a rapid escalation from a short period of 'tension' to a swift 'conventional' war leading directly to nuclear war), there will be neither the time nor the space for social conflict. By the time nuclear war is even likely, war-resistance may be largely beside the point. The resistance to nuclear war has to be successful in the period of general war-preparation. The key question is the relationship between militarism and antimilitarism, and the wider social struggles of the society in which nuclear war is prepared. Central to the argument here is that war-resistance in the nuclear age cannot easily be converted into another form of militarism, as happened to revolutionary anti-militarism in the First World War.

The growing historical redundancy of war means that the task is to develop non-military alternatives, rather than different forms of militarism. The development of warfare towards human extermination is irreversible within the terms of war; only by moving beyond them is there any hope.

NUCLEAR MILITARISM AND SOCIAL PARTICIPATION

The reasons for the development of radical politics in the first two phases of total war were mainly to do with the contradictions of military participation. Both the First and Second World Wars involved total societal mobilisation. A nuclear war, however, will mobilise society as a whole only, by delivering it to mass destruction. The mobilisation process proper is transferred back into the war preparation stage: but, as we have seen, nuclear militarism is not mass militarism in the same sense. Small professional armed forces and technologically skilled work forces in the armaments industries 'participate' more or less directly; the mass of society participate mainly in the sense of ideological mobilisation. Even this ideological mobilisation, as an active process, is limited to periods of relative crisis in international relations and the arms race.

The social contradictions of nuclear militarism are therefore very different from those of previous phases of total war. Conflicts within the military sectors of society are limited. Small, relatively well-paid professional armies do not generate revolt in the same way as mass armies of raw conscripts. Skilled arms workers, well aware of their dependence on nuclear militarism, will revolt only if made redundant, although those with trade union traditions may be open to the politics of arms conversion. By and large, however, the military sectors will provide only a flow of individual critics: disillusioned scientists, retired generals, politicised union officials and shop stewards. These are important to an anti-war movement, but they do not provide its basis. The crucial social contradictions of nuclear militarism are therefore those which affect the wider society. In general, these will arise not through anything which can seriously be called 'military participation' but through external or indirect effects. This is because of the remoteness of the nuclear arms race and society.

The arms race is best conceived of as an arch over society: its twin pillars, in the military and the military-industrial sectors, stand on the edges of society. Most members of society live for the majority of the time without being aware that the arch is there, above them, although in fact it is constantly being enlarged, with jagged edges pointing down at them as well as up at 'the enemy'.

The arch requires many of the best building materials in society, but most people do not see these being diverted from ordinary social uses.

Only when a particularly sharp international incident or escalation of the arms race occurs do most of society become aware of this overarching military reality. Because the arms race is so abstracted from everyday social life, there is little ongoing social conflict about it. Conflict is confined to various elite interest groups in the armed forces, the state and military industry. Only when extraordinary developments occur (particularly a series of international conflicts and arms race issues, such as coincided at the beginning of the 1980s) is widespread social awareness generated. This, combined with the national political situations prevailing, is also the context in which anti-nuclear weapons movements develop. Not surprisingly, such movements have considerable difficulty in maintaining their momentum.

A cycle of protest actions, even involving millions, may build up over several years, but given the abstractness of nuclear issues it is difficult to achieve concrete results. The first CND movement in Britain did not remove a single missile. The wider European peace movement of the 1980s has contributed to the removal of- intermediate nuclear forces, under discussion in 1987, but can claim no direct success. The chief cause of this is not their particular strategic or tactical weaknesses, nor their social composition, but the political intangibility of their targets. The nuclear arms race is largely the prerogative of the two superpowers; even those aspects of it which are within the control of other nation states are often carefully screened off from normal political debate-let alone control. Although, within parliamentary democracies at least, it is theoretically possible to affect decisions about military policy, it is exceptionally difficult for peace movements to sustain the momentum of forces strong enough to break through. Among political elites, the sort of consensus which lasted among British political parties until 1980 is often strongly rooted. Among the wider population, nuclear politics may have no deep roots in present military participation, but they have the force of habitual attitudes often linked-however inappropriately-to the lessons of real military participation in the Second World War. Pro-nuclear elites may use their control of political and cultural institutions to reinforce these attitudes in the population.

The seemingly intractable problems of war-resistance and radical politics in the nuclear age are therefore interlinked. Anti-war or anti-nuclear-weapons movements cannot be sustained by the social contradictions of the arms race alone. Equally, radical social movements cannot progress without confronting the military realities which constitute so much of the framework of state and ideology. The interrelationship between the two can be traced back to the basic pattern of militarism, state and economy in the nuclear phase of total war, which affects all social movements.

Nuclear militarism is about more than nuclear weapons. They are the archetype of the capital-intensive weapons systems which, as Mary Kaldor's study shows, characterise contemporary militarism as a whole. Highly sophisticated-according to Kaldor-'baroque' weaponry changes the nature of the relationship between arms, economy and society. It requires a state-supported (but not necessarily state-owned) arms industry; it does not, however, require the state to support, control or still less own much of the rest of the national economy. Although the strategic reasons for the state to retain extensive direct control over many basic national industries and services may not disappear, they are greatly weakened. Large conscript armies and mass-production munitions industries are a thing of the past, as far as the most technologically advanced military powers are concerned. State intervention and the welfare state may survive for other reasons but, to the extent that they have been based on military necessity, they are likely to be threatened.

The political consequence of this is that the state cannot now be relied upon, as it could in the second phase of total war, to provide basic social needs. This implies the danger of the state cutting services which individuals and groups cannot provide for themselves. At the same time, however, it may create a great deal more involvement for society in providing for its own needs, instead of passive dependence on the state. In discussing the social implications of military participation in the Second World War, we noted the centralised and bureaucratic character of the 'military-democratic' state. Military participation implied at best a distorted form of social participation. The relative decline of centralised state bureaucracy obviously opens up dangers of restoring large areas of economic and social life to private capitalism. But it also opens up possibilities of more genuine social participation: cooperative ownership and production, workers' self-management, involvement of consumers in the running of services, etc. Such possibilities not only involve social advance: they also have political implications, since adapting state apparatuses to different forms of social organisation modifies the state. Examples of this can be seen, at least at the local state level, in Western Europe.

The 'military-democratic' state was based on a bonding of state and society, and a relative unity within the state of its military and social apparatuses. The 'nuclear' state opens up a large gap between the military branches of the state and the underlying society; but this also tends to become a divide within the state. Lesser organs, such as the local state and educational, health and welfare services, can become arenas both for expressing social needs and for opposing nuclear militarism. The social and military contradictions become, to a certain extent, conflicts within the field of the state.

Just as Britain was a strong case of the 'military-democratic' form, so it now exhibits a particularly sharp form of nuclear militarism. A society which in living memory, was mobilised almost to the last man (and woman) is now the most thoroughly demobilised of all major states. Even the infrastructure of conscription, which remains in the US (and was activated for Vietnam), has been dismantled in the UK. Civil defence, which is a serious business in neutral states such as Switzerland, has nowhere been more thoroughly abandoned as a means of protecting citizens. Despite the strong attachment of sections of the political establishment to the traditional armed services, it is commitment to nuclear weapons which has long been a litmus test for both conservatism and right-wing social democracy. Little of the institutional basis of military participation survives, although the ideological residues may be more potent.

Britain has thus undergone a more radical transition in its relationship to militarism than other states. The British state, traditionally *laissez-faire*, became radically interventionist as a result of the first two phases of total war. In the nuclear age it has embraced the logic of nuclearisation more fully than other states, and ultimately this has been reflected in the Thatcherite attempt to divest the state of many of its no-longer strategic assets. British society has been profoundly affected by this transformation: the disciplined military-democratic culture of the early post-war years has been eroded by demilitarisation and affluence. Britain's clear decline, as world power, empire and economy, has provided fewer and fewer symbols with which to maintain national ideology and countries. Only in the superpowers is there now a real basis for militaristic nationalism. In Europe (East even more than West), national pride can no longer be based on military prowess. And yet most European societies are more disciplined by proximity to the geopolitical fault in the Continent, as well as by the surviving forms of military participation. Britain stands well to the fore of the general military demobilisation, and its economic, social and political crisis has been the more acute partly in consequence of this. It is a striking confirmation of the transformation of the relationship between militarism and society that the consistently high level of British military expenditure has done virtually nothing to offset these trends.

Implications for Social Movements

The logic of the changing relationship between state and society is that the anti-nuclear movements must see the opening up of social contradictions as necessary for their long-term success, while social groups with interests in the welfare state must be prepared to take a stand against militarism. For anti-nuclear movements the strategic options seem to be: either to remain isolated as 'single-issue' movements, in which case the lack of real social involvement in military matters is likely to condemn them to long-term ineffectiveness; or to find a way, while maintaining their specific aims and identities, to become part of a broader social process. Theoretically, there is a third option: to campaign for an alternative form of mass military participation, but this seems wholly anachronistic. If we are right about the 'dead end' of war and strategy, then the goal of peace movements must be to continue to demilitarise society, not to define an alternative militarism.

Peace movements must actually be about peace, not (primarily) defence.

The task of demilitarising society involves two main planks. One is the direct and obvious job which the peace movement has been doing, of opposing military preparations. The other, however, is to assist movements which advance social participation to reclaim for positive non-militarist purposes the social space which the limited *de facto* demilitarisation of much of nuclear society has created.

The decline of socio-economic 'participation' via the centralised welfare state has also meant the decline of the traditional, centralised labour movement. The opening of a wider social space has also seen more varied and fragmented social movements claiming it. Instead of unified trade-union movements dominated by male manual workers, we have more variegated workers' organisations in which white-collar and professional workers, and women in all occupational groups, are playing larger roles. The boom created larger ethnic minorities in all major capitalist societies: their communities are now claiming a role. Women, and sexual minority groups, no longer accept their subordination: their movements have an extraordinarily wide influence on society. The decomposition of traditional families has created new interest groups, such as single parents. The decline of cities has called forth community groups concerned with housing and urban facilities generally. The rapid advance of industrialism, often destructive of the environment, has led to the formation of ecological campaigns. And so on. A vast range of new forces represent the more varied interests of society, and demand that the state changes to meet their needs.

In confronting the state, however, social movements of all kinds meet fundamental problems. Many of these are familiar. There is the difficulty, traditionally identified by Marxists, that the state systematically favours the interests of large-scale capital. There is the problem of bureaucratisation which affects every area of state activity. There is the other main problem emphasised by Marxists, that the state exists to repress social movements: the police have been greatly expanded both in number and in the range of tasks and means of control which they adopt. But there is also, and in a sense ultimately, the problem of the military apparatus.

Traditionally, Marxists lumped together the armed forces with the prisons and police as the repressive arms of the state. So it may have seemed in the nineteenth century, when there was much military repression of the working class but little continuous warfare. In the twentieth century, however, the military have been primarily a means of inter-state conflict and only secondarily a means of internal repression. In most advanced capitalist societies, this function has increasingly become a specialised police concern. Even such a major class conflict as the 1984-85 miners' strike in Britain was dealt with by para-militarising the police, rather than by bringing in the troops. Thus nuclear militarism is increasingly pure militarism: indeed, its technology is such that it has minimal potential for policing. Even the apartheid state in South Africa might hesitate to 'nuke' its own subject population. What we are confronted with, in the end, is an immensely powerful, expensive apparatus of unprecedented destructive capacity which exists almost entirely to service real, or hypothetical, conflicts between states.

What, it may be asked, has this sort of militarism to do with the social movements which we have been discussing? The people they seek to mobilise do not on the whole participate directly in this militarism. It is remote, abstract; it may even seem to provide a space within which social movements may act. Its potential for actual war, nuclear war, catastrophically threatens the whole of society; but how directly is this threat felt by most of society? Their connection with nuclear militarism, as a form of militarism in the here and now rather than as a threat of ultimate annihilation, needs to be established.

The problem of this militarism for social movements is deep but not always easy to grasp, for it is as much a matter of culture as one of tangible social and economic facts. Nuclear militarism represents a principle of social and state organisation which is directly opposed to the life-creating, lifeexpanding, democratic impulses of most basic social movements. The essence of nuclear militarism is not only its capacity for instantaneous destruction, with its distortion of all the best imoulses of our culture and technologv. It is a fundamentally restrictive principle of social organisation, which mentally coerces society into accepting a framework of international conflict as an overriding reality. It places at the heart of the state a huge commitment of resources to military-acilities which can no longer be rationally connected to the interests of society.

The tangible effects of nuclear militarism are thus evident in the structures of the state, in militarism's privileged claims for resources. These claims have crucial social effects-the diversion of resources from social need to weaponry. But the cultural and ideological effects on society are equally real. It cannot be an accident that the period of greatest play for emancipatory impulses in our culture was from the mid-1960s through into the 1970s, when detente relaxed the Cold War and loosened its ideological hold on societies.

The 'new Cold War' can be seen as a process of re-tightening, and E.P. Thompson is right to emphasise that the peace movements must be as concerned with resisting this as with removing missiles. Indeed, as he suggests, the task for the peace movement is largely one of creating cultural links which cut across the tendency of Cold War militarism to freeze peoples in nations and blocs. When international culture is fractured by the Cold War, the responses of our culture as a whole are weakened.

If the values which sustain all the social movements for change suffer when nuclear militarism is in the ascendant, then all such movements must make the challenge to this militarism a central Part of their projects.

PEACE POLITICS AND SOCIALISM

This argument for a connection of anti-militarism and radical social movements should not be confused with the reductionist argument that nuclear disarmament can only come under socialism. Nor should it be seen as implying particular tactics, for questions of practical political intervention cannot be settled at the general level on which we have been arguing. What has been suggested is that the relationship between nuclear militarism and society implies a general strategic relationship between peace movements and wider movements for social change.

This argument, far from reproducing standard socialist arguments poses radical challenges to them. These follow from the critique of historical socialist positions which has been generated throughout this book. It has been effectively argued that socialists of all kinds have underestimated militarism and war. The primacy given to socio-economic relations has rendered socialists weak in understanding the mobilising capacity of military relations, and their implications for social change. This is reflected in specific theoretical weaknesses of early Marxism, which was very much a product of mid-nineteenth century 'peace'. The decisive proof of socialism's difficulties with war is to be found in its failure to understand the way in which the processes of total war generate the conditions in which different models of socialist itself-revolutionary, reformist and Stalinist-have been realised. It has been argued that, despite the origins of socialist ideas in the contradictions of nineteenth-century capitalism, the success of the principal forms of socialist politics has depended on their practical evolution under conditions of twentieth-century total war. It can be concluded from this that both the individual positions and the debate: between them an unlikely to be adequate in the changed conditions of nuclear militarism and society.

Traditional socialist politics, both revolutionary and reformist, have been marked, then, by experiences of war which they have little understood. One consequence of this is that, carried over into the nuclear age, they bring with then positions and attitudes which are historically anachronistic This is most obviously true of attitudes to war and politico violence, but it applies more generally to concepts of politico action and organisation. Many of the new left and feminist critiques of traditional Marxism and social reform would be greatly strengthened if they recognised the fact that what they are criticising is, effectively, the socialism of total war. It is not just that traditional socialisms are openly militaristic in one sense or another; it is also that the forms of state and social organisation which they represent are those associated with the era of mass militarism, and are in decay with it.

Although both revolutionary and reformist traditions in the twentieth century have contained important anti-militarist strands, they have been based on the fundamental idea that war may be necessary to socialism. While socialists have protested at the horrors of modem war, they have rarely questioned the basic pragmatic approach to war generated by the nineteenth-century attitudes of Marx and Engels. A particular war, or form of warfare, may have been objected to, and the objection fused with an elementary moral condemnation. But war in general has rarely become the object of systematic socialist critique-in a number of ways an understandable situation, since there were indeed many real choices within wars before 1945. Socialists recognised the opportunities which wars presented them, if not in theory then at least in practice, and the advantages which could sometimes be achieved by a war policy.

For revolutionary socialists, it has been axiomatic that the old ruling class and state will attempt to resist their overthrow, so that revolutionaries must be prepared to arm to achieve or maintain victory. In practice, revolutionary movements have not only tended to become militarised, but have often adopted military forms from the outset. For reformist socialists, it has been equally axiomatic that, where there is even a minimal identification between working-class interests and a democratic state, they have a duty to support the state's wars. Although less directly militarised in themselves, reformist movements have accepted and often positively identified with the dominant militarism of the state.

From this it has followed that socialism became an over whelmingly militarist and statist idea. Both existing 'models' of socialism have embraced the centralised, bureaucratic methods of war-mobilisation as methods of creating socialist advance. However extreme and exceptional the Russian civil war was, however much an aberration the eulogies of 'war communism' produced by later critics of Stalinism (Trotsky, Bukharin), it is the ultra-statist model then established which became the norm for revolutionary regimes. Latter-day revolutionaries may deplore this outcome and prefer the 'genuine' revolutionary alternative of socialist democracy, but they have not explained how revolutions can avoid the militarist-statist result. Similarly, however much reformist socialists recognise a problem of bureaucracy, the statist model of war mobilisation remains a key reference point for success. So long as they accept the legitimacy of the military apparatus, a key element of secretive, centralised, bureaucratic state power will remain far beyond democratic control. A politics which fails to challenge this is unlikely to move seriously beyond statism in general.

One of the major difficulties in moving beyond socialist militarist politics is the unevenness of historical trends in war. The nuclear dead-end largely closes off military means of resolving conflicts among advanced Northern industrial states. But empirically, and in the short run, it quite obviously has no such general effect in the South. Although some regional conflicts are certainly inhibited and controlled by their close connections to superpower interests, this is not universally true. Theoretically, since the superpowers are involved in virtually every part of the globe, virtually any conflict has the potential for East-West escalation. But in practice the limits often seem clear, and wars are all too possible. Socialists in the advanced world are overly inclined to see progressive, anti-imperialist content even in inter-state wars in the Third World, while revolutionary struggles receive general support. The extent to which both 'old' anti-imperialist and 'new' nuclear-age critiques of war apply to Third World wars and revolutions is often neglected.

However, many wars are actually wars of national ruling classes and budding regional imperialists. Moreover, since many advanced Third World states now possess nuclear technology, their conflicts are developing a potential for mutual destruction which replicates that of the superpowers. In the decades to come, therefore, the nuclear limit will increasingly apply to all major wars, in the Third World as much as the Northern hemisphere. Among these wars there are still genuine national revolutionary struggles. Even liberals and Christians find it difficult to deny that faced, say, with the armed intransigence of the apartheid state, armed struggle may be justified; or that faced with the invasion of the US-backed Contras, Nicaragua may need to defend its revolution. Taken in isolation, or in the context of the uneven tendency of war to become self-defeating, this is obviously true. But it is equally important not to confuse a statement that in South Africa (or wherever) armed struggle is justifiable in principle with the argument that it is actually the best, or the most important, method of struggle available. Mass social action involves more people and is more likely to lead to some form of democratic state; armed struggle may or may not assist this. One of the elements involved here is that, despite uneven development, national politics do not develop in isolation from other countries. The values, ideologies and culture of protest are worldwide, and just as armed struggle in the Third World has an (often damaging) influence on the culture of revolt in the West, so the values of our peace movements may have an indirect influence on mass movements in South Africa and elsewhere.

While the identification of sections of the Western left with movements for change in the Third World is a sign of healthy internationalism, an over-identification with the method of armed struggle is very questionable. At the very least it suggests a vicarious attachment to methods which are overwhelmingly redundant as serious political tactics in Western countries. At worst it has led to disastrous attempts to ape armed struggle in the actions of small terrorist groups. More commonly perhaps, the domestic corollary of international guerrilla struggle is a preference for aggressive modes of action and quasi-militaristic modes of organisation. Physical confrontation on the streets may be actively sought (although this is not to deny that it is also provoked by the police). Socialist organisations may borrow the structures and language of militarism. They may define themselves as 'combat organisations' locked in direct conflict with a centralised state. This justifies strict centralism, discipline and internal security, which in turn deny any prospect of democracy among their members. This was the common fate of revolutionary organisations in Western Europe after 1968.

It is not only among would-be revolutionaries that the influence of military forms can be found. The official Communist Parties have long retained hierarchical command organisations, even while advocating 'pluralism' and parliamentary roads to socialism. This situation can be traced back to the militarisation of the Russian Revolution, although it also has roots in the CP's attempts to ensure the absolute loyalty of its members in the polarised politics of the inter-war, Second World War and Cold War years. Socialist parties, too, have often become parties of state power in the context of total war. The British Labour Party experienced its most authoritarian regime in the 1940s and 1950s: the discipline of war and reconstruction was extended to party organisation. This was also the period of its greatest success. It does not follow, however, that this model can be recreated today. Our analysis would suggest that a contemporary model of political organisation should have an openness to a wide range of social movements, and should reflect the libertarian and radical democratic impulses which many of them project.

The decline of the early post-war model of the Keynesian welfare state has left political space which has been successfully occupied by 'anti-statist' forces of the right. This 'antistatism', for example of Thatcherism or Reagonomics, is of course founded on a central contradiction. It is a very selective opposition to statism: it diminishes the economic and welfare roles of the state, while increasing its policing and military roles. On the other hand, the left has not yet developed an effective non-statist, or less statist, alternative, although some of the elements of this may exist. One reason for this is that it has not y et understood that any alternative must be based on a thoroughgoing anti-militarism. This is necessary, not only to expose the contradictions of right-wing 'anti-statism', but also to develop any real momentum for the left.

The essence of a non-statist socialism, it might be quite widely agreed, is a reliance on the democratic, cooperative efforts of groups of producers, users, consumers, etc. This emphasis is quite different from the reliance on the centralised state, or on the individual enterprise in the market advocated by the right. Such an approach does not eliminate the state (but nor does the approach of any significant political force on the right). What it does is to change the basis of the relationship between social groups and the state. Where previous socialisms were based on the state's definitions of social needs, a non-statist socialism envisages that the state creates a framework of support for social groups defining their own needs and pursuing their goals.

Such an approach could not be realised by militaristic seizure of existing state power, either through revolutionary means or by a sweeping electoral victory envisaged by classical reformists. On the contrary, it must inevitably be based on a gradual process of building democratic initiative and self-oganisation in large areas of society, in tandem with a process of decentralising state power. Such an approach can be called a hegemonic strategy: attempting to build up a practical basis of support in society as a precondition for political change. The concept of 'hegemony' employed by socialists advocating this sort of approach derives from the Italian Marxist, Antonio Gramsci. The images of political struggle which are present in his work are themselves of a military kind, but they have a relevance in analysing the structures of society, militarism and state power today.

Gramsci advocated a political version of trench warfare (war of position) rather than an all-out assault on state power (war of manoeuvre). He saw state power as a repressive citadel surrounded by outer trenches and fortifications, consisting of institutions which diffused its ideological dominance in society. Writing in fascist Italy, which he saw as an 'integral state' of repressive and ideological control, he believed that only a socialist movement which struggled in the outer trenches would ever be in a position to attack political power.

Gramsci's ideas are relevant today not because, as his Eurocommunist epigones argue, they are a prescription for gradual socialist advance in a parliamentary regime; but, on the contrary, because his bleak model of the relationship of state and society has some applicability today despite parliamentary government. If our analysis is right, the repressive core of state power, and above all militarism, has become less accessible to any form of direct political assault. Pure, nuclear-centred militarism generates as a by-product extremely sophisticated means of defeating any insurrection. At the same time it dispenses with the politically vulnerable mass conscript armies on which revolutionary movements have historically relied. This militarism, with its extreme centralisation of power, also renders itself relatively immune to democratic political control. Nuclear militarism generates a small 'power elite' of top political, military and business leaders who control the key issues of war and peace. The normal processes of the party system hardly touch these issues, partly because a consensus has been constructed to defend this concentration of political-military power.

The activities of peace movements in the 1980s have amounted to a direct assault on the centres of power in nuclear militarism. They have had tremendous success in exposing the very existence of this power, and in stimulating debate on suppressed issues. They have also exposed the weakness of the social underpinning for nuclear weaponry, forcing political elites on to the defensive especially over new weapons systems. They have not, however, fundamentally shaken the centres of nuclear power. A more deeply based hegemonic social movement is necessary for this.

This is not to write off the peace movements: they have achieved more than anyone could have imagined possible just few years ago. They may yet, in alliance with particular political forces, change the military policies of a number of states, and so contribute to a process of disarmament and detente. They have made a unique contribution to opening up international political and cultural space on the left, within Western Europe, across the East-West divide, and to some extent globally.

The peace movements have, moreover, been a major focus of radical mobilisation in response to a general rightward drift in Western societies. But their longer-term impact may depend on a broader-based reversal of this rightward tendency, across a number of societies. They need to be part of a wider advance of social movements which can democratise society, give society greater control over the state, and bring to political power parties which are committed to is process. Only then are we likely to see a sustained effort to undermine nuclear militarism which has a real chance of success.

The problem, both for the peace movement and the left, is date simply that the main historical precedents for such radical popular movements are war situations. Radical social movements have generally come in the train of war mobilisation: the success of both revolution and reform has owed an enormous amount to this. We have to develop a social and political movement on a different basis. This is an opportunity well as a problem because, for the first time, radical movements can develop without carrying with them particular forms of militarism which distort or even defeat their social ideals. Both revolutionary militarism and democratic militarism have had their day, at least in the advanced industrial world

The problem is to identify situations other than war situations which will stimulate social majorities actively seeking change; and to find agencies other than the centralised state which can lead and organise them. Of course we are not simply trying to identify a different sort of crisis which can lead to the kind of seizure of power by socialist forces that has previously occurred in war conditions. As we have already seen, the process of change may be different. There is therefore no point in reinstating catastrophic economic crisis, beloved of the more traditional schools of Marxism, as the locus of change. Economic catastrophes in themselves, as the interwar slump and, more recently, the onset of generalised recession in the 1970s have shown, do not produce radical change. They are more likely to result in forms of reaction. We need, indeed, a more complex, layered, conception of the accumulation of crises which shows how economy, society, culture and politics interact-and how they create the conditions in which change may develop.

The most relevant general conceptions of crisis are those which derive, again, from the work of Gramsci. His idea of 'organic crisis'-a crisis of social relations, culture and ideology as well as of economics and state power-has been fruitfully applied by Stuart Hall to contemporary British conditions. Just as Gramsci argued that the organic crisis of early twentieth-century Italian society produced the 'integral' repression and ideology of fascism, Hall sees the specific decline of post-war Britain as stimulating the growth of 'authoritarian populism'. While the main focus of this was originally identified as the drive towards 'law and order', the Falklands war was seen as bringing out crucial dimensions of nationalism and patriotism. The 'crisis' of British society is one which encompasses the world role of the national economy and state as well as its social organisation. and culture.

Such a concept of crisis is nationally formulated, and could not be applied directly to any other society. This is a difficulty, however, only for those theories-such as many classical Marxist approaches-which start from general concepts of capitalism and fail to recognise that military and society remain largely national. An approach such as that advocated here, while trying to discuss general trends in the relationship of war and society, must always recognise that modem wars are fought between nation-states. National societies therefore have individual experiences both of war and political development. We have emphasised the uniqueness of both 'models' that we have discussed: the Russian Revolution and British social democracy. The development of political alternatives can only be discussed really concretely in a national context, although there are broad international currents at work.

The most important of these is clearly Green politics. The Green movement originated in West Germany as a successor to the extra-parliamentary opposition and an expression of the environmental and anti-nuclear-power battles of the 1970s. It became a national political force as a result of the peace movement of the early 1980s. It has developed into a significant radical presence in a number of European countries, largely as a result of the international nature of the peace movement. As a minority party, Greens clearly confront all sorts of practical problems which may make their independent political existence precarious: in Germany, the problems of coalition which follow from electoral success; in Britain, the difficulty of breaking through electorally at all.

More important than specific party developments, however, Ls the fact that Green ideas have given a general political coherence to the individual causes (nuclear weapons, nuclear power, the environment, anti-racism, feminism, etc.) around which people have become active. This coherence is relevant to activists within mainstream left-wing parties as well as to:hose who form the new Green parties. Green ideas generally contain their own version of an 'organic crisis', which includes nature as well as culture, society and state. The future certainly lies in bringing together these ideas with the understanding of economic realities which has been at the heart of socialist ideas.

Anti-militarism has been axiomatic to the Green movement, and in this sense the rethinking of war which is proposed in this book is a contribution to the development of ideas for a new Green left. At the centre of Green and peace movement practice in the 1980s have been the problems of defence policy; and it is our relationship with these that we now turn.

The Politics of Defence

We have stressed that the most active phase of Cold War ideology corresponded to the period of transition from the mass militarism of the Second World War to the nuclear-dominated militarism of the late 1950s onwards. After the early challenge to nuclear weapons (especially in Britain), the nuclear arms race was accompanied by a period of relative ideological demobilisation during which a wide range of social movements emerged. Only when new peace movements developed in the early 1980s-essentially out of the social movements of the 1960s and 1970s-was Cold War ideology reactivated in Europe. Indeed, only when challenged did political leaders find it necessary to justify to a mass audience the rapid expansion of weaponry which had proceeded throughout the 1970s. The responses of national leaders varied, of course, according to the geopolitical fractures which had appeared in the once-monolithic Cold War blocs. There was a world of difference between the evangelical anti-communism of the American New Right and the cautious strategic formulations of many Western European governments. The British Tories drew on an ideology of 'the Soviet threat' which, while falling well short of US excesses, was remarkably crude by comparison with most Western European arguments.

The nuclear disarmament movements which emerged so rapidly, and thus initially possessed an ideological advantage over most governments, saw themselves as peace movements. They were defined by their opposition to nuclear weaponry, rather than by their support for any alternative military positions. Implicitly, if not in formal policy, they were thoroughgoing anti-military movements. Only as governments and pro-nuclear political forces recovered from the initial shock of the peace movements, and began a political counter-offensive, were peace movements forced to confront difficult issues about which military alternatives they favoured. The fact that the peace movements affected major political forces quite quickly-notably opposition social-democratic parties-Lncreased this pressure, since mainstream political parties certainly could not reduce their nuclear commitments without Jarifying their 'defence' stance.

Many parties which were affected by the peace movements did not, of course, reject all nuclear weapons: the British Labour Party was altered more radically than most continental socialist parties. It moved from the 1979 Labour government's all-round pro-nuclear stance to a 1981 support for full unilateral nuclear disarmament. Those in the peace movements who recognised the importance of such shifts could not but be aware that they might at the same time cause difficulties in getting anti-nuclear parties elected. Labour's movement to unilateralism accelerated the splitting off of the pro-nuclear Social Democrats, which was obviously likely to weaken Labour's chances. Despite the mass support for peace movements, it was not always clear that even partial anti-nuclear positions, such as those widely adopted on the Continent, would prove electorally successful. Public opinion polls, which recorded consistent majorities against the new cruise and Pershing missiles (even in Britain), showed in most cases equally consistent support for maintaining existing nuclear weapons and for NATO as an alliance.

Many in the peace movements have therefore felt it necessary to develop 'alternative defence policies', both to enhance the credibility of their opposition to particular nuclear systems, and to offer a framework around which policies for sympathetic political parties might be formulated. Such policies are not acceptable to all sections of the peace movement: they are objected to by both traditional pacifists and revolutionary Marxists, who believe it is inappropriate to suggest alternative ways of defending 'capitalist' states. It is important to look at the problems involved in the light of the perspective outlined in this book.

It is not the principle of 'defence', in the abstract, which should be questioned. Even more than in the Second World War, the vast majority of society have an interest in the existing social arrangements and state. The mass of the working class and the middle class benefit from and identify with existing political arrangements; many even have a small property stake, if only in their own houses. So there should be no problem, in principle, in supporting the military defence of Western parliamentary democracies against external threats: providing that such threats can be shown to exist, and that relevant (and not self-defeating) military means are available. It is here, of course, that the problems of any meaningful defence strategy arise.

It is not, moreover, the existence of a Soviet military threat to Western Europe which is in doubt. Versions of targeting plans have been published, so that people in British cities can have some idea of the missiles directed against them. No peace campaigners who have distributed leaflets showing the effect of a bomb on their locality could deny the reality of this Soviet threat. What can be denied is, first, that this threat is any more than the symmetrical counterpart to the Western threat to Soviet and East European peoples; and, second, that there is any genuine defence against it.

Western strategic experts generally accept that there is no serious evidence of any Soviet intention, plan or interest in a military invasion of Western Europe. Unlike Nazi Germany, the Soviet Union is not aggressively expansionist in that sense, however much it would like to extend its political influence and economic access to the West. The Soviet Union keeps large land forces in Eastern Europe, partly to maintain its control there. The use of these forces against Western Europe can be envisaged if East-West issues, more likely military or political than territorial, unsettle relations to the point where the USSR sees war as likely and decides to act first. Alternatively, and more probably, this could occur if a regional war in the Third World destabilises East-West relations to the point where a general war seems likely.

In either case, it is the general pattern of East-West rivalry, rather than any specific Soviet intention or interest in conquering Western Europe, which is more likely to produce attack. Moreover, since that is the case, there would be little reason for such a war to be limited to the conventional conquest of particular European countries and resistance to that. Both superpowers and alliances are likely to see their interests as a whole as being involved; escalation of the war beyond conventional battle is highly probable. Even if the war was begun conventionally, it is likely to become nuclear (at east at the battlefield level) quite quickly. By the time it has involved attacks on Britain, some way from the East-West border, it is almost certain to have become nuclear. Indeed, since it would be obvious that any war was likely to become a major war, there would be a considerable incentive for a pre-emptive nuclear first strike which would invalidate all preparations for conventional defence. Escalation could indeed prove instantaneous.

In this context, some 'alternatives' to nuclear weapons are clearly as or more dangerous than nuclear weapons themselves. 'Strong conventional defence', if it means that NATO requires stronger offensive conventional capacities, or even a greater capacity for sustained conventional resistance, is extremely risky. On the one hand, it could enable political and military commanders to believe that it is possible to have a conventional war in Europe without nuclear escalation, so making war more likely. But any war in central Europe, however 'limited', would be catastrophic for tens of millions of people. On the other hand, the belief that there was 'space' for a conventional war could mean that a 'limited' conventional conflict would be allowed to develop into an extremely wide and destructive conventional war. Such a war would not only involve an appalling number of casualties in itself. Since escalation is a law of war, it would involve the risk that nuclear weapons would be used. Even if battlefield nuclear weapons had been withdrawn from central Europe; even, indeed, if all nuclear weapons had been withdrawn from the entire continent; or even-to take the limiting case-if the superpowers themselves had undertaken nuclear disarmament: in all these cases, an all-out conventional war could and probably would still escalate into a nuclear conflict. Nuclear weapons, as is repeatedly argued by their proponents, cannot be uninvented. The conclusion to be drawn from this truism is not, however, that we must permanently maintain and develop our nuclear arsenals. It is, much more radically, that no war should ever be contemplated between states which are nuclear-capable.

The case for 'strong conventional defence' comes from two main directions: from the generals (such as successive NATO Commanders in Europe), for whom it is a partial alternative within the context of a general nuclear defence; and from politicians (such as the leaders of the British Labour Party), for whom it is a general alternative to nuclear weapons. The motives of the two groups may be quite different, but their policies are likely to converge in practice if significant nuclear arms reductions change the military and political context.

In the context of a powerful political process of detente and disarmament, therefore, 'strong conventional defence' could just about represent an important stepping stone away from the nuclear arms race. Considered as a defence policy in its own right, however, it is a nonsense. It only exemplifies the dangers of military strategy in the nuclear age, possibly to a greater degree than a nuclear 'defence'. At least with nuclear weapons, strategists and politicians make strong distinctions between possession and use-even if these could much too easily break down. The defensive quality of nuclear weapons is widely held to lie in their deterrent value, not in their physical use which many agree would be self-defeating. Of course, as we have seen, the central contradiction of 'deterrence' is that it is only viable if use is conceivable. This has led attempts to refine nuclear weaponry, to make its use more plausible, so that battlefield nuclear weapons are in a sense more dangerous than strategic weapons, because their use can be more easily envisaged.

For precisely the same reasons that battlefield nuclear weapons are such a dangerous concept, 'strong conventional defence' is exceptionally risky. No one has even tried to make clear-cut distinction between deterrence and use in such a strategy. All the evidence is that generals and politicians believe-without much of the equivocation that affects nuclear strategy-that strong conventional forces could and should be used. If they were, it would quickly be demonstrated that, far from genuinely defending the people of Europe, they would lead to a suicidal and genocidal war. At the very least, millions of Germans would die; with any escalation, the danger of all-out nuclear extermination would not be far away.

The simple truth is that total military defence of any kind, conventional as well as nuclear, is impossible in any sense that is free from utterly unacceptable risks for the people of Europe and the world. This may be difficult to understand, in world that is still living on the myths of a world war for 'freedom' and 'democracy'. Politically and intellectually, peoples as well as states are still conditioned by past experience of war. In the case of the United States and Britain, this experience was far removed from the worst episodes of the 1939-45 period. But even the Russians, Poles, Germans, Japanese and Chinese, who saw far more of the horror of that war, would have to make huge imaginative leaps to grasp the absolutely greater horrors of nuclear war. The awareness which exists does not yet sufficiently inform the policies of any major state.

However valid politically, as we have suggested, the very concept of 'defence' is therefore extremely problematic in a military sense. Purely defensive wars are rare enough in history, and highly unlikely in the nuclear age. Defence and offence go together, and in the nuclear age produce a threat of mutual annihilation. While the other side's nuclear weapons are indeed threatening, so are 'ours, for they invite the potential enemy to target us with their missiles. The defence which people require in the nuclear age is defence against war as such: against the whole system of international relations, strategy and war-preparation which may produce war. The most important defence is not, therefore, military at all, but political. This is not playing with words, but a simple recognition of the irresolvable contradictions of any military strategy on the part of states or alliances which have entered the age of nuclear warfare. Military defence of peoples and societies as a whole is simply not possible with a reasonable degree of confidence that appalling risks can be avoided.

The politics of nuclear disarmament, detente and international cooperation are the only safe basis for defence. The main task for the peace movements is not, therefore, to propose alternative ways either of fighting wars or of maintaining deterrence. It is rather to find ways of undermining the arms race, developing cultural and political relationships between people and movements across the Cold War divide, and pushing governments into constructive measures of both disarmament and political change-within and between blocs.

Any discussion of 'defence policies' is only meaningful within this context. The main reason that the peace movement is forced into an engagement with non-nuclear military defence is that it has to start at the point of awareness of the public at large, and to a lesser extent parties and governments, if it is to have any chance of influencing events. As has already been suggested, peoples as well as governments are still thinking about war in ways which reflect the past rather than present prospects. The assumption that military defence is possible has hardly been questioned either by public or by politicians, although the whole argument for deterrence contains an implicit recognition that in reality it is very difficult to envisage conditions in which a war might rationally be fought. Politicians advocating nuclear disarmament often seem to regard it as their first task to assure the public not only that they will be defended, but that all possible non-nuclear-means will be deployed.

Peace movements should be more honest and put forward the case that there is no real military defence in the nuclear age. If we align ourselves tactically with the advocates of 'strong conventional defence', it must not be in order to foster

illusions that such a prospect is safely available, but because any form of nuclear disarmament can be used as a constructive step towards wider disengagement. If we put forward alternative defence policies' ourselves, these should be of a sort which clearly point in the direction of political change rather than alternative forms of warfare. Interestingly, in this context, proposals have recently been revived for a form of 'citizen's territorial defence' along the lines advocated by some left-wingers in Britain in 1939-45. While in one sense this seems like a constructive proposal, since it breaks down the professionalisation of the armed forces and relies on limited weaponry, it is also fundamentally anachronistic. It proposes to revive mass participation in military defence at a time when such defence is increasingly impossible and when society as a whole has largely moved beyond military involvement. Such proposals would reinforce the illusion that the next war may be similar to the last, which is one of the biggest obstacles to a breakthrough in opposition to nuclear militarism. It would, in a sense, remilitarise society, when the peace movement has the opportunity to turn a large measure of *de facto* demilitarisation into a more positive commitment to peace.

A more relevant concept is that of 'non-provocative defence' argued by a number of European writers. It is proposed that West

European countries should adopt weaponry, force levels and deployments of such a kind as would clearly indicate to the Soviet Union the lack of an offensive capability or intention. The aim, instead, would be to develop anti-weapon systems which would indicate a willingness to resist territorial incursions, without responding by offensive attacks.

Such a stance would promise to impose considerable costs on an invader, but without threatening all out war. It would represent a recognition that war of the kind pursued in 1939-45, let alone that envisaged by current strategists, is no longer feasible. But, by promising some military resistance, which could be reinforced by unarmed popular opposition, it could make a contribution to answering popular anxieties about 'leaving us defenceless' as well a posing genuine problems for a state which was considering any sort of military incursion.

While such a strategy has some plausibility, its advocacy has major problems. Although there is a clear enough distinction in principle between 'non-provocative defence' and what we have called 'strong conventional defence', it may be hard to make this distinction clear in political debate. In a context of enormous nuclear over-armament, where 'strong conventional defence' (with or without nuclear weapons) is on offer from major military and political forces, any argument for; conventional military strategy may appear as an echo of this policy.

At the very least, any alternative defence policy which the peace movements (or political forces close to them) argue for should be clearly subordinate to a political strategy. 'Non provocative defence' is only a partial military defence against partial military aggression; there can be no total military defence against the total attack of which nuclear-armed states are capable. The central thrust of any anti-nuclear politics should be that the only defence for any society in the nuclear age is political rather than military. Military attack must be prevented, not fought off; war must be permanently eliminated, not rehabilitated in 'less destructive' forms. Defence must he based, first, on establishing the political framework for regulating conflicts without war; and, second, on reversing the escalation of the arms race, so dangerous in itself, by systematic reductions in armaments.

A Philosophy of 'Historical Pacifism'

Those who claim to hold 'philosophies' of war and peace very often ground them in some variety of religious or ethical belief. They are more likely to have an absolute objection to war itself than a historical or political approach to the changing forms of war. Indeed, within peace movements there me often considerable tensions between those who hold philosophical position against war as such and those who are primarily interested in political measures against particular forms of militarism. The one major philosophy which is founded on a historical conception, Marxism, is one which is associated with a pragmatic approach to war. Neither support for, nor opposition to, war in general can be a principle for Marxism. Historical materialism determines that the means of violence should be understood, and judged, within the context of the economic, social and political relations in which they are produced and used. At its most simple, this position boils down to the argument that weapons are neither good nor bad in their own right: it depends in whose hands they are. The inadequacy of this approach can be seen in the disreputable indirect apologetics for Soviet nuclear weapons sometimes made by Stalinists and Trotskyists within the peace movements.

In this book we have made fundamental criticisms of the theoretical conceptions and historical interpretations of classical Marxism. With the benefit of late twentieth-century hindsight, we have tried to pinpoint the dominant role of the processes of war. Forces which were largely implicit when Marx wrote have since become powerfully explicit in world history. It is in the spirit, if not the letter, of Marx's approach to revise historical materialism by allowing fuller scope to the relations of war. In this sense, while there is little point in continuing to claim the label 'Marxist' we nevertheless need to maintain the goal-to which non-Marxist social theorists have also contributed-of a historically informed politics and social practice. This book can be seen as a contribution to a broadly based radical and Green critique of Marxism.

Underlying the politics of war which we have been discussing there should, then, be a historical understanding of the present phase of warfare. In a basic sense, of course, there is wide recognition that nuclear weapons alter all the rules for war and peace. Very many people who supported, indeed fought in, wars before 1945 have recognised that nuclear war is utterly inconceivable. Even the strategists, politicians and military leaders with responsibility for nuclear weapons have had, as we have seen, to acknowledge this tacitly. For many, there is the clearest possible divide, and those who perceive it sometimes call themselves 'nuclear pacifists' to convey that their refusal of nuclear weapons is as absolute as the total pacifist's rejection of war itself. E.P. Thompson, for example, has described himself in these terms.

The difficulty with a simple nuclear pacifism is that ii suggests that the problem is a particular sort of weaponry, and tries to draw a sharp line between nuclear and non-nuclear war which cannot really be made. Just as nuclear weapons developed the potential for mass killing of civilians already present in aerial bombing, so nuclear technology has beer applied to all shapes and sizes of weaponry. If lines must be drawn, a more relevant one than that between nuclear and non-nuclear weapons, or forms of warfare, is that between war involving nuclear-capable states and war which is clearly limited to non-nuclear states. But all such distinctions are relative: nuclear weapons have so altered the prospects of war that the problem can increasingly be seen to be war itself.

This is why 'historical pacifism' is better than nuclear pacifism. Nuclear pacifism tries to draw one particular line within modern warfare; historical pacifism is the belief that the problem is modem warfare in general. Nuclear pacifism is absolute but limited; historical pacifism is more conditional, but more comprehensive. Historical pacifism can be defined as the belief that war is becoming, and to a large extent has already become, redundant as a means of achieving justifiable human ends. Historical pacifism will lead us to refuse not just nuclear war, and direct preparations for it, but any war or war-preparation, however conventional, which could lead to nuclear war. Historical pacifism will lead us to ask, even of war which seems wholly non-nuclear, whether the mass killing involved can seriously be justified by the political goals or state interests which it purports to further. Historical pacifism will enable us to learn the lessons of past warfare, and ask of any war whether the means involved will not defeat or distort the ostensible aims. The idea of historical pacifism advanced here would allow very much more limited scope for legitimate military activity than the concept of nuclear pacifism. Indeed, it involves reversing the basis of the argument about war and peace. Where nuclear pacifism rests on an assumption of the general legitimacy of war, and makes a case that nuclear war is exceptional and illegitimate, historical pacifism poses things the other way round. It argues that the whole historical development of warfare, of which nuclear weapons are the culmination, has undermined the assumption of the legitimacy of war. In the nuclear age, war is becoming outmoded; it is the warfare which is still justified which has to be explained.

This seems a much better way round of posing matters. Given all that we know of the murderous, genocidal and ultimately exterminist dangers of modern warfare, it is right to ask of anyone who proposes the use of military force whether this can possibly be legitimate. We need to ask-whether it is a case of the Falklands Task Force or a PLO attack on Israel, or whatever-not only whether the political goals are legitimate in themselves, but whether there is any other means of furthering them, and whether the means proposed will really achieve what is intended without causing new problems which will outweigh any positive results. We need to ask all states, and non-state organisations, which maintain military forces and use them whether their policies and actions are contributing to the overriding goal of eliminating the danger of exterminist war. This approach gives us, I hope, a standpoint for action which is relevant to the character of our age and the overriding danger which war now poses to human society.

16 War Today

War is a profound topic—like truth, love, death, or the divine. Intellectuals from every field have cut their teeth on it: political scientists, historians, ethicists, philosophers, novelists, and literary critics. But war is not one thing, always and everywhere. People write about the wars of their own time and their own country. The current war on terror partakes of all these. When framed as a clash of civilizations or modes of life—secular and fundamentalist, Christian and Muslim, modern and primitive— the war on terror is reminiscent of the Cold War. Like the Cold War, the war on terror seems greater than the specific conflicts fought in its name.

It transcends the clash of arms in Iraq or Afghanistan. On their own, those wars resemble postcolonial and anticolonial conflicts from Algeria to Vietnam. When we link the war in Afghanistan to women's rights or the war in Iraq to the establishment of democracy, we evoke the history of military deployment for humanitarian ends. In our broader political culture, the phrase "war on terror" echoes the wars on drugs and poverty as the signal of an administration's political energy and focus. At the same time, the technological asymmetries of battling suicide bombers with precision guided missiles and satellite tracking has made this war on terror seem something new—as has the amorphous nature of the enemy: dispersed, loosely coordinated groups of people or individuals imitating one another, spurring each other to action, within the most and the least developed societies alike. Strictly speaking, of course, terror is a tactic, not an enemy.

We use the phrase "war on terror" not only to disparage the tactic, but to condense all these recollections in a single term. By doing so, we situate this struggle in our own recent history of warfare.

The phrase also frames the broader project with fear, and marks our larger purpose as that of reason against unreason, principle against passion, the sanity of our commercial present against the irrationality of an imaginary past. In this picture, we defend civilization itself against what came before, what stands outside, and what, if we are not vigilant, may well come after. It is not novel to frame a war in the rhetoric of distinction— us versus them, good versus evil—nor to evoke a nation's history of warfare each time its soldiers are again deployed.

When we call what we are doing "war," we mean to stress its discontinuity from the normal routines of peacetime. War is different. To go to war means that a decision has been taken: the soldier has triumphed over the peacemaker, the sword over the pen, the party of war over the party of peace. Differences among us are now to be set aside, along with the normal budgetary constraints of peacetime. This is serious and important—a time of extraordinary powers and political deference, of sacrifice and national purpose. The point about war today, however, is that these distinctions have come unglued.

War and peace are far more continuous with one another than our rhetorical habits of distinction and our wish that war be truly something different would suggest. A phrase like "the war on terror" can evoke so much precisely because wars of metaphor have blurred with the wars of combat on the ground. The distinction between them is far more tactical assertion than material fact. This can be easier to see in hindsight.

Take the Cold War. It was an enormous military and diplomatic—and economic and ideological—struggle, carried on by the political, military, and commercial elites of both superpowers for more than a generation.

At the same time, until the Soviet Union's surprising collapse, it was always plausible to insist that the Cold War had long ago ended, that the many proxy wars and great power interventions we now remember to have taken place in its name each had its own more specific logic, and that the long and stable peace between the blocs was itself frozen, rendering the rhetoric of "Cold War" a somewhat retro political vocabulary for justifying this or that policy priority. In this account, relations between the blocs were governed not by the law of war, but by the stable law of "coexistence." Was it war—or was it peace? Looking back, as historians, we could argue either way, for surely the Cold War was both a titanic global struggle *and* a period of remarkable stability among the great powers.

Throughout the period, however, experts and politicians, citizens and pundits disagreed about which to emphasize. And their disagreements had stakes for policy and politics. Was détente a dramatic "opening," or the belated recognition of an established order among the world's powers? Was the nuclear standoff itself the end of history, at least the history of great power military struggle?

Or would that end only come after we had accelerated our spending on arms to a level unsustainable for our adversary? As these questions have become matters for historical interpretation, it is easier to see positions about them arrayed on a spectrum, and to treat those who would argue one *or* the other as straining in a way that seems tendentious or partisan. We feel we can tell something about someone who argues one way rather than the other—something about his or her politics or personality. Distinguishing war from peace is both a serious political decision and a symbol of partisan positioning. There are parallels in our current "war on terror."

We can imagine a spectrum of positions, from insistence that the country remain on a war footing, at home and abroad, to the view that we treat the problem of suicide bombing or terrorist attacks as a routine cost of doing business, a risk to be managed, a crime to be prevented or aggressively prosecuted.

In short, the boundary between war and peace has become something we argue about, as much or more than something we cross. War today is both continuous with—and sharply distinguishable from—peace. As policy, the difference will be one of degree—what *balance* of policing and military action? What balance of offense and defense? But these differences are also matters of ideology and political commitment. War today is both a fact and an argument. The increasing continuity between war and peace, on the one hand, and the continued rhetorical assertion of their distinctiveness, on the other—to understand what makes the wars of our time and place unique.

Both threads lead to law. It has become routine to observe the omnipresence of law in our peacetime culture. The same has become true for war, and the result has knit war and peace themselves ever closer together. Warfare has become a modern legal institution.

At the same time, as law has increasingly become the vocabulary for international politics and diplomacy, it has become the rhetoric through which we debate—and assert—the boundaries of warfare, and insist upon the distinction between war and peace or civilian and combatant. Law has built practical as well as the rhetorical bridges between war and peace, and is the stuff of their connection and differentiation. To understand—and accept—these continuities between the politics and practices of war and peace, we must understand more clearly what it means to say that warfare has become a legal institution.

When we think of war as sharply distinct from peace, it is easy to imagine it also as outside of law. War is often the exception to the routine legal arrangements of peacetime; contracts, for example, routinely exempt acts of war alongside "acts of God." If we pause to think about the law relevant to war, we are likely to focus on international rules designed to limit the incidence of warfare, from the ancient "just war" tradition, to the institutional machinery set in place by the United Nations Charter to "save succeeding generations from the scourge of war."

Or the many disarmament treaties limiting the use or availability of the most heinous weapons—exploding bullets, gas, chemical, or nuclear weapons. Or the rules of humanitarian law regulating the treatment of prisoners of war or those wounded on the battlefield. We are likely to think of these rules as coming from "outside" war, limiting and restricting the military. We think of international law as a broadly humanist and civilizing force, standing back from war, judging it as just or unjust, while offering itself as a code of conduct to limit violence on the battlefield. Indeed, it is common to associate this entire legal universe with the International Committee of the Red Cross, itself borrowing something from the neutral and humanitarian image of its Swiss hosts. But law is relevant to war in many other ways.

The military, like other public and private bureaucracies today, operates in war and peace against the background of innumerable local, national, and international rules regulating the use of territory, the mobilization of men, the financing of arms and logistics and the deployment of force.

Taken together, these laws can shape the institutional, logistical—even physical— landscape on which military operations occur. Today's military is also itself a complex bureaucracy whose managers discipline their forces and organize their operations with rules. Armies have always been disciplined by rules, usually legal rules.

The national regulations by which Nelson disciplined the Royal Navy at Trafalgar were tough, parallel to those of British criminal law of the era. Under the Articles of War, a man could be hanged for mutiny, treason, or desertion. Routine discipline was to be enforced through flogging and "starting," or striking a man across the back with a rope or rattan cane. The interesting point is that in Nelson's day, these rules were distinct both from contemporaneous international legal debates about the "justice" of warfare and from the rules governing the French and Spanish fleets.

In the years since, as the military has become a more complex modern bureaucracy, linked to the nation's commercial life, integrated with civilian and peacetime governmental institutions, and covered by the same national and international media—and as our ideas about law have themselves changed—the rules governing military life have merged with the international laws about war to produce a common legal vocabulary for assessing the legitimacy of war, down to the tactics of particular battles. Was the use of force "necessary" and "proportional" to the military objective—were the civilian deaths truly "collateral?"

What is difficult to understand is the extent to which this vocabulary—of just war, legitimate targeting, proportionate violence, and prohibited weaponry—has been internalized by the military. Not every soldier—not every commander—follows the rules. Rules are bent and ignored. Rules are violated. But this is less surprising than the astonishing way the legitimacy of war and battlefield violence has come to be discussed in similar legal terms, by military professionals and outside commentators alike. As such, law today shapes the politics, as well as the practice, of warfare. The political context within which this merger of law and war has become significant.

The forms war and law assume vary with the nature of politics and statecraft. The legalization of our political culture, and the emergence of a global policy class of experts who respond to the same media and speak the same language, has altered the relationship between war and law.

It is only in this context that we can understand what it means that lawyers are increasingly forward deployed with the troops, or that planned targets are routinely pored over by lawyers. This is the context in which it seemed sensible for opponents of the Iraq conflict to frame their opposition in legal terms. The war, they said, was *illegal*.

For all his contributions to legal codification, it is hard to imagine Napoleon consulting a lawyer to discuss targeting. In the same way, it would have been bizarre to oppose Hitler's invasions—let alone the Holocaust—principally because they were *illegal*. The emergence of a powerful legal vocabulary for articulating humanitarian ethics in the context of war is a real achievement of the intervening years.

What does it mean, however, to find the humanist vocabulary of international law mobilized by the military as a strategic asset? How should we feel when the military "legally conditions the battlefield" by informing the public that they *are entitled* to kill civilians, or when our political leadership justifies warfare in the language of human rights? We need to remember what it means to say that compliance with international law "legitimates." It means, of course, that killing, maiming, humiliating, wounding people is legally privileged, authorized, permitted, and justified. At the same time, how should the U.S. military itself react to the escalating public demand that it wage war without collateral damage— or to the tendency to hold the military to an ever higher standard as its technological capabilities increase? The legalization of modern warfare has a history.

It is customary to relate changes in modes of warfare to the political history of ideas about sovereignty and the nation, and to changes in the material and technological capacities of the military profession. But the changing nature of warfare is also a function of changing ideas about law. When law saw *itself* as an autonomous discipline, external to the institutions it regulated, it was more difficult for legal ideas and rules to infiltrate the military professions, or to become the political vocabulary for assessing the legitimacy of strategy and tactic.

When the legal profession understood law as a framework of sharp distinctions and formal boundaries, it was easier to think about war and peace as sharply distinguishable legal statuses, separated by a formal "declaration of war." As late as 1941, it seemed natural for the United States to begin a war with a formal declaration, as Congress did in response to Pearl Harbor.

In the lead-up to both world wars, the United States carefully guarded our formal status as a "neutral" nation until war was declared. That Japan attacked the United States without warning— and without *declaring* war—in violation of our neutrality was a popular way of expressing outrage at the surprise attack. In the years since, the formal status of neutrality has eroded.

Moreover, when Israel launched a preemptive strike against Iraq's nuclear capability, there was plenty of outrage—but it was not expressed as a failure of warning or declaration. Something had changed. In the late nineteenth century, law provided a set of categories and distinctions whose violation could seem an outrage. These categories persisted thru the middle of the last century, and their vocabulary of distinction is with us still. Meanwhile, however, the broad legitimacy of warfare and military tactics were not evaluated in legal terms prior to the Second World War. A legal institutional process and doctrinal vocabulary for doing so had begun to be developed for that purpose by the start of the twentieth century, but it would only catch on after 1945. As a result, across the twentieth century, the legal experience of war reversed.

The categories came to seem far too spongy to be the occasion for outrage, while in a broader sense, warfare had become a legal institution. Across the twentieth century, more antiformal and flexible ideas about law joined hands with a more professional and bureaucratic idea about warfare to make the interrelationship between law and war more pronounced.

And it became far easier to think of war as a matter of "more or less," separated from peace (as belligerents were separated from neutral powers) more by the political claim to be engaged in the serious business of war than by any formal or institutional boundary. These changes had particular significance for efforts to restrain warfare through law.

The humanist legal strategy of standing outside the military while insisting upon compliance with external humanitarian standards was joined by efforts to infiltrate the military with bureaucratic legal restrictions. Today's humanitarians blend these two strategies, seeking to restrain war's violence by oscillating between external denunciation and internal partnership with colleagues in the military. In large measure, their strategies have been successful. Military professionals find the same external standards conditioning the political environment within which war is fought, and use the same internal norms of conduct to mobilize and discipline the force. Military and humanitarian professionals are speaking the same legal vocabulary. All this was in place by the end of the Cold War.

Since then, of course, the international order has been dramatically transformed. The emergence of a global economic and commercial order has amplified the role of background legal regulations as the strategic terrain for transnational activities of all sorts, including warfare. Sharp boundaries between the political and institutional cultures of the first, second, and third worlds have dissolved, heightening the significance of the shared legal language of the world's political elites. In the years after the fall of the Berlin Wall, the humanitarian institutions and professions that call themselves "civil society" quickly became more prominent players on the world stage, heightening the significance of their humanitarian and human rights vocabulary for global political and legal debate. The legacy of successful—and decidedly unsuccessful—partnerships between global humanitarian, diplomatic, and military actors over the last decade has complicated all of their relationships to an increasingly shared legal vocabulary. It is not new to observe that at the same time, the nature of warfare has itself changed.

The Second World War—a "total" war, in which the great powers mobilized vast armies and applied the full industrial and economic resources of their nation to the defeat and occupation of enemy states—is no longer the prototype.

Experts differ about what is most significant in the wars that have followed. Our wars are now rarely fought between roughly equivalent nations or coalitions of great industrial powers. They occur more often at the peripheries of the world system, among foes with wildly different institutional, economic, and military capacities. The military increasingly trains for tasks far from conventional combat: local diplomacy, intelligence gathering, humanitarian reconstruction, urban policing, or managing the routine tasks of local government.

It is ever less clear where the war begins and ends—or which activities are combat, which "peacebuilding." In combat, enemies are dispersed and decisive engagement is rare. Battle seems at once intensely local and global in new ways, as informal networks of fellow travelers exploit the financial and communications infrastructures of the global economy to bring force to bear here and there, or global satellite systems guide -precision munitions from deep in Missouri to the outskirts of Kabul. Violence itself seems to follow patterns better understood by study of epidemiology or cultural fashion than military strategy. Taken as a whole, the political, cultural, and diplomatic components of warfare, both globally and within the sphere of battle, have become more salient. The significance of war's legalization for these developments.

As many in our own military have already well understood, there are new opportunities for creative strategy. They have a term for the waging of war by law—"lawfare." In today's asymmetric wars, moreover, law can be weaponized quite differently by our own technologically sophisticated forces and by the dispersed groups of terrorists and insurgents against whom they have found themselves in combat. At the same time, the legalization of warfare offers new opportunities for those who seek to restrict the use and violence of military force. Millions of people marched against the Iraq war buoyed by the claim that the war was an illegal violation of the UN Charter.

17 Tools of Statecraft: Diplomacy and War

By their very nature, diplomacy and military force are means to the ends of statecraft as well as channels by which governments press their agendas onto others.

Neither is inherently more or less useful than the other. Diplomacy verbally communicates realities that may move nations (it is not to be confused with any particular message diplomats may carry or with its effects), while military action (not to be confused with war) physically communicates a government's wishes by trying to sweep away resistance to them.

Whereas diplomacy represents realities, military operations create them. Statecraft—with which neither diplomacy nor military action should be confused—is about managing reality, coupling ends and means in ways that advance a country's interests.

Far from being antithetical to one another, diplomacy and military force are complementary insofar as they serve the same political ends. Diplomacy is often popularly thought of as the peaceful alternative to violence, but in fact, diplomacy serves to prepare as often as to avoid war.

It is an important part of waging war, often makes the difference in who wins, and nearly always codifies wars' results. Again, diplomacy is the verbal representation of compelling international realities, and military force is one of those realities. Conventionally, major military action is called war.

The connection between means and ends determines the

character of actions. War is military operations tailored to achieve one's preferred peace. Only insofar as a military operation is so crafted as to bring about the desired peace does it qualify as an act of war as opposed to senseless violence.

The study of history helps us to see through the fog of contemporary loose talk. Persons who know the meaning of words could only cringe at the Bush administration's evasion of the central question about the outcome of the 2006 Lebanon war when it said "diplomacy won," and at the Democrats' equally meaningless claim that it would have placed greater emphasis on "diplomacy." Studying history helps us to understand the arts of diplomacy and of war for themselves and as tools of statecraft.

Diplomacy

Imagine two persons at odds over any given matter. A friend might suggest: "Why don't you resolve your differences through diplomacy? I'll set up the meetings."

But, what could each say at those meetings that would make the differences less important than they were before? If the differences remained important, why should either side accommodate the other's wishes?

Perhaps the differences were not real—mere misunderstandings. Perhaps, though real, they were small in comparison with other interests that either or both are willing to take as currency in exchange for giving up their claims in the matter at hand.

Perhaps new events have reduced the controversy's importance for either or both. Or, one side may present to the other realities of which it was ignorant that lead it to change its position.

If so, the meeting may produce agreement. But if neither side presents to the other anything it did not know before, both sides will be lucky if the meeting just leaves the controversy where it was and does not worsen it. John Quincy Adams, a student as well as a practitioner of statesmanship, believed that governments understand their own and others' interests quite well.

His involvement in diplomacy, which lasted from 1778 to the end of his presidency in 1829, convinced him not that negotiations are superfluous, but rather that they ratify the several parties' recognition of existing realities regardless of agreements or lack thereof.

Diplomacy can make it more comfortable to live with reality by clarifying mutual understanding of it. On the other hand, Adams' magisterial notes on his 1823 recommendation that America spurn the invitation to join Britain in a declaration disapproving any attempt to recover Spain's American colonies—that jointness would have added nothing to the reality of parallel British and U.S. opposition to such a venture—underlines the central fact about diplomacy: though it conveys reality, it does not amend it.

In 1968, Fred Ikle published *How Nations Negotiate*, which is used by diplomatic academies around the world. Too many graduates, however, forget its central teaching, which is that the diplomat's first task is to figure out whether agreement is possible on the basis of "the available terms"—in short, whether both sides' objectives, though different, are compatible.

Only if they are can negotiations proceed according to what Ikle calls "rules of accommodation"—making sincere proposals, honoring partial agreements, etc.

If the objectives are incompatible, the diplomats may choose to walk away, or to "negotiate for side effects"—to use the negotiations to undermine the other side's government, sow dissention among its allies, deceive it, pocket partial agreements and renege on commitments, buy time, gather intelligence, etc.

Disaster looms when one side follows the rules of accommodation while the other negotiates for side effects. The essence of Ikle's teaching is that the negotiator's primordial job is to judge correctly whether the other side is negotiating for "available terms" or is waging war through diplomatic means, and hence to choose whether to negotiate for agreement, walk away, or treat the diplomatic table as a battlefield. That choice is "perpetual," he writes, because human motives are variable.

The history of U.S. diplomacy since World War II is in too-large measure that of what happens when this judgment is made badly. Whether with regard to the Korean and Vietnam wars, the Soviet Union, or the Middle East and North Korea in our time, the default U.S. modus operandi has been to consider diplomacy as an independent factor, for diplomats to treat all interlocutors as "partners," and to treat negotiations as mutual good-faith searches for agreements.

Of course this has permitted, even encouraged and rewarded, America's adversaries to treat negotiations as instruments of conflict. Just as important, by validating the other side's *bona fides,* American diplomats have placed themselves in the awkward position of taking blame for the failure of negotiations to achieve the ends that they themselves proclaimed were at hand.

The embarrassment of revoking certifications of *bona fides* granted gratuitously has pressed American diplomats preemptively to dismiss the option of "walking away" and to worry lest the other side take it up. Hence also, American diplomats are wary of exerting pressure through "side effects" lest they "sour" the negotiations.

Thus they end up valuing less the substance of any agreement than the appearance thereof. The result has been not just the practice but also the advocacy of international agreements that are no such thing.

Most often, today's high-profile agreements are written purposely so that both sides may interpret them precisely as they wish—that is, precisely as if no negotiation had taken place. Whom does this benefit or disadvantage?

Clearly, governments who depend on public opinion and who publicly subscribe to the fiction that an agreement has been reached must realize that if and when they subsequently take action in response to the other side's undiminished pursuit of its goals, they will impeach thereby their own judgment and performance.

Moreover, make-believe successes are guaranteed to turn into real defeats that cannot be spun away. That is why—the case of U.S. negotiations with North Korea illustrates the point well — diplomats have caveated their claims of agreement by adding the word "framework." But what is a "framework agreement" other than the codification of an agenda and a pledge to agree later, maybe? Agreements to agree really advertise that no agreement exists.

Even more transparently unnatural are so-called agreements on "Processes"—e.g. "disarmament processes" and "peace processes." You wanted disarmament and peace; you have armament and war.

But you've succeeded in engaging the several parties in procedures that will overcome substantive intentions—tomorrow. Casting thin veils over unpleasant realities is not, however, diplomacy.

The ultimate in such see-through diplomatic garments is surely the 2005 agreement on the Bush administration's "roadmap" to Arab-Israeli peace. Here policymakers and diplomats cannot manage to pretend that there is any agreement even on a diplomatic agenda, much less on the fundamental issues. But they tout agreement on ambiguously phrased interim goals as tracing the road to talks leading to a process.

War

"What are we after? What are they after?" These questions

are as central to warfare as to diplomacy. Regarding them through the optic of Clausewitz' observation that war is politics by violent means, Western students of war have tended to understand the objectives of war as Clausewitz did, in terms of contemporary Western politics.

But though Clausewitz, writing after the Napoleonic wars, meant his treatise to describe the essence of what he called "total war," reality is much broader and war can be much more total than the European nineteenth-century variety.

Readers of *On War* are hard put to fit, say, the Old Testament description of Joshua's and the Judges' campaigns into Clausewitzian categories. Like the Saxon tribes' invasion of England or for that matter of the nineteenth-century Wahhabi invasions of the Shia shrine cities of today's Iraq, these campaigns aimed simply at annihilation.

Calling it "politics" takes some stretching. And while in retrospect we can see that Europe's sixteenth-century wars of religion were really about politics, that was by no means clear to the participants.

During those years also, bands of heretics fought major battles with various feudal levies. Were these wars or insurrections? It does not matter. The point is that the notion that war must be about politics leads logically to incapacity to grasp that the tribal conflicts and religiously justified violence all around us are as much war as anything mankind ever experienced.

Answering the questions "what are we after, and what are they after?" is war's primordial prerequisite. At the outset of the Peloponnesian war, Archidamus asked his Spartans " what is to be our war?—meaning, how are we going to beat Athens? The history of that war shows that neither Archidamus nor anyone asked the truly primary question: "What is to be our peace?"

What is the state of rest at which we are aiming, with which we can be satisfied? Because the war is going to end some day, we also need to know what might satisfy the other side under what circumstances.

Only then can we figure out which defeats we can inflict on them to get what we're after. It turned out that, neither side having a vision of peace, the war turned into an end in itself that ruined both. Similarly, Napoleon was a master at setting up battles and winning them but, as de Gaulle writes, "striking continually with France's sword, he broke it."

Only from the perspective of the peace you desire is it possible to identify what stands in the way, the people, the institutions, the things the removal of which will give you the peace you want. Only once you have figured that out does it make sense to think of whom to kill and what to destroy, and then, sequentially, to ask "what will it take?" and hence to design military operations.

This is the point, however, at which the arts of war and diplomacy diverge. Diplomats have the option of walking away from their engagements. But once war's killing starts, the options narrow to two: victory or defeat.

That is why it is so important, before entering into a war, to calculate "what it will take" to pay the price for victory and whether you are ready, willing, and able to pay it. If you are not, Machiavelli tells us in his *Discourses*, you should avoid fights, even by negotiating preemptive surrenders.

Keeping your forces out of situations they can't or won't handle, avoiding routs, maintaining some control over the situation, is worth the price. Once the fighting starts, the passions and hatreds that it excites eliminate that option. Pericles made that clear to the Athenians after misfortunes had made them regret having gone to war. "To recede is no longer possible… For what you hold is to speak somewhat plainly a tyranny; to take it perhaps was wrong but to let it go is unsafe."

In the course of war, any limits you may set on your pursuit of victory are actually limits on your commitment to your peace.

If you are not willing to contemplate wholesale slaughter, or want a negotiated solution, remember: once it becomes clear that you will do what is needed to win, those negotiations become about the price you must pay for defeat.

Note however that the price of defeat is even less calculable than the price of victory. In November 1918 Germany did not imagine the political and economic price that Versailles would impose on it.

But, having given up its defenses as the price of armistice, it was at the winners' mercy. This can happen informally as well, because retreats tend to turn into routs, embolden winners and whet their appetites. Moreover, assorted jackals feast on losers as freely as lions. As in the case of Germany, the price of surrender is not merely giving up one's own peace, but above all giving the winner the unrestricted power to change the terms of surrender ex post facto.

So, what will it take to remove the enemy's obstruction to our peace? How much killing any side has to do to end the war depends first of all on what the enemy's after, on his character, and on one's own objectives.

Few peoples have ever fought "to the last man." Even the Japanese on Okinawa surrendered after the futility of resistance had become obvious, they sickened of suicide, and noticed that the Americans were sparing captives. Japan's emperor and his people eventually accepted the shattering of their sacred myths. But Germany's Nazis chose *Gotterdamerung* for themselves and their people.

At best we can control what we are after. A county bent on exterminating peoples from which enmity arises must expect all its victims to die fighting.

One that is bent on desecrating another's way of life must expect having to kill more than one that aims to undo an enemy regime—simply because fewer people have a life or death investment in regimes than in sacred ways.

And of course since regimes' roots run unequally deep, eradicating them will be more or less bloody business. Usually, putting an end to interference in one's own affairs takes less blood and treasure than interfering in others'. When, however, one's reputation inflames enemies' passions, only much blood can quench them.

Bad performance by diplomats or generals may foul up a good plan. But no amount of brilliance at the conference table or on the battlefield can rescue a bad plan or make up for neglect of the principles underlying each craft.

18 Rights of Neutrals Under International Law

The word "law" had tricked us into thinking of something clearly defined and accepted by those to whom it applied, and something backed by force to compel obedience. Now what we considered international law consists mainly of a great body of precedents of different nations, some of them conflicting. These precedents represent certain immunities granted by belligerents to the commerce of neutrals in time of war.

To be, sure, the immunities are an advance over the days when a belligerent proceeded like a pirate against lives and property on ships trading with the enemy. But the advance, when we consider it closely, is seen in no way to have kept pace with the growth of the vast interests it was designed to protect. International law at the best is an inadequate recognition of the rights of those who keep the peace at the hands of those who break it. Yet even such law as there was has been disregarded. Blinded by self-interest, the belligerents have inaugurated a return to the practices of piracy from which this law has been designed to save us. When we turn to a power sufficient to compel obedience to the law, we find that behind it there is nothing but international morality, the public opinion of the world. Especially in the last fifteen years this public opinion has been enlightened as to the great interests dependent upon an uninterrupted flow of peaceful commerce in war times.

True, in the process of public enlightenment there has been more emphasis upon the horrors of war in general. The strongest of the forces forming public opinion on international matters has been the peace movement. Today we can say that more good might have been accomplished if the greater emphasis had been not upon preventing all war but upon confining its damage to those who fight. But a valuable by-product of the peace movement has been the spread of information on the rights of peaceful nations compared with belligerents and the need to extend those rights, not restrict them. It was hoped that in time of war this international public opinion as to the rights of neutrals would exercise a strong moral force upon the belligerents to stay within the limits of law. That is, it was expected that the conscience of belligerents, fearing the disapproval of neutrals, would compel respect for the established order of things. We were doomed to disappointment.

The disapproval of neutrals has not been lacking, expressed most clearly in the protests of their governments directed to both belligerents. But a belligerent conscience, that is, fear of this disapproval or even any large respect for it, is lacking in the parties to the war. Perhaps it was too much to expect that international morality alone would suffice to give sanction to international law. Within national boundaries we do not trust to morality alone. The prime interests of life and property are safeguarded by definite, clearly understood laws, accepted by all, and backed by force. Morality supplements force and does not supplant it. Withdraw the force of the law in any nation and its observance would disappear. Could we expect international morality alone to be any more able to supplant force in compelling observance of international law? Whatever our expectations were, regarding the binding force of morality upon warring nations, we can have them no more.

It is necessary to find some form of peaceable compulsion that will bring the belligerents back to the limits of law. Everyone recognizes the necessity of doing this at the end of the war. As a sequel to the peace, men are planning a new sort of international law with sharp power to enforce it. But the return to legal limits must be now, in the midst of the war. For neutrals to forfeit their rights will be a victory for the forces of international immorality and disorder. Respect for international law will be permanently weakened. Moreover, no one can with certainty say that the end of the war will see established the formal system of international law of which we dream.

It may be that this law will still be largely a matter of precedents, enforced by nothing stronger than the morality of nations. What security will there be in our relations if those precedents, hard won in the past, are now effaced and if that international morality notoriously proves unequal to its task? Apart from this matter of principle, the great interests of trading nations, injured by the actions of belligerents, and the constant peril to innocent lives upon the high seas, both call for a return to freedom of neutral trade and travel now, before the end of the war, whose end we cannot foresee. Now is the time to put an end to the sacrifices of life and property demanded of those who choose to remain aloof from the conflict. From the very beginning this war went beyond the limit of military and naval actions.

It became an "economic war"; namely, a process of interrupting the flow of commerce between neutrals and belligerents and even between neutrals themselves. The purpose was to deprive the interrupted belligerent of necessities of military, industrial and civil life and so bring upon the enemy nation "pressure" sufficient to end the war. But an economic war of this sort is also an economic war against neutrals, for the same pressure is brought to bear upon them as upon the belligerent attacked, perhaps even greater pressure. It may be that the belligerent can find or develop a substitute for the neutral's product more easily than the neutral can find a substitute for the belligerent's market. There are two parties to all trade. It is impossible to interrupt the trade without striking them both. The economic war began in August, 1914.

Soon after the outbreak of the military war England's sea power drove German naval vessels from the ocean. Since then, Germany's navy upon the high seas has been unable to do more than carry on a sort of guerrilla warfare beneath the waves. England, after driving German cruisers from the Atlantic, proceeded to inaugurate measures designed to withhold from Germany the importation of most commodities that come to her by sea. Germany retaliated by a submarine campaign that endangered not only neutral property but also neutral lives on vessels sailing to or from England. Through this policy of action, retaliation and counter-retaliation the seas have become a battlefield where the commerce and citizens of neutral countries venture at peril of capture or sudden destruction. The effect of belligerent violations of neutral trade rights upon the agriculture, industries and commerce of the United States, could be written about any nation now at peace. Our wrongs and losses are merely types of what has been forced on other neutrals as well. The sum of these wrongs and losses is an argument demanding that nations which plan to work and trade be led to dismiss now, and for all time, the aggressions of those that plan to devastate and slay. It happens that the United States is the only great power remaining neutral, the only force today that is able to assert the rights of the world of peace.

If we fail in the objects we seek, in the negotiations we carry on with both belligerents, the hope of all neutral nations is gone. It is worth while briefly to review that body of neutral rights which we called international law and the successive measures by which those rights were abolished. By common consent the seas are the public highways of nations; outside a zone three miles from shore they are not the domain of any one nation. They belong to peaceful commerce, not to belligerents who roam their surface seeking to destroy each other. As a remnant of marine barbarism, a belligerent has the right, if it has the power, to capture or drive from the ocean the merchant vessels of its foe. To the extent of its command over the sea, a belligerent may prevent contraband of war from reaching an enemy in any vessels; and, if capable of blockading the enemy's seacoast, may put a stop to all ocean commerce of the blockaded country.

Under international law, these were the limits and conditions of interfering with commerce between neutrals and a country at war. Only within much narrower limits, according to modern conceptions of international law, can a belligerent interfere with commerce between neutrals themselves. This commerce may be interrupted only when it consists of contraband of war—the actual tools of fighting—demonstrably in transit to enemy territory. These are the rights of commerce on the seas. The rights of travel are as well understood. Though a belligerent may capture and in certain cases destroy a merchant vessel of the enemy, this may not be done without providing for the safety of crew and passengers. All passengers on neutral vessels, wherever bound, are immune from interference, excepting members of the armed forces of the enemy traveling home. The laying of mines at sea is not permitted except for defensive purposes and then only in the territorial waters of the warring power that lays them. With these main exceptions, which are burdensome enough, the sea must be free for the uses of commerce. While this is international law as generally understood, it has not been in form to give nations a sense of security.

The law is mainly in the form of precedents, such as proclamations of belligerents in previous wars, decisions of the prize courts of captors, and treaties between individual nations. Some of the precedents of different countries are conflicting. Therefore civilized powers have made several attempts to reduce the law of the sea to a form acceptable to all and accepted by all. One such attempt resulted in the brief Declaration of Paris, adopted as a sequel to the peace negotiations following the Crimean War. More recently in the Hague Conferences efforts were made to form treaties which all nations were to sign. Most important for our present purposes is the Declaration of London. The British Government in 1909 called the London Conference to codify the law of the sea. All the leading nations took part. The result was the Declaration of London, signed by all national representatives who attended the Conference. It is true that not all the Hague Conference agreements, called Conventions, were accepted by all civilized nations.

It is true that for reasons partly selfish and partly technical the Declaration of London was not *ratified* by many home governments and so did not become officially binding upon them. But it was signed by the representatives of all great powers. The Preliminary Provision reads: "The Signatory Powers are agreed that the rules contained in the following Chapters correspond in substance with the generally recognized principles of international law." Hence it is that neutrals felt that the Declaration of London was morally binding.

Hence it is that nations at peace looked forward to seeing the judgment of civilized nations as to the rights of neutrals upon the sea, expressed particularly in the Declaration of London, proclaimed as sea law by all belligerents at the outbreak of the war. We were disappointed. The disregarding of legal limits was first in evidence when either Germany or England began laying floating mines upon the high seas, forbidden in a Hague Convention. Each took the alleged action of the other as the excuse for retaliation. Because of these floating mines in the North Sea, literally scores of vessels were lost, mostly belonging to the Scandinavian countries or Holland. Three American vessels were included, the Greenbriar, Carib and Evelyn. Because of the danger of mines, ocean freights and war risk insurance rates became a heavy burden on shippers and buyers and, in the case of some commodities, became prohibitive of commerce.

A pall of uncertainty and fear was thrown over the commercial world. Unfortunately, as it would seem in the light of later events, America refused to join the North Sea neutral countries in a protest against the mining of the North Sea. Such action might have made more effective the protest of all neutrals against the later German War Zone about the British Isles. Yet the effect of mines upon the high seas was small compared with the paralysis of trade effected by a practical abolition of the rights of neutrals to trade with Germany and a severe restriction of their right to trade with each other. England brought this about by certain amendments to international law through its Orders in Council. Germany, with her retaliatory submarine warfare, designed the same paralysis of English trade. That the object was not attained is due solely to the fact that German submarines are less omnipresent and less able to intercept all trade than British cruisers are. The exact process of this abolition of the freedom of commerce is easy to follow.

At the very opening of the war the American Secretary of State, with a view to protecting neutral rights while allowing the belligerents all lawful freedom of action, suggested to them that they adopt during this conflict the unratified Declaration of London as their code of action towards neutrals. Germany and Austria agreed. Russia and France delayed their answer until they could hear from Great Britain, and then joined that country in its policy announced by the Order in Council of August 20, 1914, accepting the Declaration of London with modifications. The modifications were subversive of the principles of the Declaration to which they were attached. These modifications, supplemented by an unexampled extension of the British contraband list, and finally by what our government calls an illegal blockade, have been England's method of exercising economic pressure upon Germany and, necessarily, upon all neutral nations that trade with her. In the Declaration of London the articles classed as *absolute contraband* of war-that is, articles which Great Britain might properly shut out of Germany altogether, were restricted to the actual tools and equipment of fighting nations.

Conditional contraband was a more comprehensive list, including such merchandise as food, clothing, coal, harness and saddlery, horseshoes and barbed wire. These articles, capable of direct use by the armed forces of the enemy, might be stopped only if the interfering belligerent could prove that they were destined for those forces. Finally, the Declaration specified a list of *free goods*, articles which might not be molested because only distantly related to warfare, necessary to the civilian population, and contributing a very important portion of the commerce of peaceful neutrals. Such articles were cotton, wool, hides and skins, and rubber. This was law as codified in the Declaration of London. The British Order in Council had the effect of adding the conditional contraband list (food, clothing, etc.) to the absolute list, by decreeing that conditional contraband would be presumed to be moving to the German military, and hence subject to capture, if the goods were "consigned to or for an agent of the enemy state or to or for a merchant or other person under control of the authorities of the enemy state." That is, goods could be consigned to no one in Germany; they could not be shipped to Germany at all. It is obvious that after this action any addition to the British conditional contraband list was as complete a ban on commerce as an addition to the absolute contraband list.

The two henceforth were identical. This action stopped our direct trade with Germany. It might appear that goods on the free list could still move. Some of them did move, from free to contraband. People feared to ship the others lest they should be so listed while ships were on the ocean, and the goods made subject to seizure. Practically nothing has been shipped to Germany from this country but cotton, and it was not shipped until

December. In belated response to the insistence of southern senators and of American business interests which had found themselves gravely embarrassed by the cessation of cotton shipments, Great Britain finally made a clear statement that this particular commodity would not be considered contraband. So much for direct trade with Germany.

There was still a method by which we should have been able to export our goods and discharge our neutral obligations to trade with Germany as with England. We might have carried on this trade via neutral ports like Rotterdam or Copenhagen, from which the goods might have been shipped to Germany. The Declaration of London allows a belligerent to interfere with a shipment between two neutral ports only when it consists of absolute contraband for enemy territory. Conditional contraband so moving may not even be suspected. The Order in Council changed this. It extended the new intention of capturing conditional contraband to goods moving to Germany even through a neutral port. And, as explained, conditional contraband was seizable if destined to anyone in Germany; it was not conditional but absolute. The British action, besides stopping our trade with Germany, barring only a certain amount of indirect trade carried on with much difficulty and danger, subjected to grave peril our commerce with other neutrals.

The British contraband lists were extended so rapidly that soon almost no important article of commerce with neutrals was free from seizure by England, who suspected everything on these lists as being of possible German destination. The shipper to a neutral country then had the prospect of a British prize court passing judgment as to whether shipments were destined for Germany and, in the case of an affirmative judgment, whether any compensation should be paid the shipper, or his cargo simply confiscated. The uncertainty was a risk against which no one could insure. As for the British contraband lists, a few instances will illustrate how they grew. On September 21, copper, lead, rubber, hides and skins were added; on October 29, motor vehicles, motor tires, mineral oil and leather. On December 23, naval stores and cottonseed oil went on the list. On March 11, raw wool was banned. The Germans have retaliated and published a contraband list containing articles that have nothing to do with war, like lumber and flax. The protests against the British August 20 Order in Council resulted in the substitution of an Order dated October 29. But when we came to observe the operation of the October 29 Order, we found that it did not lift the ban on our trade with Germany either direct or via neutrals, and that it added to the existing difficulties of the trade with neutrals a prohibition of shipments "to order." This prohibition dislocated the ordinary methods of foreign trade. Our protest to England of December 26 against interference with our trade with Europe failed to secure any modification of that interference. At last a real test was made of the possibility of provisioning Germany.

In January a St. Louis firm tried to get a cargo of foodstuffs to Germany on the American steamer Wilhelmina. The provisions were consigned to no one in Germany but to a member of the American firm who went to Hamburg to receive the cargo and distribute it to the civilian population. The British stopped the vessel. Unable to find any law for continuing the detention, they made law through a new Order in Council, enabling England to requisition, without trial, the cargo of any neutral ship brought into port. The Wilhelmina's cargo was so requisitioned. On February 4 Germany, claiming that its act was a reprisal against an unlawful British attempt to starve a civilian population, declared the waters around the British Isles a War Zone where British merchant ships would be destroyed by German submarines—if necessary, without search—and where the submarines might endanger neutral vessels by mistake. Neutrals were warned to keep away.

It was stated that it might be impossible to provide for the safety of passengers or crews of the British steamers destroyed. When the War Zone was announced, our government recognized the danger, and addressed a sharp note to Germany, warning that country to be careful not to strike at American vessels or American lives. At the same time, we seemed to recognize in a degree the German point of view; so we sent a joint note to Britain and Germany suggesting that Britain give up its policy of stopping foodstuffs for German civilians, that Germany abandon its submarine warfare, and that both belligerents desist from mining the high seas. With certain reservations Germany accepted the proposal. Great Britain rejected it and, indeed, instead of accepting, proceeded to more radical measures than before. On March 1, stating its action to be a retaliation against the submarine war and other alleged breaches of international law by the Germans, England instituted a "blockade" of Germany. The authorities at London announced that all vessels carrying cargoes to or from Germany, whether direct or via neutral ports, would be subject to seizure. This was the culmination of the British lawlessness. The culmination of the German lawlessness was the Lusitania horror. The British "blockade" terminated our cotton trade with Germany, virtually the only trade that had moved. Whatever even of cotton thereafter found its way to Germany was involved in a smuggling operation. The third largest buyer from America became as distant from us as another world, barring some dangerous, indirect trade. Moreover, all our shipments to European neutrals adjacent to Germany now became tainted with suspicion and detention.

Scores of cotton cargoes bound for neutrals have been held up in British ports. For the first time American importers of German goods saw their supplies endangered; until March 1, the flow of commerce from Germany had been unhindered. Our Federal Government faced a loss of $20,000,000 per year in customs revenues levied on German goods. The most striking circumstances in this extraordinary situation is the fact that Great Britain has at no time maintained a genuine blockade. British warships, fearing submarines, dare not undertake a close blockade of German ports. The Admiralty merely intercepts all traffic passing by Scotland or through the English Channel. Thus the blockade does not bear equally on all neutrals, for Scandinavian countries ship undisturbed to German Baltic ports, from which American products are barred. This whole process of gradually damming the currents of trade to and from one of the members of the comity of nations has been attended with huge financial loss to the neutrals. More important than this, these neutrals, because the British operations have been contrary to the accepted interpretations of international law, have been put in a position where they ask themselves seriously whether, without violating their neutrality, they may lawfully continue to trade with one belligerent which unlawfully prevents them from trading with another. Above all, they question the possibility of silent acquiescence in the policy of both belligerents in abandoning decent restraints in their treatment of the lives and property of neutrals. The time has arrived to revive the restraints and reassert international law and morals. The lifting of the British "blockade" will not suffice, for we neutrals should then find many of the products of peaceful industry each burdened with an individual blockade. That is, these, products would be found included in the British contraband lists, with all that, that means in the hindrance of trade between neutrals as well as between a neutral and a belligerent. If the "blockade" were lifted and the October 29 Order in Council and the British contraband lists kept in force, the relief to neutrals would be small. What we need is a code of law and morals so simple in its terms that the self-interest of neither belligerent can evolve a quibbling interpretation of it different from that which neutrals hold. In this code must be determined what may be contraband and what may not; and it must define the entire method of procedure against merchant ships at sea. There is no time now, in the midst of the war, for neutral nations to meet and devise such a code. The best we can do is to point to one already in existence: the Declaration of London.

Formed by the best legal talent of all nations, it is fair and it is clear. Along with the removal of England's illegal practices against the goods of neutrals must go the removal of Germany's illegal practices against their goods and lives. Germany must restrict her swollen contraband list and likewise return to the Declaration of London. "She must not use submarines against unresisting merchant vessels except to stop and search them in the approved legal way. Nor may English merchant vessels under any conditions be sunk until the safety of crew and passengers has been provided for. Floating mine fields must be removed by those who laid them. It is in America's power, as it is her duty, to restore international law on behalf of the neutral world.

19 The Future of War and Peace

The 20th century was the most murderous in recorded history. The total number of deaths caused by or associated with its wars has been estimated at 187m, the equivalent of more than 10% of the world's population in 1913. Taken as having begun in 1914, it was a century of almost unbroken war, with few and brief periods without organised armed conflict somewhere. It was dominated by world wars: that is to say, by wars between territorial states or alliances of states. The period from 1914 to 1945 can be regarded as a single "30 years' war" interrupted only by a pause in the 1920s-between the final withdrawal of the Japanese from the Soviet Far East in 1922 and the attack on Manchuria in 1931.

This was followed, almost immediately, by some 40 years of cold war, which conformed to Hobbes's definition of war as consisting "not in battle only or the act of fighting, but in a tract of time wherein the will to contend by battle is sufficiently known". It is a matter for debate how far the actions in which US armed forces have been involved since the end of the cold war in various parts of the globe constitute a continuation of the era of world war. There can be no doubt, however, that the 1990s were filled with formal and informal military conflict in Europe, Africa and western and central Asia. The world as a whole has not been at peace since 1914, and is not at peace now. Nevertheless, the century cannot be treated as a single block, either chronologically or geographically.

Chronologically, it falls into three periods: the era of world war centred on Germany (1914 to 1945), the era of confrontation between the two superpowers (1945 to 1989), and the era since the end of the classic international power system. We can call these periods I, II and III. Geographically, the impact of military operations has been highly unequal. With one exception (the Chaco war of 1932-35), there were no significant inter-state wars (as distinct from civil wars) in the western hemisphere (the Americas) in the 20th century. Enemy military operations have barely touched these territories: hence the shock of the bombing of the World Trade Centre and the Pentagon on September 11. Since 1945 inter-state wars have also disappeared from Europe, which had until then been the main battlefield region.

Although in period III, war returned to south-east Europe, it seems very unlikely to recur in the rest of the continent. On the other hand, during period II inter-state wars, not necessarily unconnected with the global confrontation, remained endemic in the Middle East and south Asia, and major wars directly springing from the global confrontation took place in east and south-east Asia (Korea, Indochina). At the same time, areas such as sub-Saharan Africa, which had been comparatively unaffected by war in period I (apart from Ethiopia, belatedly subject to colonial conquest by Italy in 1935-36), came to be theatres of armed conflict during period II, and witnessed major scenes of carnage and suffering in period III. Two other characteristics of war in the 20th century stand out, the first less obviously than the second.

At the start of the 21st century we find ourselves in a world where armed operations are no longer essentially in the hands of governments or their authorised agents, and where the contending parties have no common characteristics, status or objectives, except the willingness to use violence. Inter-state wars dominated the image of war so much in periods I and II that civil wars or other armed conflicts within the territories of existing states or empires were somewhat obscured. Even the civil wars in the territories of the Russian empire after the October revolution, and those which took place after the collapse of the Chinese empire, could be fitted into the framework of international conflicts, insofar as they were inseparable from them. On the other hand, Latin America may not have seen armies crossing state frontiers in the 20th century, but it has been the scene of major civil conflicts: in Mexico after 1911, for instance, in Colombia since 1948, and in various central American countries during period II. It is not generally recognised that the number of international wars has declined fairly continuously since the mid-1960s, when internal conflicts became more common than those fought between states. The number of conflicts within state frontiers continued to rise steeply until it levelled off in the 1990s. More familiar is the erosion of the distinction between combatants and non-combatants.

The two world wars of the first half of the century involved the entire populations of belligerent countries; both combatants and non-combatants suffered. In the course of the century, however, the burden of war shifted increasingly from armed forces to civilians, who were not only its victims, but increasingly the object of military or military-political operations. The contrast between the first world war and the second is dramatic: only 5% of those who died in the first were civilians; in the second, the figure increased to 66%. It is generally supposed that 80 to 90% of those affected by war today are civilians. The proportion has increased since the end of the cold war because most military operations since then have been conducted not by conscript armies, but by small bodies of regular or irregular troops, in many cases operating high-technology weapons and protected against the risk of incurring casualties. There is no reason to doubt that the main victims of war will continue to be civilians. It would be easier to write about war and peace in the 20th century if the difference between the two remained as clear-cut as it was supposed to be at the beginning of the century, in the days when the Hague conventions of 1899 and 1907 codified the rules of war.

Conflicts were supposed to take place primarily between sovereign states or, if they occurred within the territory of one particular state, between parties sufficiently organised to be accorded belligerent status by other sovereign states. War was supposed to be sharply distinguished from peace, by a declaration of war at one end and a treaty of peace at the other. Military operations were supposed to distinguish clearly between combatants-marked as such by the uniforms they wore, or by other signs of belonging to an organised armed force-and non-combatant civilians. War was supposed to be between combatants. Non-combatants should, as far as possible, be protected in wartime. It was always understood that these conventions did not cover all civil and international armed conflicts, and notably not those arising out of the imperial expansion of western states in regions not under the jurisdiction of internationally recognised sovereign states, even though some (but by no means all) of these conflicts were known as "wars".

Nor did they cover large rebellions against established states, such as the so-called Indian mutiny; nor the recurrent armed activity in regions beyond the effective control of the states or imperial authorities nominally ruling them, such as the raiding and blood-feuding in the mountains of Afghanistan or Morocco. Nevertheless, the Hague conventions still served as guidelines in the first world war. In the course of the 20th century, this relative clarity was replaced by confusion.

First, the line between inter-state conflicts and conflicts within states-that is, between international and civil wars-became hazy, because the 20th century was characteristically a century not only of wars, but also of revolutions and the break-up of empires. Revolutions or liberation struggles within a state had implications for the international situation, particularly during the cold war. Conversely, after the Russian revolution, intervention by states in the internal affairs of other states of which they disapproved became common, at least where it seemed comparatively risk-free. This remains the case.

Second, the clear distinction between war and peace became obscure. Except here and there, the second world war neither began with declarations of war nor ended with treaties of peace. It was followed by a period so hard to classify as either war or peace in the old sense that the neologism "cold war" had to be invented to describe it. The sheer obscurity of the position since the cold war is illustrated by the current state of affairs in the Middle East. Neither "peace" nor "war" exactly describes the situation in Iraq since the formal end of the Gulf war-the country is still bombed almost daily by foreign powers-or the relations between Palestinians and Israelis, or those between Israel and its neighbours, Lebanon and Syria. All this is an unfortunate legacy of the 20th-century world wars, but also of war's increasingly powerful machinery of mass propaganda, and of a period of confrontation between incompatible and passion-laden ideologies which brought into wars a crusading element comparable to that seen in religious conflicts of the past.

These conflicts, unlike the traditional wars of the international power system, were increasingly waged for non-negotiable ends such as "unconditional surrender". Since both wars and victories were seen as total, any limitation on a belligerent's capacity to win that might be imposed by the accepted conventions of 18th-and 19th-century warfare-even formal declarations of war-was rejected. So was any limitation on the victors' power to assert their will. Experience had shown that agreements reached in peace treaties could easily be broken.

In recent years the situation has been further complicated by the tendency in public rhetoric for the term "war" to be used to refer to the deployment of organised force against various national or international activities regarded as anti-social-"the war against the Mafia", for example, or "the war against drug cartels". In these conflicts the actions of two types of armed force are confused. One-let's call them "soldiers"-is directed against other armed forces with the object of defeating them. The other-let's call them "police"-sets out to maintain or re-establish the required degree of law and public order within an existing political entity, typically a state. Victory, which has no necessary moral connotation, is the object of one force; the bringing to justice of offenders against the law, which does have a moral connotation, is the object of the other. Such a distinction is easier to draw in theory than in practice, however. Homicide by a soldier in battle is not, in itself, a breach of the law. But what if a member of the IRA regards himself as a belligerent, even though official UK law regards him as a murderer? Were the operations in Northern Ireland a war, as the IRA held, or an attempt in the face of law-breakers to maintain orderly government in one province of the UK? Since not only a formidable local police force but a national army was mobilised against the IRA for 30 years or so, we may conclude that it was a war, but one systematically run like a police operation, in a way that minimised casualties and the disruption of life in the province. Such are the complexities and confusions of the relations between peace and war at the start of the new century. They are well illustrated by the military and other operations in which the US and its allies are at present engaged. There is now, as there was throughout the 20th century, a complete absence of any effective global authority capable of controlling or settling armed disputes. Globalisation has advanced in almost every respect-economically, technologically, culturally, even linguistically-except one: politically and militarily, territorial states remain the only effective authorities. There are officially about 200 states, but in practice only a handful count, of which the US is overwhelmingly the most powerful. However, no state or empire has ever been large, rich or powerful enough to maintain hegemony over the political world, let alone to establish political and military supremacy over the globe. A single superpower cannot compensate for the absence of global authorities, especially given the lack of conventions-relating to international disarmament, for instance, or weapons control-strong enough to be voluntarily accepted as binding by major states. Some such authorities exist, notably the UN, various technical and financial bodies such as the IMF, the World Bank and the WTO, and some international tribunals. But none has any effective power other than that granted to them by agreements between states, or thanks to the backing of powerful states, or voluntarily accepted by states. Regrettable as this may be, it isn't likely to change in the foreseeable future.

Since only states wield real power, the risk is that international institutions will be ineffective or lack universal legitimacy when they try to deal with offences such as "war crimes". Even when world courts are established by general agreement (for example, the International Criminal court set up by the UN Rome statute of July 17 1998), their judgments will not necessarily be accepted as legitimate and binding, so long as powerful states are in a position to disregard them. A consortium of powerful states may be strong enough to ensure that some offenders from weaker states are brought before these tribunals, perhaps curbing the cruelty of armed conflict in certain areas. This is an example, however, of the traditional exercise of power and influence within an international state system, not of the exercise of international law.

There is, however, a major difference between the 21st and the 20th century: the idea that war takes place in a world divided into territorial areas under the authority of effective governments which possess a monopoly of the means of public power and coercion has ceased to apply. It was never applicable to countries experiencing revolution, or to the fragments of disintegrated empires, but until recently most new revolutionary or post-colonial regimes-China between 1911 and 1949 is the main exception-emerged fairly quickly as more or less organised and functioning successor regimes and states. Over the past 30 years or so, however, the territorial state has, for various reasons, lost its traditional monopoly of armed force, much of its former stability and power, and, increasingly, the fundamental sense of legitimacy, or at least of accepted permanence, which allows governments to impose burdens such as taxes and conscription on willing citizens. The material equipment for warfare is now widely available to private bodies, as are the means of financing non-state warfare. In this way, the balance between state and non-state organisations has changed.

Armed conflicts within states have become more serious and can continue for decades without any serious prospect of victory or settlement: Kashmir, Angola, Sri Lanka, Chechnya, Colombia. In extreme cases, as in parts of Africa, the state may have virtually ceased to exist; or may, as in Colombia, no longer exercise power over part of its territory. Even in strong and stable states, it has been difficult to eliminate small, unofficial armed groups, such as the IRA in Britain and Eta in Spain. The novelty of this situation is indicated by the fact that the most powerful state on the planet, having suffered a terrorist attack, feels obliged to launch a formal operation against a small, international, non-governmental organisation or network lacking both a territory and a recognisable army. How do these changes affect the balance of war and peace in the coming century? I would rather not make predictions about the wars that are likely to take place or their possible outcomes. However, both the structure of armed conflict and the methods of settlement have been changed profoundly by the transformation of the world system of sovereign states.

The dissolution of the Soviet Union means that the Great Power system which governed international relations for almost two centuries and, with obvious exceptions, exercised some control over conflicts between states, no longer exists. Its disappearance has removed a major restraint on inter-state warfare and the armed intervention of states in the affairs of other states-foreign territorial borders were largely uncrossed by armed forces during the cold war. The international system was potentially unstable even then, however, as a result of the multiplication of small, sometimes quite weak states, which were nevertheless officially "sovereign" members of the UN.

The disintegration of the Soviet Union and the European communist regimes plainly increased this instability. Separatist tendencies of varying strength in hitherto stable nation-states such as Britain, Spain, Belgium and Italy might well increase it further. At the same time, the number of private actors on the world scene has multiplied. What mechanisms are there for controlling and settling such conflicts? The record is not promising. None of the armed conflicts of the 1990s ended with a stable settlement. The survival of cold war institutions, assumptions and rhetoric has kept old suspicions alive, exacerbating the post-communist disintegration of south-east Europe and making the settlement of the region once known as Yugoslavia more difficult.

These cold war assumptions, both ideological and power-political, will have to be dispensed with if we are to develop some means of controlling armed conflict. It is also evident that the US has failed, and will inevitably fail, to impose a new world order (of any kind) by unilateral force, however much power relations are skewed in its favour at present, and even if it is backed by an (inevitably shortlived) alliance. The international system will remain multilateral and its regulation will depend on the ability of several major units to agree with one another, even though one of these states enjoys military predominance. How far international military action taken by the US is dependent on the negotiated agreement of other states is already clear. It is also clear that the political settlement of wars, even those in which the US is involved, will be by negotiation and not by unilateral imposition. The era of wars ending in unconditional surrender will not return in the foreseeable future.

The role of existing international bodies, notably the UN, must also be rethought. Always present, and usually called upon, it has no defined role in the settlement of disputes. Its strategy and operation are always at the mercy of shifting power politics. The absence of an international intermediary genuinely considered neutral, and capable of taking action without prior authorisation by the Security Council, has been the most obvious gap in the system of dispute management.

Since the end of the cold war the management of peace and war has been improvised. At best, as in the Balkans, armed conflicts have been stopped by outside armed intervention, and the status quo at the end of hostilities maintained by the armies of third parties. Whether a general model for the future control of armed conflict can emerge from such interventions remains unclear.

The balance of war and peace in the 21st century will depend not on devising more effective mechanisms for negotiation and settlement but on internal stability and the avoidance of military conflict. With a few exceptions, the rivalries and frictions between existing states that led to armed conflict in the past are less likely to do so today. There are, for instance, comparatively few burning disputes between governments about international borders. On the other hand, internal conflicts can easily become violent: the main danger of war lies in the involvement of outside states or military actors in these conflicts.

States with thriving, stable economies and a relatively equitable distribution of goods among their inhabitants are likely to be less shaky-socially and politically-than poor, highly inegalitarian and economically unstable ones. The avoidance or control of internal armed violence depends even more immediately, however, on the powers and effective performance of national governments and their legitimacy in the eyes of the majority of their inhabitants. No government today can take for granted the existence of an unarmed civilian population or the degree of public order long familiar in large parts of Europe. No government today is in a position to overlook or eliminate internal armed minorities.

Yet the world is increasingly divided into states capable of administering their territories and citizens effectively and into a growing number of territories bounded by officially recognised international frontiers, with national governments ranging from the weak and corrupt to the non-existent. These zones produce bloody internal struggles and international conflicts, such as those we have seen in central Africa. There is, however, no immediate prospect for lasting improvement in such regions, and a further weakening of central government in unstable countries, or a further Balkanisation of the world map, would undoubtedly increase the dangers of armed conflict. A tentative forecast: war in the 21st century is not likely to be as murderous as it was in the 20th. But armed violence, creating disproportionate suffering and loss, will remain omnipresent and endemic-occasionally epidemic-in a large part of the world. The prospect of a century of peace is remote.

20 Germany's Purpose and Method in Making War

German Warfare System.—From the very first days of the war, during the rush across Belgium to reach Paris, the German army systematically carried out a horrible method of making war. The stories told were at first disbelieved by the world at large, and even when irrefutable proofs were gathered, it was months before it became clear that these were not irresponsible crimes of drunken soldiery, but an organized system of crime directed by the General German Staff, aimed at the destruction of the occupied territory of the enemy nation both in its property and population. The Kaiser himself sanctioned, if he did not plan it, as is proved by his letter to the Emperor of Austria. To understand the real purpose of Germany in making war as she has, and to connect this purpose with all her methods is much more important than remembering exactly the various events, the names of battles, and the way in which the tide of war flowed backward and forward.

We want to understand Germany's "Will to Destruction," the philosophy back of it, and the many ways in which it sought to blast mankind. Science for its own sake had been superseded in many places in Germany by science in the service of Pan-Germanism. Discoveries in chemistry, physics, aeronautics, were applied to new instrumentalities of warfare. It was poison gas that almost carried the Germans through to Paris; and would have, it is thought, had it been used in as large quantities and as efficiently then as later. This gas, liquid fire, and all the variety of containers and throwers of these new deadly chemical compounds, were contributions of German scientists, as were also the use of deadly microbes and bacteria. A vast majority of the professors at the universities were ardent Pan-Germans and stood shoulder to shoulder with the political, industrial, financial and military leaders who planned the war. What must here be made clear is that the German people were systematically prepared for it by their Government and all its agents, through a carefully planned system which excited the more cruel and depraved instincts in both the people and the army, playing on their fears and their lowest desires. Unless we understand this we shall miss one of the fundamental explanations of German frightfulness. The atrocities in Belgium probably would not have been committed by the German soldiers so readily if their officers, acting on superior orders, had not falsely told them of all manner of things that the Belgians would do to them and had done to others—gouging out eyes, cutting off ears and noses, breaking arms and legs, treacherous attacks by civilians, poisoning wells and food. The German soldiers when they themselves did these things in Belgium, simply thought they were doing unto the Belgians as the Belgians would do unto them.

This use of false statements was just as common in the highest German diplomatic as in the military sphere. The Austrian Government before the war forged documents (Friedjung trial and conviction, 1909, Zagreb), in order to condemn by their false evidence the most prominent leaders of the Austrian Slavs. The German Government falsified documents from the Belgian archives to prove that Belgium had broken her neutrality by an alliance with England. (See Second Belgian Grey Book.) The Germans promised Cardinal Mercier that, if the Belgian men who had fled the country would return, they would not be forced to work for Germany, but when they did return they were deported or enslaved. Our own government has shown that the German and Austrian governments initiated in America an elaborate propaganda of spying, corruption, and business penetration, which employed, when possible, the same methods used all over the world, of forgery, perjury, felony and conspiracy. As Dernburg and Delbrueck say (*Deutsche Politik*, Sept. 28, 1917), "Our lies are coarse and improbable, our ambiguity is pitiful simplicity, and our intrigues are without salt and without grace."

The same methods were used in Germany itself in order to control the opinions, the information, and the moods of the people. It has been thought that the leading spirit in the system both inside and outside of Germany was General Ludendorf. The carrying out of his plans in the countries occupied by the German army was largely in the hands of the General Staff, and what this system is has been disclosed in their War Book, which will now be considered.

Teachings of the German War Book.—In 1902, many years before the war, the General Staff of the German army issued its official guide and handbook. It has been described as follows by writers quoted in Morgan's translation of the book: "This cynical and terrible book has been written specially for the instruction of German officers, with the result that it has poisoned the very wells of thought and feeling, not only of the German army itself, but of the entire German people. It gives the highest official sanction to principles and to practices which are in flat contradiction to those of all civilized people. The German officer is required to terrify the helpless into betraying their own people, to murder prisoners, to retain women and children under fire, to levy blackmail upon surrendered cities, to compel the civilian to prepare works for the destruction of his country, to suborn incendiaries and assassins."

The principle on which it is based is terrorism and recourse to all means for attaining the object of the war. This is an old and familiar Prussian axiom, laid down by Clausewitz, their first and foremost military writer, elaborated since his day by Generals Hartmann and Bernhardi, and adopted as the obvious necessity by not only all civilian Pan-Germans but by the rank and file throughout the land. Even leaders in the clergy urged the massacre of the entire civilian population in enemy countries. (Vorverk, Baumgarten, etc.) Although the War Book ostentatiously forbids many of the most hideous crimes, they have been actually committed by the German army; such as the poisoning of wells, streams, and food, the propagation of infectious diseases, the killing of wounded and prisoners, the use of prisoners of war in work against their own country or work that is prejudicial to health, the general taking of private property, wholesale incendiarism, forced levies, etc.

The teaching given to the army, therefore, may be safely said to have gone far beyond the precepts of the War Book. The German army has repeatedly and officially broken every one of the laws which it pledged itself in its own War Book to respect. It is therefore condemned out of its own mouth.

Varieties of German Crimes.—It is not easy to catalogue the varieties of German criminal practices in common use, but for convenience the. following are mentioned:

(1) Bombing of hospitals and attacking Red Cross units.

(2) Firing on stretcher-bearers.

(3) Murdering of civilian population by poison gas. Burning alive or otherwise murdering entire innocent populations of villages in Belgium and Northern France.

(4) Wholesale killing of the wounded, including burying alive innocent civilians.

(5) Wholesale killing of prisoners and hostages.

(6) Bombing of open towns,

(7) Torpedoing hospital ships.

(8) Torpedoing passenger ships.

(9) Sinking boatloads of people saving themselves from sinking ships.

(10) Mutilating soldiers and civilians, including women and children and wounded.

(11) Torturing soldiers and civilians, including women and children.

(12) Exposing men, women, and children to death by using them as screens in attacking the Allied forces.

(13) Torturing, starving, and killing in prison camps.

(14) Systematic and wholesale violating of women.

(15) Destruction of the children to remove a future menace to Germany.

(16) Use of starvation on large scale for destruction or compulsion of entire populations.

(17) Complete destruction of the public and private property of the occupied territory, with removal of all valuables to Germany.

(18) Deliberate destruction of public buildings of historic value

or beauty, and looting or destruction of libraries, galleries, and other collections.

(19) Attempts to completely break the life, pride, honour, and fortunes of the population of all occupied lands.

(20) Attempts to destroy all industrial, commercial, and national life that might interfere with German domination.

(21) Wholesale incendiarism.

No adequate idea of some of these classes of crime is given by the title. In the case of torturing and mutilating, there are instances of deliberate breaking of arms and legs, cutting off of hands and breasts, skinning alive, burning alive, burying alive. In this chapter the atrocities committed by the allies of Germany (Austrians, Bulgarians, and Turks), are included. It is a well-known fact that in all these matters they were "coached" by Germany.

Mental Tortures.—The teachings of the German War Book and other Pan-German writings lay stress upon terrorization, on breaking the spirit of alien populations. The ingenious cruelties employed to accomplish this are shown in many authenticated documents and accounts of witnesses, These cruelties included: Taking out batches of hostages and other civilians and announcing that they were to be executed in the presence of their families; then taking them back to prison; repeating this several times, going so far as to put the firing squad in position. Announcing that one-third of a large group were to be executed, but not saying which, so that all of these unfortunates and their families remained in the anguish of uncertainty. Many were driven crazy, to the delight of the German soldiers. The degradation of women in public was also a common method. The holding of hostages for execution in case there was the slightest trouble in the town made their lives depend on whether a drunken German discharged his gun. The separation of husbands from wives, grown daughters from their parents, of little children from their mothers, was largely to break the hearts of the people. The return of thousands of unidentified little children, through Switzerland, proves this. Thousands of young girls were farmed out to officers and regiments of privates. In the destruction of all material things in Belgium, Northern France, and parts of Poland, as well as in Serbia, there is shown not only the aim to make the country so poor and desolate that it could not for half a century compete with Germany—an aim publicly and authoritatively stated (Rohrbach, etc.)—but also the aim to destroy everything that attached the people to the land, namely: the church, the home, the resting place of their dead, the heirlooms, and all the belongings associated with their past and present lives. The destruction of Rheims Cathedral, the national shrine of the French people, was a venomous attempt to break the national spirit.

Plan to Crush the Economic Life of the Allies.—The devastated area of France occupied by Germany seemed quite small compared with the whole country, but it represented a large part of the wealth of France and almost the whole of her mining industry and her manufactures. All raw materials, all manufactured articles, all machinery was shipped to Germany; also all drawings, files, contracts, business records and other papers. What could not be shipped or could not be used was destroyed. The great coal mines of Lens were demolished to such an extent that it will be years before they can be again in full operation. The same system was carried out in Belgium. Big establishments like the Cockerell Iron works were completely wrecked. Usually the skilled mechanics and operatives were forcibly deported to Germany.

In countries like Spain, Sweden, Holland, and in Italy and America (before they entered the war), the process of industrial supremacy was to go on if possible under strictly legal conditions. In Poland, Russia, the Ukraine, Lithuania, the Baltic provinces and Rumania, the Germans denuded the country of everything, even after the Russian armistice. In Bolshevist Russia the Germans obtained practically complete control by so-called purchase, and counted on running all Russian economic life as soon as order was partly reestablished. Their Bolshevist agents turned over to German hands sufficient of what Germany wanted to enable her to eventually control raw material and manufactured articles as well as means of transportation. How much was done in the United States has been disclosed by the Bureau of Alien Property and by the Senate's (Overman) committee on German propaganda. The same propaganda was extended to Central and South America and Mexico.

The German Government's Plan to Keep the Slavs Ignorant.—The ingenious idea of using ignorance as a weapon was a big German asset. It was applied both at home and abroad. Ignorance of the truth in general and of the outside world in particular, except as distorted, was fostered in Germany and Austria.

Another kind of ignorance was promoted among the Slavs, both in the Central Empires and in Russia. It was a complete ignorance; an ignorance that left the Slavs helpless in the hands of better educated Germans. In this way business, industry, trade, and commerce could be kept without competition in German control. The strong German influence in Russian governmental and court circles before the war was used to prevent the adoption of any adequate scheme for educating the masses of the Russian people. Austria carried out the same idea in Bosnia and Herzegovina.

The Prussian Horror in Poland.—This can best be expressed in Mr. Walcott's words: "A year ago I went to Poland to learn the facts concerning the remnant of a people that had been decimated by war. The country had been twice devastated. First the Russian army swept through it, and then the Germans, Along the roadside from Warsaw to Pinsk, the present firing line, a distance of 230 miles, near half a million people had died of hunger and cold. The way was strewn with their bones picked clean by the crows. With their usual thrift the Germans were collecting the larger bones to be milled into fertilizer, but finger and toe bones lay on the ground with the mud-covered and rain-soaked clothing.

"Wicker baskets were scattered along the way—the basket in which the baby swings from the rafter in every peasant home. Every mile there were scores of them, each one telling of a death. I started to count, but after a little while I had to give up, there were so many..... "In the refugee camps, 300,000 survivors of the flight were gathered by the Germans, members of broken families. They were lodged in jerrybuilt barracks, scarcely waterproof, unlighted, unwarmed in the dead of the winter.... "In Warsaw,... a city of one million inhabitants, one of the most prosperous cities of Europe before the war, the streets were lined with people in the pangs of starvation.... Day and night the picture is before my eyes—a people starving, a nation dying.

"In that situation, the German commander issued a proclamation. Every able-bodied Pole was bidden to Germany to work. If any refused, let no other Pole give him to eat, not so much as a mouthful, under penalty of German military law.

"This is the choice the German government gives to the conquered Pole, to the husband and father of a starving family; leave your family to die or survive as the case may be. Leave your country, which is destroyed, to work in Germany for its further destruction. If you are obstinate, we shall see that you surely starve.

"... Germany will set him to work that a German workman may be released to fight against his own land and people. He shall be lodged in barracks, behind barbed wire entanglements, under armed guard. He shall sleep on the bare ground with a single thin blanket. He shall be scantly fed and his earnings shall be taken from him to pay his food.

"That is the choice which the German government offers to a proud, sensitive, high-strung people. Death or slavery.

"When a Pole gave me that proclamation, I was boiling... I asked Governor-General Beseler, 'Can this be true?'

"'Really, I cannot say,' he replied. 'I have signed so many proclamations; ask General Kries.'

"So I asked General Kries. 'General, this is a civilized people. Can this be true?'

"'Yes,' he said, 'it is true'—with an air of adding, Why not?
"I dared not trust myself to speak; I turned to go. 'Wait,' he said. And he explained to me how Germany, official Germany, regards the state of subject peoples.

"Even now I find it hard to describe in comprehensible terms the mind of official Germany, which dominates and shapes all German thought and action.... I saw it in Poland, I saw the same thing in Belgium, I hear of it in Serbia and Rumania. For weeks it was always before me, always the same. Officers talked freely, frankly, directly. All the staff officers have the same view.

"Let me try to tell it, as General Kries told me, in Poland, in the midst of a dying nation. Germany is destined to rule the world, or at least a great part of it. The German people are so much human material for building the German State, other people do not count. All is for the glory and might of the German State. The lives of human beings are to be conserved only if it makes for the State's advancement, their lives are to be sacrificed if it is to the State's advantage. The State is all, the people are nothing.

"Conquered people signify little in the German account. Life, liberty, happiness, human sentiment, family ties, grace, and generous impulse, these have no place beside the one concern, the greatness of the German State.

"Starvation must excite no pity; sympathy must not be allowed, if it hampers the main design of promoting Germany's ends.

"'Starvation is here,' said General Kries. 'Candidly, we would like to see it relieved; we fear our soldiers may be unfavorably affected by the things that they see. But since it is here, starvation must serve our purpose. So we set it to work for Germany. By starvation we can accomplish in two or three years in East Poland more than we have in West Poland, which is East Prussia, in the last hundred years. With that in view, we propose to turn this force to our advantage!

"'This country is meant for Germany,' continued the keeper of starving Poland. 'It is a rich alluvial country which Germany has needed for some generations. We propose to remove the able-bodied working Poles from this country. It leaves it open for inflow of German working people as fast as we can spare them. They will occupy it and work it.'

"Then, with a cunning smile: 'Can't you see how it works out? By and by we shall give back freedom to Poland. When that happens Poland will appear automatically as a German province.'

"In Belgium, General Bissing told me exactly the same thing. 'If the relief of Belgium breaks down we can force the industrial population into Germany through starvation, and colonize other Belgians in Mesopotamia where we have planned large irrigation works. Germans will then overrun Belgium. Then when the war is over and freedom is given back to Belgium, it will be a German Belgium that is restored. Belgium will be a German province and we have Antwerp—which is what we are after.

"In Poland, the able-bodied men are being removed to relieve the German workman and make the land vacant for Germany. In Belgium the men are deported that the country may be a German colony, In Serbia, where three-fourths of a million people out of three millions have perished miserably in the last three years, Germany hardens its heart, shuts its eyes to the suffering, thinks only of Germany's gain.

In Armenia, six hundred thousand people were slain in cold blood by Kurds and Turks under the domination and leadership of German officers—Germany looking on, indifferent to the horror and woe, intent only on seizing the opportunity thus given. War, famine, pestilence—these bring to the German mind no appeal for human effort, only the resolution to profit from them to the utmost that the German State may be powerful and great. "That is not all.... Women left captive are enslaved. Germany makes all manner of lust its instrumentality... —(From the Prussian Horror in Poland by F. R. Walcott, U. S. Bureau of Public Information.)

The German Army in Belgium and Northern France.—After reading the reports of the Belgian, British, and French Commissions of Inquiry, the letters and diaries of German soldiers and officers and the official German proclamations, one is forced to the conclusion that the German army in its invasion acted in every part of its organization in a way that would shame the human race to put it into words.

There was usually but one excuse. Some one would call out: "A shot has been fired." This was the signal. There is not a single case in which it has been proved that a German was fired upon by a civilian of any of these towns. Their arms had all been given up and everything was done everywhere to keep the peace and prevent atrocities. But this had no bearing on the result, because of the prearranged Prussian scheme of destruction. In a number of cases where shots were actually fired, it has been proved that they were fired by German soldiers themselves.

In the case of Huy the usual accusation against the inhabitants was even contradicted by the German officer in charge, Major Bassewitz (see illustrative extracts), who puts the blame where it belongs, on drunken German soldiers. Another German officer acknowledges in his diary (Oct. 15, 1914): "This way of making war is purely barbarous.... On every occasion, and under no matter what pretext, there is incendiarism and pillage. But God is just and sees all: His mill grinds slowly, but it grinds exceedingly small."

In the massacre of the innocent inhabitants the men were the principal sufferers, quite a common practice being to shoot one-third of the males. But women and children were quite commonly murdered.

Take the case of Dinant, where about 650 people were murdered, more than 100 were women, children, and old men. And in this case the German Military Governor, General Longschamp, declared the innocence of the inhabitants saying: "The result of the inquiry I held was that no civilian fired at Dinant." In this case the premeditation of the German officer is also proved by the warning given several days before the destruction (Aug. 23, 1914).

The prisoners sent to Germany for internment testify to the brutal cruelty of the German civilians on the way, including women and children. This shows how universal was the state of mind brought about in Germany by the educational system of lies and hatred. Pitilessness, a gloating cruelty, an ingeniousness in inventing torments, were the almost universal characteristics of all classes of Germans. Though German commanders have acknowledged that the alleged shooting by Belgian civilians was really the work of drunken or frightened German soldiers, this, confession comes invariably *after* the inhabitants of the innocent town have suffered.

After the first few weeks we have the frank German statement that the burning, looting, and murdering, was carried out according to a prearranged plan in order to so frighten the entire country back of the line that only a few old territorials would be required for garrison purposes, and to keep the communication lines and supply depots safe.

Therefore it was arranged to divide the country into districts and to pick out one village in the center of each district in which to carry out this scheme of destruction, thus terrorizing all the other villages in the neighborhood, whose inhabitants would live in fear of similar frightfulness and so be abjectly cowed. The Use of Deadly Microbes.—It will never be known to what extent Germany attempted to poison and infect human beings and animals in both enemy and neutral countries, breeding epidemics and diseases.

There are several well-known cases from which a great deal may be inferred. Two of them have a particularly official character; one in Rumania and the other in Sweden, when both of these countries were neutral. The deadly microbes were found in the luggage of an official representative of the German government to Sweden, which he had sent on to Norway. One of his instructions was to infect horses and other livestock to be shipped to Russia. The Bucharest (Rumanian) case will now be given at length.

The Deadly Microbes at Bucharest.—The evidence given by the U. S. State Department shows that before Rumania had declared war against Austria-Hungary, and was observing strict neutrality, German official agents clandestinely introduced into Bucharest, the capital of Rumania, packages containing powerful explosives and vials containing deadly microbes destined to infect domestic animals and susceptible of producing terrible epidemics among the human population of the country. The vials contained anthrax microbes and the bacilli of glanders. The box of disease germs bore the seal of the German consulate at Kronstadt. Inside of this box, above a layer of cotton wool, this typewritten note in German was found:

"Inclosed 4 small bottles for horses and 4 for cattle. Utilization as formerly stipulated. Each phial suffices for 200 head. If possible, to be administered directly into the animals' mouths, otherwise into their fodder. We ask for a small report about successes obtained there, and in case of good results the presence for one day of M. K. would be required."— (The boxes of explosives and vials were first in the German consulate in Bucharest and then in the German legation, where they were discovered after the U. S.—being still neutral—had taken over German interests in Rumania. *N. Y. Times, Current History*, Nov., 1917.)

Desecration and Destruction of Churches—The Germans have shown a particular hatred of churches, of religion, of the clergy, of all religious emblems, and works of sacred art. Calumnies of every description were circulated among the German soldiers directed against the Belgian priests, with the result that many were abused, imprisoned, and shot. Especial pains were taken to desecrate the churches, especially the altars, with every kind of filth. Also, in forced evacuations of towns, pains were taken to mine the churches, so as to blow them up when full of people.

German Filthiness.—The picture would be incomplete without calling attention to the unspeakable filthiness of the Germans when they were able to give free rein to their churlish characteristics. It was a disgusting filthiness of mind and body, a perverted gross sensuality and bestiality. The "high-born" officers in a beautiful French castle took pains to personally defile the curtains, hangings, tapestries, furniture, ornaments, and dishes. (See Madame Huard, "My Home on the Field of Battle.")

Murder Traps.—The greatest ingenuity was shown in the variety and kind of death traps left behind by the Germans for wholesale and retail murder. They traded on the humane and religious sentiments that would make a Frenchman or an Englishman free a tied-up cat or dog, or bury a dead body, or attend service in a church.

Germany's Submarine Warfare.—The purpose of Germany's unrestricted submarine warfare was not merely the immediate one of starving out England and preventing communication between the Allies, but also the ultimate purpose of destroying as much as possible of the non-German world's tonnage. It was not at first understood why the shipping of neutral nations was sunk just as persistently as that of enemy nations, but at last the world knew that Germany was aiming at a monopoly of the sea after the war.

Therefore she was planning to sink every non-German ship afloat, not only French, British, Russian, and Italian, but Norwegian, Dutch, Swedish, Danish, Spanish, and American. If the crew perished also, so much the better; so many non-German sailors the less. It would be entirely false to German ideals to allow any regard for the rules of international law and humanity to lead to the sparing of any ship whatsoever because it was a Hospital Ship or a Passenger Ship. Two birds could be killed with one stone. The acknowledged Pan-German plan to kill off as many as possible of every non-German race except where they could be of use, made the sinking of such ships especially acceptable: "Sunk without leaving a trace" *(Spurlos versenkt).* In his "Submarine Warfare" Frost, the U. S. Consul at Queenstown gives first-hand testimony as to the murders at sea, and such special cases as the turning adrift of boatloads of survivors without food or clothing, and the tying of a boatload to a submarine and by submerging, pulling them under.

Bibliography

Arend, A.: *International Law and the Use of Force*, London, Routledge, 1993.

Chandra, R.: *Judicial System in India, Lucknow*, Print House (India), 1992.

Damrosch, L.F.: *Law and Force in the New International Order*, Boulder, Westview Press, 1991.

Friedman, G.: *The Future of War: Power, Technology and American World Dominance in the 21st Century*, N.Y., Random House, 1996.

Gray, C.H.: *Postmodern War: The New Politics of Conflict*, N.Y., The Guilford Press, 1997.

Heimanson, Rudolph: *Dictionary of Political Science and Law*, N.Y.: Oceana Publications, 1967.

Holsti, K.: *The State, War, and the State of War*, Cambridge, Cambridge Univ. Press, 1996.

Huntington, S.P.: *The Soldier and the Indian Army*, N.Y., Vintage Books, 1964.

Jones, W.H.: *The Government and Politics of India*, London, Hutchinson, 1971.

McInnes, Colin: *Hot war, Cold War: the British Army's way in warfare 1945-95*, London, Brassey's, 1996.

Murray, W.: *The Making of Strategy*, Cambridge, 1994, Cambridge Univ. Press.

Nair, A. M.: *An Indian Freedom Fighter in Japan*, Bombay, Orient Longman, 1983.

Posen, B.R.: *The Sources of Indian Military*, Cornell Univ. Press.

Roseneau, J.: *Along The Domestic-Foreign Frontier*, Cambridge, 1997, Cambridge Univ Press.

Ruggie, J.G.: *Winning the Peace*, N.Y., 1996, Columbia Univ. Press.

Van Creveld, M.: *Technology and War*, N.Y., 1991, The Free Press.

Holsti, K.: The State, War, and the State of War, Cambridge, Cambridge Univ. Press, 1996.

Huntington, S.P.: The Soldier and the Indian Army, N.Y., Vintage Books, 1964.

Jones, W.H.: The Government and Politics of India, London, Hutchinson, 1971.

Kelly, John B.: India and the Pakistan War, Oxford, Clarendon Press, 1968.

McInnes, Colin: Hot war, Cold War: the British Army's way in warfare 1945-95, London, Brassey's, 1996.

Murray, W.: The Making of Strategy, Cambridge, 1994, Cambridge Univ. Press.

Nair, A. M.: An Indian Freedom Fighter in Japan, Bombay, Orient Longman, 1983.

Posen, B.R.: The Sources of Indian Military, Cornell Univ. Press.

Roseneau, J.: Along The Domestic-Foreign Frontier, Cambridge, 1997, Cambridge Univ Press.

Ruggie, J.G.: Winning the Peace, N.Y., 1996, Columbia Univ. Press.

Van Crevèld, M.: Technology and War, N.Y., 1991, The Free Press.

Index

□□□